Transitions from Authoritarian Rule: Prospects for Democracy,
edited by Guillermo O'Donnell, Philippe C. Schmitter, and
Laurence Whitehead, is available in separate paperback editions:

Transitions from Authoritarian Rule: Southern Europe,
edited by Guillermo O'Donnell, Philippe C. Schmitter, and
Laurence Whitehead

Transitions from Authoritarian Rule: Latin America,
edited by Guillermo O'Donnell, Philippe C. Schmitter, and
Laurence Whitehead

Transitions from Authoritarian Rule: Comparative Perspectives,
edited by Guillermo O'Donnell, Philippe C. Schmitter, and
Laurence Whitehead

Transitions from Authoritarian Rule:
Tentative Conclusions about Uncertain Democracies,
by Guillermo O'Donnell and Philippe C. Schmitter

CONTRIBUTORS

Marcelo Cavarozzi   Centro de Estudios de Estado y Sociedad, Buenos Aires

Julio Cotler   Instituto de Estudios Peruanos, Lima

Manuel Antonio Garretón   Facultad Latinoamericana de Ciencias Sociales,
Santiago

Charles G. Gillespie   Amherst College

Terry Lynn Karl   Harvard University

Abraham F. Lowenthal   University of Southern California

Luciano Martins   Universidade Estadual de Campinas, São Paulo

Kevin J. Middlebrook   Indiana University, Bloomington

Guillermo O'Donnell   Helen Kellogg Institute, University of Notre Dame

Laurence Whitehead   Nuffield College, Oxford

Transitions from Authoritarian Rule

Latin America

edited by
Guillermo O'Donnell,
Philippe C. Schmitter, and
Laurence Whitehead

The Johns Hopkins University Press
Baltimore and London

Fourth printing, 1993

The Johns Hopkins University Press
2715 North Charles Street, Baltimore, Maryland 21218-4319
The Johns Hopkins Press Ltd., London

Library of Congress Cataloging-in-Publication Data

Transitions from authoritarian rule. Latin America.

    Papers originally commissioned for a conference sponsored by the
Latin American Program of the Woodrow Wilson International Center
for Scholars between 1979 and 1981.
    Bibliography: p.
    Includes index.
    Contents: Introduction to the Latin American cases / Guillermo
O'Donnell—Political cycles in Argentina since 1955 / Marcelo
Cavarozzi—Bolivia's failed democratization, 1977–1980 / Laurence
Whitehead—[etc.]
    1. Representative government and representation—Latin
America—Case studies.   2. Authoritarianism—Latin America—Case
studies.   3. Democracy—Case studies.   I. O'Donnell, Guillermo
A.   II. Schmitter, Philippe C.   III. Whitehead, Laurence.   IV.
Woodrow Wilson International Center for Scholars. Latin American
Program.
JL966.T74   1986   321.09′ 098   86-2711
ISBN 0-8018-3188-1 (pbk.)

A catalog record for this book is available from the British Library.

Contents

Foreword

Abraham F. Lowenthal

The three coeditors of *Transitions from Authoritarian Rule* have kindly invited me to introduce this effort because it resulted from the Woodrow Wilson Center's project on "Transitions from Authoritarian Rule: Prospects for Democracy in Latin America and Southern Europe."

The "Transitions" project was the most significant undertaking of the Wilson Center's Latin American Program during the seven years I had the privilege of directing its activities. The resulting four-volume book contributes substantially on a topic of vital scholarly and political importance. I want to highlight both these points, to underline some of its strengths, and finally to say a bit about what is still left to be done.

The Woodrow Wilson International Center for Scholars was created by an act of the United States Congress in 1968 as a "living memorial" to the twentieth president of the United States, a man remembered for his idealism and for his commitment to democracy, for his scholarship, for his political leadership, and for his international vision, but also for his interventionist attitudes and actions toward Latin America and the Caribbean. The Center supports advanced research and systematic discussion on national and international issues by scholars and practitioners from all over the world. It aims to bring together the realms of academic and public affairs, as Wilson himself did.

The Latin American Program was established early in 1977, within the Center's overall framework, to focus attention on the Western Hemisphere. The Program has tried, from the start, to serve as a bridge between Latin Americans and North Americans of diverse backgrounds, to facilitate comparative research that draws on the Center's special capacity to bring people together, to emphasize the highest standards of scholarship, to stress privileged topics that merit intense cooperative efforts, and to help assure that opinion leaders in the United States and Latin America focus more attentively and more sensitively on Latin America and the Caribbean and on their relation with the United States.

In all its undertakings, the Program has been striving to assure that diverse viewpoints—from men and women with varying national, professional, disciplinary, methodological, and political perspectives—are presented, and that complex issues are illuminated through the confrontation of different analyses. But the Program's orientation has never been value-free; it has stood for vigorous exchange among persons who disagree about many things but who fundamentally respect the academic enterprise and who share a commitment to the core values all the nations of the Americas profess. The Program has sought diversity of many kinds, but not artificial balance. It awarded fellowships in the same semester to writers exiled because of their convictions from Argentina and from Cuba, for example, but it has never invited their censors on an equal basis. It has sponsored research on human rights from many different standpoints, but never from the perspective of the torturers. And it sponsored the project on "Transitions from Authoritarian Rule" with a frank bias for democracy, for the restoration in Latin America of the fundamental rights of political participation.

The "Transitions" project was begun in 1979 on the initiative of two charter members of the Latin American Program's nine-person Academic Council: Guillermo O'Donnell (then of CEDES in Buenos Aires) and Philippe Schmitter (then of the University of Chicago), with the active encouragement and support of the Council's chairman, Albert O. Hirschman, and of Council member Fernando Henrique Cardoso of Brazil. During the project's first phase, I served as its coordinator. As the project grew in scope and complexity, it became clear that another Center-based person was needed to focus more fully on it; we were fortunate to recruit Laurence Whitehead of Oxford University, a former Wilson Center fellow, who then worked closely with O'Donnell and Schmitter and became coeditor of the project volume.

The "Transitions" project illustrates the Wilson Center's aspirations in several respects:

Its leaders are recognized as among the world's foremost academic authorities in Latin America, the United States, and Europe.

It attracted the participation of other top-flight scholars from all three continents and encouraged them to work closely together in a structured and linked series of workshops and conferences.

It emphasized comparative analysis, and sharpened the focus on Latin American cases by putting them into a broader perspective.

In its various workshops, the project drew on the perspective not only of scholars but of several persons—from Latin America and from among former U.S. government officials—experienced in politics and public affairs.

Its findings have been made available to opinion leaders from different sectors through specially organized discussion sessions in Washington.

It maintained a creative tension between its normative bias, its theoretical ambitions, and its empirical and case-oriented approach. The project's animus, as I had occasion to say at its first meeting, was never wishful thinking but rather "thoughtful wishing," that is, it was guided by a normative orientation that was rigorous and deliberate in its method.

Finally, the project illustrated a point the Wilson Center's director, Dr. James H. Billington, has often emphasized: to seek tentative answers to fundamental questions rather than definitive responses to trivial ones. All the project's participants know that the complex issues involved in transitions to democracy have not been dealt with conclusively in this volume, but they can take great satisfaction in what they have contributed.

Transitions from Authoritarian Rule

Ultimate evaluations of this book's import, obviously, will have to come from analysts less involved in the project's inception and management than I. I would like, however, to suggest some of the reasons why I think *Transitions from Authoritarian Rule* is important.

It is the first book in any language that systematically and comparatively focuses on the process of transition from authoritarian regimes, making this the central question of scholarship as it is today in Latin American politics.

Its analytic and normative focus on the prospects of building democratic or polyarchic politics in the wake of an authoritarian transition provides a vantage point that organizes the materials in ways useful not only to scholars and observers but to political actors as well.

Its comparisons of cases in Latin America and in Southern Europe and of cases of transition from bureaucratic authoritarianism, military populism, and sultanistic despotism allow for considering several different variables.

Transitions from Authoritarian Rule is rich in nuanced, contextually sensitive analysis, and each of the case studies is written by a leading authority. Although the methods, perspectives, and styles of the various authors understandably differ, their agreement on shared assumptions makes this a coherent volume. The book is filled with subtleties, complexity, and a keen sense of paradox.

Throughout, disaggregation is emphasized. All authoritarian regimes are not equated with each other. No authoritarian regime is regarded as monolithic, nor are the forces pushing for democratization so regarded. Distinctions are drawn between "democracy" and "polyarchy"; between "democratization" and "liberalization"; between "transition" and "consolidation"; between "hard-liners" and "soft-liners" or accommodationists within the authoritarian coalition; and among "maximalists," "moderates," and "opportunists" in the coalition supporting *abertura* (liberalization).

From the various cases, several points emerge that deserve special mention here. These cases show that, although international factors, direct and indirect, may condition and affect the course of transition, the major participants and the dominant influences in every case have been national. They demonstrate the importance of institutions, of mediating procedures and forums that help make the rules of political discourse legitimate and credible in a period of change. They illustrate the vital significance of political leadership and judgment, of the role of single individuals in complex historical processes. They point out, again and again, the importance of timing, the complexity of interactive processes carried out over extensive periods, the various ways in which transitions produce surprises, and some of the ironies and paradoxes that result.

Above all, the cases analyze the ways in which transitions from authoritarian rule are conditioned and shaped by historical circumstances, unique in each country but patterned in predictable ways, by the way in which a previous democratic regime broke down, by the nature and duration of the authoritarian period, by the means the authoritarian regime uses to obtain legitimacy and to handle threats to its grip on power, by the initiative and the timing of experimental moves toward *abertura*, by the degree of security and self-confidence of the regime's elites and by the confidence and competence of those pushing for opening the political process, by the presence or absence of financial resources, by the counseling of outsiders, and by the prevailing international *fashions* that provide legitimacy to certain forms of transition.

The Tasks Ahead

I do not wish to detain the reader longer before he or she enters the reading of *Transitions from Authoritarian Rule*. It remains only to concede, as all the authors would, that this book is incomplete, and that much remains to be done. The cases of transition are still few in number, and each one merits a much more detailed and sustained analysis. The processes of consolidation, so important if these transitions are to be meaningful, are barely considered in this volume, and require separate treatment. The sensitivity that the authors in their chapters show to the dilemmas and choices faced by opposition groups pressing for *abertura* needs to be matched by equally empathetic and well-informed assessments of the choices made by those within authoritarian regimes who permit *abertura* to occur and push for its extension. Some of the categories of analysis—of hard-liners (*duros*) and soft-liners (*blandos*), for example—need to be further specified and refined.

All this and more needs to be done. No doubt the editors and authors of *Transitions from Authoritarian Rule* will be among the leaders in carrying out this research. Some of them will be leaders, as well, in the very processes of building democracies. They, and many others, will go much further than this volume can, but they will build upon a solid foundation.

Preface

Between 1979 and 1981 the Latin American Program of the Woodrow Wilson International Center for Scholars, in Washington, D.C., sponsored a series of meetings and conferences entitled "Transitions from Authoritarian Rule: Prospects for Democracy in Latin America and Southern Europe." As this project grew in scope and complexity, Abraham Lowenthal, program secretary from 1977 to 1983, provided indispensable encouragement that enabled us to turn it into the present four-volume study. We wish to acknowledge our special debt of gratitude to him, and also to thank the Woodrow Wilson Center, the Aspen Institute for Humanistic Study, the Inter-American Foundation, the Helen Kellogg Institute of the University of Notre Dame, the European University Institute in Florence, and Nuffield College, Oxford, for their financial and logistical support. Louis Goodman, acting secretary of the Latin American Program in 1983–84, also gave us much-needed assistance. Needless to add, only those named in the table of contents are responsible for the views expressed here.

All of the papers published in these four volumes were originally commissioned for a Woodrow Wilson Center conference or were circulated, discussed, and revised in the course of the "Transitions" project. They have, therefore, some commonality of approach and outlook, but it was never our intention to impose a uniformity of interpretation and terminology. On the contrary, we deliberately set out to widen the range of serious discussion about regime transitions in general, and to promote informed debate comparing specific cases. In Volume 4, O'Donnell and Schmitter present the lessons they have drawn from this experience of collaboration among scholars working on Latin America and Southern Europe. Volume 3 contains a series of discussion papers analyzing common themes from different perspectives. Volume 1 (on Southern Europe) and Volume 2 (on Latin America) contain country studies, some of which were written during or immediately after the launching of a democratic transition, and some even before it had begun. Two cases (Uruguay and Turkey) were added to our sample at a later stage in the project as developments in these countries called for their inclusion, whereas the chapter on Italy refers to a transition completed more than thirty years earlier. Because of these differences in timing, and the delay in publication, readers should be warned that not all chapters carry the analysis right up to date (end of 1984).

Although the three editors are listed alphabetically in volumes 1, 2, and 3, they, of course, established some division of labor among themselves. Primary responsibility for Volume 1 rests with Philippe C. Schmitter; Laurence Whitehead took the lead in editing Volume 2; and Guillermo O'Donnell had first responsibility for Volume 3. This has been very much a collective endeavor, however, and all three of us share credit or blame for the overall result.

Transitions from Authoritarian Rule

Latin America

1 •

Introduction to the
Latin American Cases

Guillermo O'Donnell

In *Transitions from Authoritarian Rule: Tentative Conclusions*, Philippe Schmitter and I discuss processes and problems typical of the demise of authoritarian rule, based on a set of Southern European and Latin American cases. In several of those cases the pretransitional regime fits the category of "bureaucratic authoritarianism," which I have elaborated in previous writings.[1] With some exceptions, Schmitter and I do not pay specific attention to geographical location, cultural area, or previous regime type; rather, we attempt to generalize across them. In the present chapter I shall discuss certain characteristics of the Latin American countries from the perspective of their chances for democratization.[2] For this purpose, I shall draw some comparisons with the Southern European cases. Two caveats are in order. First, I shall not repeat here analyses and arguments that Schmitter and I present in the Conclusions. Second, the present discussion is closely related to Chapter 1 in Volume 3, where Laurence Whitehead analyzes variations attributable to the diverse geopolitical as well as economic international contexts in which contemporary Southern European and Latin American countries find themselves. The reader will find in Whitehead's chapter the persuasive argument that international factors are more favorable to democracy in Southern Europe than in Latin America. In the present chapter, I focus on domestic characteristics of the latter cases which differ and, in some important aspects, contrast with conditions present in Southern Europe. Those differences and contrasts also support a more optimistic assessment about the prospects of democratic installation (and, probably even more so, of democratic consolidation) in Southern Europe than in Latin America. In the last part of this chapter, however, I argue that in most of contemporary Latin America some important subjective changes have occurred that, even in the midst of a bleak configuration of "objective" factors, offer new grounds for hope about democratization.

We may begin by noting the greater heterogeneity of Latin America as compared to Southern Europe: not all the Latin American cases included in this volume fit the category of bureaucratic authoritarianism before initiating their respective transitions. When designing the project which eventuated in the present volumes, we thought it important to include cases that covered various types of authoritarian rule in the contemporary capitalist societies of Latin America. Our intent was to broaden our understanding of the processes of demise and transition by allowing rather wide variations in the type of preceding authoritarian regime. (In this sense the reader will find it useful to consult the chapters by Robert Kaufman and Alfred Stepan in Volume 3, in which diverse paths of eventual transition to democracy from Latin American bureaucratic-authoritarian regimes and from a wide range of European and Latin American authoritarian regimes, respectively, are discussed.)

One such regime type is what, for want of a better term, could be called "traditional." It has strong patrimonialist (in the Weberian sense), and in some cases even sultanistic, components. This is the kind of regime most prone to revolutionary transformation. Somoza's Nicaragua fitted this category, as did Batista's Cuba; Stroessner's Paraguay is the last remnant of what used to be a quite common form of rule in the region.

Another kind of authoritarianism, which may be termed "populist," is represented by the case of Peru, analyzed in Chapter 7 by Julio Cotler. Although the central role played by the armed forces differentiates the Peruvian case from older, more typical forms of Latin American populism (where the central role was played by civilian political movements led by strongly personalized leadership), in my opinion the former also belongs to the populist "family" of regimes. On the one side, the institutional, as opposed to the personalistic, role that the armed forces played suffices to set the Peruvian case apart from traditional forms of military dictatorship. On the other side, the Peruvian military-populist regime contrasts in several important aspects with bureaucratic-authoritarian ones. Among these differences are the anti-oligarchic orientation of the policies of the Peruvian regime; its intention to rapidly expand industry and the economic role of the state in a country that had advanced little in these directions; and its intention not to exclude coercively the popular sector (as in the bureaucratic-authoritarian regimes), but to activate and incorporate politically various segments of this sector. This is significant even if this effort, in typical populist fashion accentuated by the "antipolitical" biases inherent in the armed forces, coexisted with attempts to corporatize and control from above the representation of the popular sector. As a consequence of these orientations, the military-populist experiment in Peru, in contrast to bureaucratic-authoritarian regimes, did not have the support of the large fractions of urban capital, or of the more dynamic agrarian sectors (most of which, in fact, it expropriated). Furthermore, even if, as Cotler points out, political repression was not absent, its level and intensity did not entail a significant change in relation to previously prevailing patterns. In any case, the Peruvian regime was much less systematic and harsh in the use of repression than were the bureaucratic-authoritarian ones. Among other important consequences, this meant that the Peruvian military and their civilian allies had less to fear than their bureaucratic-authoritarian counterparts in terms of eventual reprisals from future civilian governments. Another important difference between this case and that of the bureaucratic-authoritarian regimes is that, in reaction to the quite radical policies implemented initially by the military populists, the dominant Peruvian classes rapidly demanded a return to political democracy. This contrasts with the support that those same classes have lent to bureaucratic-authoritarian regimes until a late stage in their existence.

The differences just sketched are important in many respects. In relation to the respective transitions, however, most of the predicaments and uncertainties that Schmitter and I discuss in our Conclusions can also be observed in the Peruvian case. This suggests that, irrespective of the previous type of authoritarian rule, our concluding arguments may apply to all cases of nonrevolutionary regime transition in countries that have a more than minimally activated popular sector and a reasonably complex capitalist economy. Those conclusions are less relevant for societies with less differentiated stratification systems, as well as extensive patrimonialist practices and scarcely capitalist economies. These societies seem more likely to follow a different transition path (i.e., a revolutionary one), as illustrated by Nicaragua[3] and, earlier, by Cuba. But that this is not necessarily the pattern is shown by the recent transitions to constitutional democracy of the Dominican Republic and Ecuador, which, even though they were already socially more complex and less patrimonialist than Cuba and Nicaragua at the moment of the respective transitions, resembled the latter more closely than the Latin American countries discussed in this volume.

Even with such caveats, these observations suggest a high degree of commonality (certainly higher than we had expected) in the processes of transition once a certain threshold of stateness and socioeconomic complexity has been reached. This is supported by two cases of earlier democratization, Venezuela and Colombia. Here, the preceding authoritarian regimes were a mixture of traditionalist and—especially during their first stages—populist features. The transition in these two countries, as Chapter 9 on Venezuela by Terry Karl and the literature on Colombia cited in the Conclusions make clear, also shared most of the predicaments and uncertainties we have found in the processes of bureaucratic-authoritarian demise. Venezuela and Colombia, however, are exceptional in one significant respect, to which I shall return: they have been the only two cases of carefully pacted political democratization in Latin America.

Another case—a type in itself—that we thought important to include in our project is that of Mexico. It is discussed in this volume by Kevin Middlebrook, in a chapter which maps patterns of change very different from all the other cases. Considerable changes have occurred within a regime that has nevertheless exhibited remarkable continuity of structure and leadership. Its "institutionalized revolution" resembles bureaucratic-authoritarian rule in many ways, and certainly is not a political democracy as we define it in the Conclusions. Yet the Mexican regime differs from the bureaucratic-authoritarian ones in its relatively high degree of institutionalization and, hence, in its ability to deal with the one problem that plagues the latter: presidential succession. It also differs in the relatively minor role that the armed forces play in its power structure and in its significant support from the popular sector. These facets derive from the distinctive historical origin of the Mexican regime as a mass revolutionary movement, in sharp contrast with the strong component of dominant-class support for the coups that originate the bureaucratic-authoritarian regimes. Thus, the patterns of change in the Mexican regime provide a useful contrast to the more discontinuous, often dramatic changes observable in our other cases.

On the other hand, Chile remains, as it has been from the time of its inclusion in the project, a case of bureaucratic-authoritarian rule. In Chile only very limited, reversible, and uncertain steps toward liberalization have been made. The regime is showing abundant signs of exhaustion, but is not willing to surrender to the broad opposition it has generated. Nonetheless, as argued in our Conclusion, the limited liberalizing moves undertaken by the Chilean regime seem to indicate that it has passed the point of no return as far as restabilization of bureaucratic-authoritarian rule, or even its fundamental continuity through *democradura*, is concerned. At any event, the chapter on Chile by Manuel Antonio Garretón allows us to observe some typical changes and tensions internal to bureaucratic-authoritarian regimes, as well as some initial movements by defecting regime supporters and mobilizing regime opponents which prefigure the alliances and dynamics of an eventual (and increasingly likely) transition.

Uruguay, another case of extremely repressive bureaucratic-authoritarian rule at the time that our project was launched, has recently inaugurated a democratic government. This was a rather protracted transition, tightly controlled by the authoritarian rulers until close to its culmination. Those rulers attempted to exclude some important parties and political actors from the elections and to establish institutionalized controls by the armed forces over future civilian governments. Those controls would have greatly restricted the actual policy-making capabilities of those governments, and damaged their chances of being perceived by the electorate as its authentic representatives. These attempts were formalized in an explicit political pact (the "Acuerdo del Club Naval" of November 1984), signed by representatives of the armed forces and of most of the opposition parties. But—supporting our argument in the Conclusion about the dynamics that transitions tend to develop once fully launched—in spite of such an agreement and the solemnities with which it was surrounded, the pact was not implemented. The important but practically sole exception was the imprisonment until the elections of Washington Ferreira Aldunate, a leading member of the opposition (and his proscription from running as a presidential candidate). The "Acuerdo" practically became a dead letter from the day of the inauguration of the present democratic government in Uruguay.

In the Conclusion we make several references to Brazil, and to the chapters by Luciano Martins in the present volume and by Fernando Henrique Cardoso in Volume 3; not much needs to be added here. Suffice it to say that, among the

Latin American bureaucratic-authoritarian regimes, the Brazilian regime stands out as the only one which, despite the present social and economic crisis, can claim with some credibility to have achieved significant developmental successes. Furthermore, the Brazilian popular sector, for various historical reasons, is weakly organized and scarcely activated politically. These factors were crucial for the high degree of control that the Brazilian regime was able to exert over the transition. This transition took an exceptionally long time (no fewer than ten years) and, as we shall see below, in an important sense it cannot yet be considered truly complete. Furthermore, the "regime's party" enjoyed significant electoral support during the period. Only in 1982, after extensive liberalization had been in effect for several years and under the impact of a severe social and economic crisis, did demands for democratization become intense and widespread. These events slackened the grip that the bureaucratic-authoritarian regime had maintained on the transition since 1974 and deepened the cleavages between hard-liners and soft-liners in the regime and the armed forces. Although fears of a regressive military coup and spectacular episodes of violence instigated by recalcitrant hard-liners were not lacking, the last period of this regime was, as compared with the other cases in this volume, relatively tranquil. Undoubtedly this was related to the fact that the armed forces and the dominant classes felt scarcely threatened by the main opposition party and party currents. A contributory factor was the emergence during 1984, the crucial last year of this transition, of Tancredo Neves as the leader who, coming from the more moderate wing of an already moderate opposition, could make an implicit (or, perhaps, explicit but secret) political pact with the soft-liners in the government and in the armed forces, as well as with some leaders of the regime's party. In this sense, like Greece's Karamanlis, Neves had many of the characteristics of the "notables" whose role in some transitions we discuss in the Conclusion. Neves's success in playing this pivotal role led to an outcome that shortly before would have been almost as unimaginable as the Spanish *Cortes* voting their own extinction: an electoral college rigged with nonelected regime appointees made him president by an overwhelming majority. Neves's death before assuming the presidency made his constitutional successor, José Sarney, the first civilian president of Brazil since 1964. Even though by most criteria Brazil today is a political democracy, a crucial component is lacking: the authority of the executive was not established by a general election (either directly or indirectly by means of an electoral college specifically voted to that effect). This entails the unusual situation of a transition that for most purposes must be considered complete but that has, nonetheless, sidestepped around the issue of holding reasonably fair and competitive elections for the highest executive offices. This situation must be understood in the context of deep-seated Brazilian traditions, expressed—and reinforced—by the numerous interelite negotiations that this very sequential transition has fostered; perhaps nothing illustrates this point better than the fact that President Sarney was, until early 1984, one of the most important leaders of the regime's party. In this sense, Brazil may soon offer the closest contemporary resemblance to pacted democracies à la Venezuela and Colombia.

In all these respects, the contrast of Brazil with Argentina and Bolivia could hardly be stronger. The latter were cases of authoritarian rule (bureaucratic authoritarianism in Argentina and a volatile hybrid of bureaucratic authoritarianism, populism, and traditionalism in Bolivia) which could never claim anything close to the economic achievements of the Brazilian regime. To this factor must be added the phenomenal corruption of their respective governments and armed forces and, in the case of Argentina, humiliating defeat in an external war and, mostly in Bolivia but also to a significant extent in Argentina, a "gangsterization" of the armed forces that brought them close to predatory sultanism. The combination of these elements led to the spectacular collapse of these regimes. In Southern Europe this democratization by collapse occurred only in Portugal (and then without the element of widespread corruption). To a lesser extent Greece is also a case in point. There, after the Cyprus fiasco the "regime of the colonels" was ousted by the higher-ranking military establishment, which was able to hand over the transition to Karamanlis. Karamanlis, to be sure, had been in exile during the colonels' regime and had emerged as the main leader of the opposition, but he was also a "reliable" Center-Right politician, both for most of the high command of the armed forces and for the Greek dominant classes. This contrasts with the Argentine and Bolivian transitions, where the armed forces became virtually incapable of acting collectively, much less of ensuring that subsequent elections were not won by parties and candidates far away from the military's preferences.

In such conditions of regime collapse, liberalization barely precedes democratization, as we can see in the respective chapters on Argentina and Bolivia by Marcelo Cavarozzi and Laurence Whitehead. There is no phased or guided interaction between these two processes, as can be observed elsewhere. Moreover, in further contrast to the relatively successful authoritarian regime of Brazil (and Spain), parties in Argentina and Bolivia which claimed— or were even suspected of—some continuity with the preceding regime made a dismal showing in the electoral arena. In such circumstances, there are few inducements for the opposition to enter into agreements with a rapidly collapsing and almost unanimously rejected authoritarian regime. With the social forces and political institutions that had supported the defunct regime in a state of profound (if often temporary) disarray, countries such as Argentina and Bolivia are literally precipitated into democracy. This is much more of an all-or-nothing situation than the more usual pattern, where transitional regime incumbents, defectors, and democratic opponents engage in numerous rounds of pressures, counterpressures, and eventual agreements. As we argue in the Conclusion, the case of transition by regime collapse is the one most likely to lead to a fuller, less restricted type of political democracy. It may also be the one which presents less formidable obstacles to advances in social and economic democratization. But for the same reasons (i.e., because it leaves the dominant classes and the armed forces heavily underrepresented in the institutional arenas of political democracy), the pattern of democratization by collapse is also more likely to lead to the emergence of strong disloyal oppositions and to unmediated confrontations between parties, factions, and organized interests. Consequently, this pattern seems more prone to lead to severe authoritarian reversals. The hectic political history of Argentina and Bolivia, where the more recent democratizations by collapse have by no means been the first, illustrates this risk all too well.

Finally, in this volume Venezuela represents the case of a political democracy which emerged in a world context quite different from the present one. It is also, by Latin American standards, an enduring democracy, consistent with the series of carefully crafted political and economic pacts that have punctuated its recent history. The counterpart to these deliberate restrictions on arenas and policies has been, as Terry Karl argues in her chapter, the neglect of opportunities for solving or alleviating that country's deep social and economic inequalities. Thus, intermittently eloquent signs remind us of rather widespread dissatisfaction with the confining conditions of Venezuelan (and, for that matter, Colombian) political arrangements. Pacted democracy may enhance the probability that a given polity will not revert to authoritarian rule; but such not inconsequential achievement seems to have serious costs in terms of social and economic equity.

As stated above, the main interest of this volume is with transitions from bureaucratic-authoritarian regimes. This offers some interesting similarities with the authoritarian regimes of Southern Europe, although in Latin America this form of rule has emerged more recently and, with the exception of Spain in the aftermath of its civil war, has involved significantly more violence and repression. Moreover, in Europe those authoritarian regimes emerged at the margin of the region's dynamic center; in Latin America, along with the Mexican regime and its unique characteristics, the bureaucratic-authoritarian regimes emerged in some of the socially more complex and "modern" countries of the region: Argentina, Brazil, Chile, and Uruguay.[4] Around this central interest, we decided to include the socially conservative pacted democracy of Venezuela, Peru's military populism, and Mexico's "institutionalized revolution," because we considered them important in themselves, and because they highlight some issues more generically involved in regime transition.

Despite the rather broad scope of our project, there are some important issues on which we have not focused our attention, except for some brief and tentative observations in Volumes 3 and 4. Each of these issues deserves detailed study. The first concerns the consolidation of political democracy and its expansion in the areas of demilitarization and broader political participation, as well as its eventual extension to various social and economic arenas. The second issue is that of revolutionary regimes (Cuba and Nicaragua), their dynamics and probable direction of change. These cases are especially interesting with regard to the significant advances they have achieved (at the cost of being more or less participatory but not democratic regimes) in terms of social and economic equity—an accomplishment especially remarkable given the very poor record of Latin American democracies in this domain. The focus of our project resulted from the analytical need to avoid encompassing too wide a range of variation, and to allow reasonably detailed discussion of what is a very complex (and understudied) subject: nonrevolutionary transitions from authoritarian regimes.

Another reason for limiting ourselves to nonrevolutionary transitions to democracy was that, as admitted in Volume 4, our project had from the outset a normative bias, coupled and reinforced by an empirical generalization. We have considered political democracy as desirable per se, even after recognizing the significant tradeoffs that its installation and eventual consolidation can entail in terms of more effective, and more rapid, opportunities for reducing social and economic inequities. The empirical generalization reinforcing this normative preference is that the Latin American experience of the last three decades has shown that there is not, nor is there likely to be in the foreseeable future, a *vía revolucionaria* open for countries that have reached some minimal degree of stateness and social complexity and, concomitantly, of expansion of capitalist social relations. Except for the few Latin American countries which are subjected to some variation of patrimonial rule (and which, therefore, face not only the task of establishing a new political regime, but also and perhaps more so, of completing the creation of a national state), all attempts at revolutionary transformation have not merely failed; they have been a powerful factor leading to the emergence of authoritarian regimes. Most of these regimes have been brutally repressive, and extremely regressive in terms of social and economic inequalities. Furthermore, it seems clear that any such attempt in the foreseeable future will be much more likely to induce similar authoritarian reversals than to achieve whatever egalitarian goals may be claimed by revolutionary movements. Simply, the conditions conducive to the success of efforts at a violent and comprehensive rupture are absent in countries where the armed forces are reasonably professionalized and have overwhelming superiority in the control of violence in their territory; where the local bourgeoisie has strong roots in the domestic productive structure and intimate (if subordinated) links with international capital; and where any revolutionary attempt is likely to be actively "discouraged" by the United States and by most European and Latin American countries while having little hope of receiving the never unmixed blessing of active support from the Soviet Union and its satellites.

Having thus cleared the way for focusing on nonrevolutionary Latin American transitions from authoritarian (basically bureaucratic-authoritarian) regimes, it is worth comparing them further with their Southern European counterparts. The most salient difference between the Latin American cases and most Southern European ones is the central role played in the former by the armed forces. A high degree of militarization of the authoritarian regime increases the difficulties of the transition in at least two respects: with regard to the repercussions during the new democratic regime of repression used by the preceding authoritarian rulers, and with regard to the broad range of issues and institutions that the armed forces usually "conquer" during a highly militarized regime. Both hinder seriously the assertion of authority and the effectiveness of decision-making by a new democratic government.

A second difference between the two regions—which converges with the international factors discussed by Laurence Whitehead in Volume 3—is the more ambiguous meaning that the very idea of political democracy has had in Latin America. With the partial exception of Chile, Uruguay, and Costa Rica, political democracy in Latin America has often been identified by leftist and populist parties alike more as a mechanism for the containment of their followers and for the manipulation of their aspirations than as an institutional arrangement amenable to the representation, processing, and eventual satisfaction of such aspirations. Furthermore, the ideological rooting of democracy has not been helped by the restrictive (when not openly fraudulent) nature of past democracies in most Latin American countries. Neither has such rooting been helped by the repeated opportunistic recourse by dominant classes in Latin America to the mechanisms and discourses of political democracy whenever this seemed expedient for blocking the activation of popular and even middle sectors. Moreover, they were prepared to abandon those same mechanisms and discourses in favor of openly authoritarian "solutions" when democratic institutions no longer seemed useful for maintaining the restrictive characteristics of political life.

Shifting the comparison to a third level, we find another set of factors more favorable to the prospects for democracy in Southern Europe than in Latin America. With the partial exceptions of Argentina and Uruguay, now less exceptional after the extremely regressive social, economic, and educational policies of their respective authoritarian regimes, inequality is significantly higher in Latin America than in Southern Europe. The continuation of acute, pervasive, and blatant inequalities—sharpened by the severe economic crisis and the monumental foreign debt inherited in many countries from the preceding authoritarian regimes—may be one of the outcomes of the socially restricted and/or shaky democratic regimes that already exist, and will exist in the near future, in Latin America. The inability of these regimes to deal with at least the more extreme or more politically demanding inequalities, or their inability to persuade the population that, even if they can do little for the moment, they are firmly committed to tackling those problems in the not-too-distant future, would augur poorly for their medium- and long-term chances of consolidation.

Another characteristic is the infrequent recourse to formal and explicit political and economic pacts as transitional devices in Latin America. As already mentioned, the exceptions are Venezuela and Colombia several decades ago. A partial exception, also already noted, is Uruguay; but the "Acuerdo del Club Naval" was barely implemented, if at all. An even weaker exception is Brazil, where, as we saw, an implicit or perhaps explicit but secret political pact was apparently made between the armed forces, some regime incumbents, and some leaders of the regime's party on the one side and, on the other, the sole person of Tancredo Neves. But the very existence of this pact is not entirely certain and its contents, in any event, are a matter for speculation—including the crucial question as to what extent it may be construed as binding by President Sarney. Thus, in contemporary Latin American transitions, no formal, explicit political pacts have been made, with the exception of the extremely short-lived one in Uruguay. Furthermore, there is not even one case of the economic pacts we discuss in the Conclusion.

What accounts for this lack of formal and explicit pacts? The cases studied in our project, as well as those of earlier transitions, suggest that political or economic pacts are greatly facilitated when either of the following conditions applies: when civil society (especially its popular sector) is weakly organized and politically inactive, or, conversely, when the levels of social organization and political activation are quite high *and* there exists a reasonably strong and representative party system, especially in relation to the popular sector. The first condition is conducive to narrow and exclusive elitist agreements, undisturbed by "demagogic" eruptions. The second in principle allows more comprehensive compromises to be worked out and implemented by institutionalized political actors.

The first condition prevailed at the time of the emergence of the pacted democracies of Colombia and Venezuela, even though massive, but short-lived, urban demonstrations preceded the demise of authoritarian rule in both countries. With the already noted (and partial) exception of Brazil, and eventually in the future Paraguay, elsewhere in South America the requisite conditions for transitions under such elitist arrangements do not exist: the political and social presence (at various levels and modes of organization) of a quite active and organized popular sector, as well as of parties claiming to represent this sector (but often unable to control it), makes the realization of such pacts difficult, and, as we saw in Uruguay, their implementation even more difficult.

The other condition conducive to pact-making during the transition seems to be the existence of a rather strong party system, and/or the survival of strong partisan identities and organizational networks during the authoritarian "interlude." This must include a party or parties which effectively represent the popular sector and which can, as a result, exert significant control over this sector. In such conditions, pact-making remains an elitist affair by its very nature, but, in contrast with the preceding scenario, agreements that include strong, popularly based political parties cannot fail to take into account some of the more actively voiced popular demands and, even more so, the need to obtain the acquiescence to the pact of the main organizations of the popular sector, especially unions. In Spain after Franco and, in a more oblique manner, in Italy after Fascism, the role of class-based, ideologically articulate parties of the Left—that is, Communist and Socialist parties—was crucial.

In exchange for greater access to electoral competition and to politico-administrative posts, those parties delivered the compliance of the popular sector and its main organizations to the agreements the parties concerned had reached with other actors. The willingness of parties to take such steps depends in no small measure on their estimate of the danger of an authoritarian regression. Their ability to do so depends on deep and multifold roots in their social bases, territorial as well as functional. Only then are those parties likely to believe that, despite the unpopularity of some of the items usually included in such agreements (for example, various forms of wage and salary restraints, or electoral arrangements which permit the overrepresentation of conservative interests in order to keep them in the electoral game), they will not be dispossessed of the allegiance of their voters by competing parties. This also requires firm discipline in the decision-making patterns of the pacting parties. With the—to my mind not very likely—exception of Chile, this set of conditions has not been met, nor is it likely to be met, in the Latin American transitions. In these transitions populist or loosely organized popular- and middle-sector-based parties dominate the electoral arena. This kind of party is much less likely (and is perceived to be less likely) to persuade its followers to comply with the eventual pact. As a consequence, both the leaders of those parties and their prospective counterparts in a pact tend to see formal and explicit agreements as too risky. They prefer informal and often secret agreements which are continually violated and renegotiated, the whole process being punctuated by open confrontations that both sides have serious difficulty in controlling. A different possibility is that pacts may come *after*, rather than during, the transition. Once a political democracy has been installed, the perception of serious threats to the survival of the regime may provide a powerful motivation for party leaders and followers to reach such agreements, even if this does little to guarantee more than short-term compliance with the terms of the agreement.

Therefore, with the exceptions noted, contemporary transitions in Latin America have neither ultraelitist characteristics nor a strong party system rooted in the popular sector—the two alternative contexts that seem most conducive to explicit pact-making as a transitional device. Moreover, political pacts also are likely to occur where the existing authoritarian regime has been reasonably successful in attaining its policy goals, is self-confident in its public image, and is capable of attracting considerable electoral support. In such cases, the outgoing regime's incumbents are likely to have enough leverage to obtain various guarantees for themselves, for the armed forces, and for their own social bases. Then, imposed rather than freely agreed upon pacts may ensue, especially if either of the two above-stated conditions also holds. In contemporary Latin America, however (again with the partial exception of Brazil, where this component of imposition may have been important in the last stages of the transition), there has been no such case of a reasonably successful, self-confident, and electorally supported authoritarian regime entering into transition.

These factors help us to understand the absence of formal and explicit political and economic pacts during the contemporary Latin American transitions. If in this matter my analysis has been tentative, discussion of the medium- and long-run consequences of the absence of such pacts leads us into an even more uncertain terrain. This is due to the usual problems posed by trying to assess consequences derived from events (and nonevents) that are mediated by numerous, poorly understood processes. It is also due to the fact that in the cases of recent democratization we do not yet have a sufficient time perspective to gauge those consequences. Thus, I shall limit myself, first, to some rather dismal empirical observations and then to some more hopeful speculations about the possible incidence of certain developments which have recently become discernible in contemporary Latin American politics.

The dismal observations to which I refer are the following: (1) Two of the three political democracies which have so far endured more than ten years, and which have survived the great wave of authoritarianism that swept Latin America after 1964, are Venezuela and Colombia; they are the two cases of carefully pacted and rather restrictive democratic regimes. (2) The other "survivor" is Costa Rica, not a case of *pactismo*, but one in which the regular armed forces were suppressed—a condition not likely to be repeated in the future. (3) None of the preexisting "nonpacted" democracies survived the post–1964 wave of authoritarianism, not even the two which were considered especially firmly rooted; rather, Chile and Uruguay became cases of the more repressive and destructive bureaucratic-authoritarian regimes of the period. The political landscape of Latin America (aside from the revolutionary experiments of Cuba and Nicaragua) has been formed by a dismal collection of various types of authoritarian regimes, sparsely relieved by pacted, not very competitive, and socially restrictive democracies—and, underlying this uninspiring surface, the corpses of many abortive, nonpacted democracies.

In another bleak aside, it should be noted that, in the long run, these variations in regime type (except for the revolutionary experiments) do not seem to have had any significant effect on the great and increasing inequalities which characterize the economies and societies of Latin America. Neither a stable, well-institutionalized, and even popular regime like the Mexican, nor the pacted democracies of Colombia and Venezuela, have in that respect a better record than those countries which have alternated between various forms of authoritarianism and democracy. Admittedly, the social-equity record of nonpacted, demilitarized Costa Rican democracy has been better, but I must confess my inability to differentiate between the relative contributions of these competitive political institutions and those of other economic and social factors, such as the relatively egalitarian distribution of land that preceded the installation of democracy in Costa Rica.

It follows from the domestic dimensions I have discussed here that the prospects for political democracy in Latin America are not very favorable, certainly less so than in Southern Europe. Having said this, and having recognized that in most Latin American countries the dice are probably loaded in favor of repeated iterations of shaky and relatively short-lived democracy and ever-uglier authoritarian rule, I shall now allow myself to speculate in a more optimistic vein. My hopes are rooted in a subtle, but potentially powerful, factor. It consists of the fact that today, in most Latin American countries— especially those that have recently undergone or are still undergoing harsh authoritarian rule—there has emerged a new element. Largely as a consequence of the painful learning induced by the failures of those regimes and their unprecedented repression and violence, most political and cultural forces of any weight now attribute high intrinsic value to the achievement and consolidation of political democracy. This is indeed a novelty, and its consequences deserve to be explored.

To begin with, low probability does not mean impossibility. After all, many of the democratic regimes of the advanced capitalist countries, today so highly institutionalized and seemingly "natural" when seen from an ahistorical perspective, also had only a small a priori probability of emergence and consolidation. *Post facto* we can assess the factors that led to such an outcome, but contemporary actors were often far from recognizing or relying on them. Rather, what is striking in the emergence of today's consolidated democracies is the great uncertainty in which all actors had to function, the numerous unexpected and frequently unintended consequences that ensued from their choices, and, quite often, the pessimism they exhibited with regard to the likely direction in which their actions seemed to take them.

Most of these democracies emerged from a context well described in a model proposed by Robert Dahl.[5] After long and often violent struggles, the main political, social, and religious forces concluded that the costs of trying to eliminate each other exceeded the costs of tolerating each other's differences. This minimal agreement led to various institutional inventions which subsequently became the main channels for the mediation and attenuation of conflicts that previously had appeared to be unsolvable. Moreover, many of the actors involved in the transition were far from wishing such a democratic outcome, nor did they have what one could call a democratic set of attitudes. Simply, they had learned the high cost of trying to suppress their enemies and had concluded, in many cases with obvious reluctance, that it was in their own interest to try to achieve more cooperative forms of political and social interaction. It is also clear that, at the time, few people actually wanted political democracy or were aware of what it could mean. A majoritarian consensus, much less a deep understanding of political mechanisms and consequences, was not then—nor is it now—either a sufficient or a necessary condition for the emergence of democracy, although it may be a necessary condition for its consolidation and expansion.

These remarks suggest that it would be misleading to expect from contemporary cases of transition more than the low probability that we can recognize *post facto* accompanied the earlier emergence of democracy in Western Europe. However, the same historical hindsight teaches us that such outcomes were infrequent. There were many other instances where the contestants remained locked in conflict without reaching cooperative institutional arrangements. What made the difference? Without going into details that would greatly exceed the scope of this chapter, one necessary condition was met in those cases where enduring political democracies were installed. This condition is difficult to pin down empirically but not too hard to recognize: the ideological climate of the period was profoundly transformed by the forceful emergence of modes of thinking that postulated some pluralistic institutionalization of political life. Those discourses contrasted with the previously prevailing traditional and authoritarian views, which postulated unity or homogeneity as the exclusive basis for political order. The new world views may never have enjoyed majority support and were ambiguous with respect to specific institutions, but they gained in acceptance and prestige. Although they had many roots in the classic and medieval past, these ideas were one of the radical novelties introduced by the Enlightenment in Western Europe. They also influenced the foundation of democracy in the United States, even though it had to go through many avatars in both continents before finding recognizable and stable embodiment in political institutions and practices. Today, a similar ideological climate is no less of a radical novelty in Latin America.

The importance of the recent emergence of many "democracy-oriented" discourses in Latin America should not be underestimated. To insist on a point already made, until now this has not been a normal (or even a frequent) component of the cultural-ideological climate within which Latin American politics have unfolded. It is not surprising that, aside from structural factors unconducive to political democracy (basically those related to the acute social and economic inequalities in these countries), in the already-mentioned ideological climate, political democracy did not grow firm roots in Latin America. Indeed, this was true even during the previous "waves of democratization" that occurred after World War II and in the early 1960s. In those periods, as well as in earlier ones, even though in various Latin American countries democratic parties governed after winning reasonably competitive elections, they were continually weakened by two ideological factors. One of them was that most intellectuals—in what they wrote, said, and taught—both from the Left and the Right, were actively hostile to those exercises in political democracy. The second factor, closely related to the first, was the ambiguity and opportunism with which the parties of the Right, the Left and the Populists, and not few of the Centrists and Liberals assessed the very idea of political democracy. Thus, in Latin America, the field of prevailing ideas and symbols—with its crucial impact on what actors want and may be willing to try—was dominated until recently by discourses that diverged sharply in many respects but coincided in a profoundly authoritarian view of political and social life. This has changed in the last decade.[6]

Two interrelated facts offer Latin America an unprecedented (and profoundly paradoxical) opportunity in the present context. The first is that most of its countries have recently undergone, or are still undergoing, experiences of authoritarian rule that have been unusually repressive and socially regressive. The second refers to the no less unusually profound crisis that the economies of the region are suffering in the aftermath of (and, to a significant extent, as a consequence of) those same authoritarian experiences. Objectively, probabilistically, and trivially, these factors can only be seen as leading, at best, to the emergence of frail democracies, soon to be succeeded by the usual pendular return to authoritarianism.

There is no truly persuasive way to argue against this view. That the characteristics and experiences of the last wave of authoritarian rule are interpreted, for the first time, from a democratic perspective by most political and ideological currents in Latin America is certainly a major innovation; but this realm of ideas, understandings, and images may weigh less in the balance of forces than the "objective" factors I have reviewed in this chapter. Yet the profound and widespread discrediting of the recent authoritarian experience—as well as of the armed forces and of the reactionary ideologies that inspired them—together with the discrediting of the discourses and groups that propose an immediate and violent leap forward to some form of socialism, has made possible the sort of shift in outcome I am suggesting here. In other words, never has the ideological "prestige" of political democracy been higher in Latin America than now. Authoritarian ideas and institutions are now discredited. This is the terrain where that unpredictable combination of *virtù* on the part of leaders, and *fortuna* in the combination of circumstances, may make the crucial difference.

On the other hand, it should be pointed out that positive evaluation of political democracy per se and, especially, the fear of relapsing into authoritarian rule, may make democratic leaders excessively cautious on some crucial issues. These include how civilian governments select and implement policies aimed at alleviating the more pressing inequities of their countries, and how they maneuver the armed forces into a situation of reasonably effective subordination to their authority. Excessive caution in these domains may facilitate the transition to limited democracy (*democraduras*), but for the same reason it is likely to generate regimes too weak and too devoid of popular support to be viable in the medium and long run. In other words, there are no ready-made prescriptions for walking the narrow path that meanders between the risk of provoking an authoritarian reaction, on the one hand, and the risk of alienating most of the potential supporters of democracy, on the other.

It should be obvious that the reasons I have given for a moderate optimism about the prospects, both for the installation and the consolidation, of democracy in Latin America do not, and could not possibly, rely on the probabilistic logic normally used in the social sciences. But the present emphasis on "possibilism,"[7] with its consideration of the potentialities of purposive human action, is supported (or, at least, is not contradicted) by the conditions of emergence of what today are many of the more solidly established democracies in the world. Nothing better fits the spirit and intent of the argument presented in these pages than Max Weber's metaphor concerning levers on a railroad switch where a timely and purposive, but not superhuman, effort can change the direction of trains running at full speed. It seems to me that, in the unabashed mood of "thoughtful wishing" in which we approached our project, this is what the issue of democratization in contemporary Latin America is all about.

2 •

Political Cycles in Argentina since 1955

Marcelo Cavarozzi

Introduction

The civilian-military insurrection in Argentina that brought down the Peronist government in 1955 began a period characterized by political instability. None of three constitutional governments managed to complete its term, while four military administrations clearly failed either to accomplish their objectives or to impose their candidates for succession. With the repetition of a cycle of rise, crisis, and disintegration of both civilian and military governments, the surface of Argentine politics acquired a uniform texture in which each cycle was distinguished from its predecessor only by the increased violence and intensity it provoked. Explanations tend to characterize Argentine society as locked in a stalemate between social forces of similar strength capable of blocking the political projects of their antagonists but incapable of imposing their own. Thus, the images of blockage and social impasse are common to a group of interpretations, among which the most profound and suggestive is that put forward by O'Donnell in his "Estado y alianzas en la Argentina."[1]

This chapter presents a different level of analysis. It starts from the premise that the orientations, interests, and values of social forces do not exist in a vacuum, but in a specific field, which is a historically defined political system. Each political system has its own laws, which are not the result simply of the interrelation of attributes of the different social forces in the system. The "code" must be deciphered through an approach that recognizes the specific characteristics of the political system but also sets out to expose it, not by reducing it to the status of a mere reflection of "structural factors," nor by considering it as an inert field.

Analysis of the convulsive formation of new modes of political activity from 1955 onwards requires recognition of the complexity of a process which included, but was not limited to, a sequence of cycles of disarticulation and reformation of social alliances. The series of precarious balances thus generated were alternately broken and reestablished. Without this recognition, the images of stalemate and impasse might suggest an absence of change and, from a long-term perspective, a situation of immobility or even of complete circularity.

Argentine society after 1955 was characterized by a dynamic equilibrium composed of two distinct stages. The first, from 1955 to 1966, corresponded to the establishment of a dual political formula that helped give birth to a political balance in which impasses were generated mainly because each government represented a precarious compromise (and not because of antagonism between civilians and the military). Each government's ability to survive was in check from the very moment of its inauguration. In practice, each instituted mechanisms designed mainly to limit the actions of the various social contenders. A state of impasse was inherent in each government, as each was conditioned by external pressures and limited by its own internal heterogeneity. The second stage, from 1966 onwards, was dominated, in contrast, by successive attempts to unite the field of politics, which had been rent by schism during the previous decade. The failure of these attempts produced catastrophic outcomes resulting from each successive failure to break the impasse. As a consequence, the deployment and later blocking of successive initiatives brought the alteration and even collapse of basic patterns of organization and social interaction.

The two sections of the present chapter explore the characteristics of both stages. In the first stage, "weak" governments, civilian and military, predominated and attempted to found a semidemocratic regime. In some cases this was done by the proscription of Peronism; in others, by not questioning the proscription previously imposed.

The consequences of those semidemocratic government projects are noteworthy. A distinct style of societal functioning was defined during this period, in which the most profound economic, cultural, and corporate-institutional processes were fairly autonomous from transformational initiatives "from above." Rather, the dominant social tendencies resulted from the interrelation of the pressure, resistance, and struggle of the different actors of civil society. As a consequence, the different social actors perfected their ability to stifle actions from above during each new cycle. All this finally contributed to the constitution of a dual political system. In this system the non-Peronist parties and Parliament operated on one side. Neither these parties nor Parliament could, however, channel the interests and orientations of the fundamental social actors. On the other side, a system of extraparliamentary and extraparty negotiation and pressures operated; in this system, agreements were made and obligations were contracted. That is, the various actors often accepted cuts in their original demands while nevertheless letting it be known that their support for substantive agreements had been given reluctantly, and that they would not hesitate to break these agreements even at the risk of provoking a rupture in the institutional system. The dual political system was characterized by the fact that parliamentarianism and the party system generated their opposite pole by proscribing the Peronists and condemning them to work "outside," and by the fact that the participants in extraparliamentary negotiations used Parliament and the parties as a blackmail weapon, threatening through them to destabilize the government.

The second stage saw the predominance of "strong" governments, or at least governments which were inaugurated or defined themselves thus; these were governments which proposed radical changes in Argentine politics, and even in Argentine society, and which at the moment of their installation (in contrast to the governments of the previous period) enjoyed fairly broad support. Invariably these "strong" governments ended catastrophically. This was not a uniformly negative circumstance, however, for these failures generally expressed the ability of Argentine society to block authoritarian and repressive rule.[2] But in contrast to the previous period, the costs of preventing the consolidation of authoritarian systems far exceeded the costs provoked by the unstable political dualism of the period 1955–66.

Why were the political and social costs so much higher after 1966? There were two reasons. In the first place, as has already been suggested, the reformers and "revolutionaries" after 1966 were much more radical than their predecessors. This extremism was exacerbated from 1976 onwards, when the Argentine "problem" was diagnosed as a sick society, unresponsive to the cures applied to its "inadequate" political system. From 1966, in fact, "surgical" analyses predominated, identifying different illnesses—the crisis of authority (in society as well as the state), labor unrest, lack of class discipline. All agreed that the "cure" would require very deep incisions. Argentine society was then subjected to brutal "treatments" in which the generalization and extension of state repression, often conducted in violation of legal norms, was only one of the "remedies" applied. To state repression were added the drastic impoverishment of daily life experienced by the most diverse groups in civil society, in large part due to the fear that impregnated interpersonal relationships; the destruction of vast segments of the productive structure; and the dismantling of many basic cultural, professional, technical, and academic circuits. It should be pointed out, however, that the image of the need for "shock treatment" as the only viable prescription to overcome Argentina's problems was not simply the product of a fevered and barbaric political imagination. It was also efficiently reinforced by a society which increasingly conceived of itself as incapable of producing consensual solutions between counterposed interest groups. This collective abdication was often linked to the almost mythical belief that problems would be resolved through the magical appearance of some providential political force or actor. After 1966, the protagonists changed: the military, the guerrillas, and the liberal technocrats became the central players. Perón and even those behind the military adventurism of 1982 were elevated temporarily to leadership positions by various social sectors. Several of these leaders adopted a strategy which either ignored the underlying conflicts or tried to resolve them voluntaristically, disregarding the ability of social actors (generally of the opposition) to resist or block such approaches.

The second reason for the tragedy of the last fifteen years had to do with the conclusions drawn by the dominant political actors from their correct diagnoses of the dualism which had characterized Argentine politics prior to 1966. In effect, the political formulae from 1966 on proposed overcoming that dualism by unifying the political scene—channeling back into the institutional framework negotiation processes which had developed outside those institutions in the preceding period. The effect of these attempts was contrary to expectations. The military governments were unable to contain politics within the narrow limits of a corporatist framework; the Peronist government was unable to channel diverse pressures and interests in an orderly fashion through the Parliament or the Social Pact. Nevertheless, the consequences of the projects of 1966, 1973, and 1976 were to block those channels through which politics had flowed prior to 1966. Political activity was once again transferred outside the institutions and conducted in an increasingly savage manner. The different actors rapidly dispensed with previously accepted "rules of the game" and adopted strategies in which progressively less attention was paid to the destructive consequences of their individual actions (both in relation to "others" and to the collective whole).

Let us now examine the characteristics of the two stages involved.

The Failure of "Semidemocracy" and Its Legacies

In 1955, a civilian-military insurrection put an end to ten years of Peronist government. The insurrection did not just overthrow Perón: it also dismantled the political model which had prevailed throughout the preceding decade. The Peronist model, based on the direct relationship between leader and masses, had made Perón the sole trustee of popular representation. Perón's personalism produced a permanent demotion of the parliamentary and party channels of political expression. Moreover, Peronism in power tended to consider the activities of the opposition parties (and of non-Peronist unions and professional organizations) as manifestations of illegitimate sectoral interests. Consequently, the government increasingly blocked such activities, both within and outside Parliament.

The leaders of the 1955 *coup* characterized the Peronist regime as a totalitarian dictatorship and raised the banners of democracy and liberty, putting forward as their objective the reestablishment of parliamentary rule and the party system. This objective, however, was repeatedly frustrated: in 1957 the Constituent Assembly, controlled by the non-Peronist parties, could not agree on a new constitution and dissolved without achieving any reform of the outdated nineteenth-century document; in 1962 the military, with the support of several parties, deposed President Frondizi, who had been constitutionally elected four years earlier; in 1966, the military intervened again to overthrow another constitutional government, this time of President Illía.

In 1955–58 and 1962–63, the interregnum between constitutional governments was occupied by military governments. These, however, did not propose to replace parliamentary democracy with an alternative political regime, nor to postpone it until a distant future, reached only after certain social or economic changes had been achieved. Rather, the main and self-proclaimed objectives of these governments were the imposition of measures to proscribe Peronism while simultaneously attempting to eradicate it. Peronism was seen as a phenomenon which was inherently and irremediably opposed to democratic values and institutions: if allowed to act freely, it would deform and even destroy them.

The application of a new political formula after 1955 was a truly convulsive and frustrating process. However, the failure to achieve institutional stability during these years did not prevent the emergence of new modes of political activity which implied a profound redefinition of the processing of socioeconomic conflicts. These new modes of political articulation unfolded gradually during the decade following Perón's fall, but they did not give rise to an institutional formula which could produce political stability. Rather they left a political-ideological legacy with which old and new political actors were obliged to struggle from 1966 onwards.

This section analyzes the way in which these new modes of political activity developed. Three of the most important elements are explored: (1) the appearance of significant imbalances between socioeconomic interests on one side, and political blocks on the other; (2) the formation of a Peronist union movement with new characteristics, which constituted an autonomous political force and progressively articulated a defensive and oppositionist strategy; (3) the entry of the military into the political arena, where initially it assumed a tutelary role in the framework of semidemocratic regimes, and later expanded its sphere of intervention, intending to dispense with democratic practices and parliamentary institutions.

Argentina after 1955: A Disarticulated Political Community

The overthrow of the Peronist government was supported by a broad political front which included all the non-Peronist parties, the corporate and ideological representatives of the urban and rural middle classes and bourgeoisie, the armed forces, and the church. The various members of the anti-Peronist front all sought different objectives. Nevertheless, the front was able to maintain its unity for a time under the flag of "democracy," which was raised in contrast to the dictatorial or totalitarian character attributed to the Peronist regime.

Many anti-Peronists shared the rather naive notion that Peronists had subscribed to their particular political creed as a result of demagoguery, illusion, and force. Consequently, the anti-Peronists believed that mere denunciation of the "crimes of the dictatorship," accompanied by collective reeducation, would result in the gradual reabsorption of ex-Peronists into "democratic" parties and unions. This illusion was short-lived; Peronism survived the fall of its government and became the source of a vigorous opposition movement. In the short term, however, this illusion effectively allowed the anti-Peronists to proclaim that the proscription of Peronism was an essentially democratic act. Indeed, this was the justification for the electoral proscription of Peronism, which placed between one third and one half of all Argentine citizens beyond the political pale.

The corollary of Peronism's exclusion, both from the electoral field and from that of legal political action, was particularly complex. It introduced a profound disjunction between society and the working of politics in Argentina which resulted in the gradual emergence of a dual political system. Parliamentary mechanisms operated in conflict with extrainstitutional modes of political activity. The main result of this dualism was that the two principal social "blocks"—the popular sector and the anti-Peronist front, made up of the bourgeois and middle-class sectors—rarely shared the same political arena. Thus, the popular sector—particularly the working class, which had been represented primarily through Peronism—was left without representation either in the semidemocratic parliamentary institutions or in the state's institutional machinery. By contrast, their social adversaries, who had been the victims of a partial political ostracism during the Peronist era, had access both to parliamentary and extrainstitutional mechanisms, exercising decisive influence in policy decisions. The popular sector exerted pressure mainly through extrainstitutional channels and the Peronist union movement progressively transformed itself into the most powerful organized expression of that sector.

Ultimately, however, popular pressure was limited to its ability to destabilize, from outside the official political framework, each of the civilian and military regimes of the period. This destabilization was achieved both by the presentation of economic demands which contradicted and undermined the viability of stabilization policies launched between 1956 and 1963, and also through the support given to antiofficialist candidates in national, provincial, and local elections.

The term "disjunction" can be used to describe the limited rapport between social alignments and conflicts on the one hand, and institutional modes of political activity on the other. To this state of disjunction was added an exacerbating "twist." Originally, the social block which opposed the popular sectors expressed itself through the non-Peronist parties and the "democratic" military that had triumphed in 1955. Gradually, however, non-Peronist parties and the military became antagonistic toward one another, for two reasons.

First, the "democratic" officers of 1955 increasingly shed their "democratic vocation" and favored the establishment of authoritarian regimes. This authoritarian "slide" on the part of the military led it into increasing confrontation with the parties. Despite the fact that the parties had not renounced their anti-Peronist stance, they came to oppose the military because their own *raison d'être* was linked to a democratic-parliamentary system and the conservation of a minimum of public liberties. The second factor which complicated relations between the military and the politicians was that non-Peronist parties became the main filter for two central controversies which arose in 1955, after Perón's fall. In that year, the anti-Peronist front had coalesced around the purpose of destroying the Peronist regime. This front began to collapse, however, when the time came to exercise power.

The first of the controversies which was to dominate the political scene developed around the government's role in the eradication of Peronism. Positions ranged from "integrationism"—which favored the gradual reabsorption of Peronism into political life, while stressing the need to purge it of its most "damaging" aspects, including Perón himself—to *gorilismo*, which demanded "the total extirpation of the Peronist cancer" from Argentine society. The second controversy evolved around the socioeconomic model that would presumably replace the 1945–55 model. In 1955, the victorious anti-Peronist front was united in condemnation of the economic problems which Argentina had faced since the late 1940s; initially the front found it easy to identify a series of ineffective policies and a corrupt administration as the main sources of the difficulties facing the country. However, this ephemeral unity died when contradictory diagnoses of the Argentine economic crisis began to emerge.

From 1956 three different positions within the anti-Peronist camp gradually emerged: reformist populism, developmentalism, and liberalism. The first of these did not question the premises of the economic model of the Peronist decade. On the contrary, it encouraged the possibility of simultaneously promoting the interests of the working class and those of the urban bourgeoisie, while also proposing a moderately nationalist policy to limit foreign capital in sectors such as energy, communications, and the production of capital goods. This position made only two important criticisms of the Peronist government's economic policies. On the one hand, pointing to the stagnation in agricultural production during Perón's regime, reformist populism held that his policies had discouraged production in that sector. On the other hand, this position argued that there had been a failure to promote heavy industry and to develop the economic infrastructure, while a disproportionate increase in the state's current expenditures had resulted in delaying investment in public works.[3]

The slogans of reformist populism were promoted by the Radicales, who had become the only organized party opposition after 1946. That party divided in two in 1956: one wing, the Intransigente or Frondizista, favored the gradual legalization of Peronism; the other wing, the Radicales del Pueblo (the Popular Radicals), remained close to the hardline, proscriptive position of the military. In any case, the majority factions of both new parties maintained their adhesion to the Radical party program, which proposed a series of nationalist and reformist measures.

When the Intransigente leader, Arturo Frondizi, was elected president in 1958, he radically redefined the party's economic orientation, articulating a "developmentalist" position. The other wing of the party, the Popular Radicals, however, continued to support the tenets of reformist populism.

By comparison with reformist populism and developmentalism (depicted below), the liberal position went much further in its criticism of the process of industrialization and of the social and political practices associated with it, not only criticizing the model of class conciliation, but also questioning the premise that industrial development should constitute the dynamic nucleus of a closed economy. Liberals argued that since the 1930s, and particularly after 1946, Argentina had been faced with two critical problems: the progressive deterioration of labor discipline and the inefficiency of large portions of the industrial sector. They traced the root of the problems to two sources: the policies which had closed the economy—thus favoring the proliferation of "artificial" industries—and the excessive growth of the state. The image of the market became, in two ways, the cornerstone of the liberal position. First, it implied the opening of the Argentine economy and its reentry into the international market, by reducing tariffs and eliminating other "distortions" that protected the "artificial" sectors. Second, it proposed a drastic reduction of state intervention in the economy and the restoration of important incentives for private-sector initiative.

As has already been pointed out, each of these three positions was in favor of dissimilar and frequently opposing economic policies. Such political divisions and alliances naturally responded to the calculations made about the impact of economic policies on each social class. The presence of the proscribed Peronist movement influenced the political arena in indirect and contradictory ways. The implicit Peronist presence was the key to determining the positions taken during this period by the social and political organizations of all three anti-Peronist groups.

After 1955 the political parties, corporate organizations, and ideological currents through which reformist populism, developmentalism, and liberalism found expression entered numerous alliances and conflicts. Two factors in particular, as we have suggested, determined both the support which these parties and organizations enjoyed, and the opposition they provoked: (1) the predictions about the consequences of the implementation of the alternative economic policies in relation to each class or social sector's economic interests; and (2) the way in which each party's rhetoric, platform, and ideology alluded to the Peronist question. Such allusions, in turn, referred to the two main political-institutional manifestations of the Peronist identity of the popular sectors: the political exclusion that they suffered as citizens and their strong adhesion to a union movement that defined itself as a part of Peronism and not just as a network of working-class organizations.[4]

Argentine politics in 1955–66 were further complicated by the predicted effects of applying alternative economic policies and by the debate over strategies to exclude or reincorporate Peronism into the legal political system. The interests of respective members of political coalitions were sometimes at odds on one of the two issues. This complex interrelation was determined mainly by the swings of those parties, business organizations, and military sectors which adhered to the liberal position.

These liberal swings responded, in part, to a relatively accidental circumstance: from the liberal perspective, the programs of the parties which had given birth to reformist populism (Radicales del Pueblo) and to developmentalism (Radicales Intransigentes) combined politics and the economy in a contradictory and unsatisfactory way. From as early as 1956, significant sectors of the Popular Radicals had defended reformist and nationalist economic policies no different from those applied during the first stage of the Peronist regime. With respect to the Peronists, however, the Popular Radicals tended toward *gorilismo:* they supported the electoral proscription of Peronism until the beginning of the 1960s and favored a system of union affiliation which would have meant the atomization of the working-class corporate organization. The latter policy was naturally opposed by the predominantly Peronist union leadership. The formula of the Intransigentes was almost diametrically opposed to that of their old comrades-in-arms. Beginning in 1958, when Frondizi assumed the presidency, the Intransigentes advocated expansion of industries producing consumer durables and capital goods, as well as the modernization and increasing privatization of the energy, transport, and communications sectors, reserving a strategic role for foreign capital and initially imposing a drastic reduction in real wages. The Intransigentes, however, never abandoned the "integrationist" aims they had announced in 1956. They tried to reinforce Peronist predominance in the union movement while also inducing union leaders to act "responsibly," which meant controlling the "excessive" wage demands of the rank and file, and distancing themselves from Perón's leadership.

With the Peronists excluded, the two Radical parties were the only significant electoral forces in the late 1950s and early 1960s. The liberal position lacked the possibility of expression through a strong Conservative party with a real chance of winning a presidential election, or even of obtaining a significant parliamentary representation. The internal coherence of the liberal programs was offset by its tremendous electoral weakness. The three proposals at the core of the liberal program had won wide support from the Argentine bourgeoisie: (1) to eradicate Peronism and pulverize Peronist unionism; (2) to reduce state interventionism drastically; and (3) to eliminate inefficient industrial sectors. This platform did not, however, win votes. After 1955, consequently, the liberals faced the fact that the defeat of Peronism would not alone resolve their political problems. Thus they were continually forced to choose between two lesser evils—developmentalism and reformist populism—and to modify their assessment repeatedly.

In periods like 1959–61, when the liberals chose to give priority to their economic objectives, they tended to form alliances—albeit unstable ones—with developmentalists. Although both liberals and developmentalists agreed on the need to apply stabilization programs based on sharp devaluations and wage freezes, they could not agree on long-term economic strategy. Therefore, the very success of the stabilization program implemented during those years made their deeper conflicts more manifest. Moreover, since the developmentalists never abandoned their "integrationism," the liberals were frequently offended by the conciliatory attitudes of the developmentalists toward Peronist union leaders. The Frondizi government's refusal to dismantle the CGT, and its machinations over the proscription of the Peronists in legislative and provincial elections, sharpened the tension between liberals and developmentalists. The liberals, as a consequence, were often inclined to emphasize their anti-Peronism, as they did in 1956–58 and, less clearly, in 1962–63—which led them into alliance with reformist populists. But this was also a less than satisfactory alternative. Both in 1958 and in 1962 the Popular Radicals' platform was anti-Peronist and anti-integrationist, but their economic policy was diametrically opposed to the liberals. Each time the reformist populists applied their economic program—as happened partially in 1956 and more clearly between 1963 and 1966—the liberals were alienated by its resemblance to Peronist policies.

Consequently, the alternating direction of the liberal swing constituted one of the determining features of the disjunction affecting the anti-Peronists throughout this period. At the same time, however, the liberals exercised only minimal influence on the political and economic course. Although they were initially able to impose stabilization programs, they were later obliged to renounce their long-term objectives. Furthermore, they were successful in achieving the proscription of Peronism, but they failed to gain control of the semidemocratic regime they had founded.

The liberals became increasingly aware that their long-term goals—the eradication of Peronism, and the rectification of the statist and proindustrialist economic orientation—were not well served by their continuous swings. Toward the mid-1960s, this growing awareness was a decisive factor in inducing the liberals to opt for an openly antidemocratic strategy. Such a strategy emphasized the need to eliminate those political mediations, parties, and parliamentary mechanisms which had supposedly prevented the implementation of the liberal program for more than a decade. Thus, between 1964 and 1966, in contrast with the Frondizi period, the liberals' renewed emphasis on their economic objectives did not lead to a new alliance with the developmentalist wing of the political spectrum. By that time the liberals were convinced that they had to sever their links with the non-Peronist parties in order to attain both their economic and political objectives.

The Peronist Unions in Opposition

The attempt by the military regime in 1955–58 to found a political regime based on parties and the strengthening of parliamentary mechanisms failed completely. Nevertheless, the attempt had significant consequences for Argentine society. In the policies of the 1955–58 government toward the working class and in labor relations, a similar situation arose: the military regime failed in its attempts to eradicate Peronism from the working class. Likewise, the regime did not manage to create a multiple union affiliation and representation system to replace that established by Peronist law in the 1940s. Despite this failure, these attempts did produce important changes within the labor movement after 1955.

In the first place, the style of political control of the working class established during the Peronist era was radically modified. This style had been based on the state's benevolent tutelage of the working class and on the union movement's ideological subordination to Perón. Moreover, the Peronist leaders who had controlled the unions until 1955 were, with a few exceptions, effectively displaced and never regained their earlier influence. In the second place, the military's frustrated project created the conditions for an entirely different Peronist union movement which gained a certain amount of independence from Perón and was able to develop its own political strategy.

Although neither Perón nor Peronism disappeared from the Argentine political scene after 1955, Perón's role did shift significantly. On the one hand, the nature of Perón's link with the popular masses changed, since he could no longer satisfy their demands nor appeal directly to them. Instead, Perón himself emerged as the main symbol of a return to a better past and constituted Peronism's greatest attraction for the masses, and in particular for the working class. On the other hand, Perón was less able to control the Peronist leaders. Some provincial politicians (especially in zones away from the metropolitan areas and the pampa region) and union leaders generated their own power bases, giving them the space to challenge occasionally the authority of the "leader." Although the most explicit challenges to Perón's authority failed, his power to prevent expressions of rebellion within Peronism was considerably reduced.

Open challenges to Perón's authority were not the only manifestation of the changes which his leadership suffered after 1955. The always ambiguous Peronist ideology increasingly began to reflect the correlation of forces within the movement. A Peronism less subordinated to Perón's authority and reflecting more directly the relative weights of its constituent social forces became an increasingly proletarian Peronism. This gradual transformation was assisted by an additional factor: Whenever the electoral proscription was lifted—even if only partially—the union leaders' sphere of influence was considerably expanded through the ballot box. The workers' vote was thus transformed into an instrument of pressure and negotiation comparable to strikes and stoppages. Moreover, in contrast to Perón and the Peronist politicians, the union leaders retained the option of collective bargaining. As a result, the Peronist union leaders developed a skill which they had lacked before 1955: the ability to negotiate with non-Peronist groups such as parties, business organizations, and the military.

Thus, after 1955, the Peronist union movement's power was both more extensive and distinctly based. But how did the union movement use its redefined and increased power? The Peronist union members of the post-1955 era operated in a society which resembled less and less the Argentina of the 1945–55 period. Yet the discourse of Peronist unionism continued to demand the restoration of conditions which had reigned prior to 1955. These conditions were, in part, real features of Argentina in the 1945–55 period and also, in part, a distillation of Peronism's ideological vision: the alliance between the national bourgeoisie and the working class under the protective tutelage of the state; redistributive economic policies; nationalism; the definition of the (agrarian) oligarchy as the main social adversary of the "popular and national" forces; and Perón's power to arbitrate.

The unifying symbol of the recovery of the lost Golden Age was, of course, Perón's return to Argentina . . . and to power. However, the return of Perón, and of Peronist Argentina, was transformed from the fundamental political objective of the Peronist union movement into a myth which fulfilled two functions. First, it allowed the union leaders to address workers as Peronists, thus salvaging a base for their collective identity that was not erased by successive post-Peronist regimes. Second, the proclaimed adhesion to a political objective which, in the context of Argentina between 1955 and 1966, was considered unattainable by all the major political actors—including Peronist—freed the unionists from the responsibility of recognizing the consequences and the more concrete political corollaries of their strategy. Such a recognition would have forced them to moderate their own economic demands. In this sense, Peronist unionism was not merely economistic, as some have argued; in it, rather, economic and political objectives were intertwined in a peculiar way.

Although the demands made by the Peronist unions were economic and corporate, they often carried political overtones. The unions argued that the economic and labor policies of the non-Peronist regimes not only damaged the immediate interests of workers but also undermined the possibility of a return to the Peronist Golden Age. The Argentine bourgeoisie made the appropriate connection between the Peronist union's economic and corporate program and the possible resurrection of an era, but attached very different connotations to the message.

The political practices of the union movement combined two elements: (1) a pattern of sporadic penetration into the mechanisms of parliamentary representation which was manifested through the limited but not insignificant ability of the union leaders to influence the electoral behavior of workers; and (2) a long-term process of attrition, intended to cast doubts on the political legitimacy of those political regimes which excluded Peronism.

The governments of the 1955–66 period, civilian and military, were weakened by the effects of one of their own operating axioms: Peronism's exclusion from the legal political scene. In effect, this exclusion meant that the political ability of the working class to obtain concessions increased in proportion to the formal rules it broke. As a result, the Peronist union movement became, as some of its opponents complained, a subversive force. This subversion, however, was not concerned with questioning capitalist social relations; it was, rather, a reflection of the fact that the unions, like other groups, broke the system's formal rules as a last resort. In reality, the destabilizing effect of union actions was always indirect and impacted especially upon the armed forces. The unionists were instrumental in creating circumstances which, in some cases, persuaded the military to depose civilian administrations. In other cases, they frustrated the aims of military regimes, thereby leading the military to abandon power in order to avoid situations which appeared to require the application of massive repressive measures.

The Peronist union movement's strategy had one important advantage: its power materialized, to a large extent, through the actions of other groups, allowing the unionists to dissociate themselves from the undesirable consequences of the repeated cycles of military coups and withdrawals from power between 1955 and 1966. The union strategy had, moreover, two other characteristics. On the one hand, the use of other actors as "intermediaries" through which the unions' objectives were achieved created conflicts which in turn led to changes in the union position. On the other hand, the union movement's power concealed its inability to formulate a coherent diagnosis of, and a response to, the structural crisis that had affected the Argentine economy since the late 1940s.

Finally, this defensive capacity allowed the union movement to block the implementation of economic stabilization policies which reduced real wages and encouraged an increase in private investment. From 1959 on, the unions mustered their forces only after the stabilization policies had achieved some "success" in reducing real wages and repressing workers' demands. Consequently, the union movement's defensive capacity was manifested mainly through "counterattacks." The success of these counterattacks may have prevented the complete execution and consolidation of the projects of stabilization and growth of the late 1950s and early 1960s, but they could not reverse the significant transformations in the Argentine economy that occurred after 1959.

The Military of the Post-1955 Period: New Styles of Political Intervention

The military was the third important element of the political formula to emerge after 1955. The success of that year's military insurrection started a new pattern of military intervention in Argentine politics. Before 1955 the military's involvement in public affairs had not normally extended beyond leadership of certain state enterprises. Nor had military leaders proposed to institutionalize nondemocratic regimes permanently controlled by the armed forces. From 1955 on, the military gradually modified that pattern of intervention. To begin with, they developed a style of tutelary intervention which resulted in Peronism's exclusion from the electoral process and from the state's representative institutions, and in the exercise of their power to veto the political measures and initiatives of the constitutional government installed in 1958 and to impose their own preferences. The military therefore restricted democratic practices and principles in two ways. They denied a significant part of the electorate the right to elect candidates of their own choice, and they repeatedly threatened to depose the constitutional authorities if their demands were not met. Peronism and, after 1959, Communism were equated with "antidemocracy," and the actions taken against Peronists, Communists, and those politicians and public functionaries who supported or tolerated them were justified with the argument that such actions were necessary to protect democracy.

In the early 1960s, important sectors of the armed forces began to realize that the benefits obtained through tutelary intervention did not justify the costs involved. The military call to support "democratic" political organizations had limited the armed forces to the political alternatives offered by the parties thus classified. At the same time, the armed forces bore the responsibility for the distortion of democratic practices in the public eye, while they could not claim the compensatory benefit of having achieved their aims. Moreover, the high degree of military involvement in public matters implied that they frequently adopted specific positions on matters of economic policy, political repression, labor legislation, and similar questions which generated deep internal fragmentation. Internal dissent and fragmentation most often emerged when different sectors of the armed forces could not agree on the type of pressures to be exerted on the constitutional authorities, or on the policies to be applied in relation to the Peronist unions and party. Military fragmentation reached its most crucial point between 1959 and 1963, when, on two occasions, disagreements culminated in armed confrontations. The victory of one of these military factions in 1963—the *azules* (the "blues")—and General Onganía's emergence as the unquestioned strongman of the army, cleared the way for a profound reevaluation of the military's political strategy.[5] As a consequence, the practice of tutelary intervention was abandoned. From 1963 on, with the advent of the Popular Radicals to power, the military largely suspended their interference in government affairs. However, as events would soon demonstrate, the armed forces had not suddenly decided to subordinate themselves strictly to the constitutional authorities. On the contrary, the "professionalist" interlude of 1963–66—and the parallel reunification of the army, and of all the armed forces around Onganía—paved the way for the doctrine of "national security." As a corollary of this doctrine, the armed forces assumed sole responsibility for the interpretation of the national interest, with the consequent exclusion of the political parties and the abolition of elections and of parliamentary mechanisms.

At some point in the mid-1960s, Onganía and his associates decided that the semidemocratic experiment begun in 1955 should be concluded. From a military point of view, the experiment had two drawbacks: (1) it encouraged military fragmentation, and (2) it inhibited sustained economic growth because it led politicians to limit themselves to the advance of short-term demands from the various social sectors. In addition, it was argued that military fragmentation and the unchecked proliferation of social conflicts provided a fertile ground for subversion.

The diagnosis made by the military factions predominant in 1966 had deep repercussions in the whole of Argentine society. The liberal groups, in particular, welcomed the antiparty position adopted by the armed forces, since by the rules of electoral politics, the liberals were forced to choose between equally unsatisfactory alternatives. Therefore, the option of a military coup and the possibility of founding a permanent and stable nondemocratic regime were tempting. This option might not only resolve the problem of their endemic lack of votes, but might also enable them to deal a final, decisive blow to the Peronist unions.

In 1966 the messages of the military led by Onganía were welcomed not only by the liberals but also, paradoxically, by the Peronist union movement—and in particular by its dominant current, the followers of the powerful leader Augusto Vandor (Vandoristas). The support by both the liberals and Peronist unionists for the 1966 military coup reflected two things: the initial ambiguity of Onganía's proposals on questions of economic policy, and the possibility—which the Vandoristas found particularly attractive—of establishing an authoritarian corporatist regime. One of the principal Peronist leaders of 1957–66 alluded graphically to these coincidences:

> The union movement in developing countries should be verticalist like the structured bodies—the Church, the Army, the family—as this is the only effective way to lobby and avoid disorder, which can arise both from the businessman's uncontrolled desire for profit and from the worker's unchecked demands. Moreover, in Argentina, a verticalist movement recovers the *caudillo* tradition. The union movement, therefore should operate under the official aegis. The state should be the protecting father, just as it is for industry, commerce and agriculture.[6]

A political agreement with the *golpista* military became increasingly tempting for union leaders, linked to a political movement whose electoral proscription was becoming an established fact of Argentine politics. The "workers' intervention in the country's future economic orientation," which the Peronist unionists had been demanding since 1957, seemed attainable only through channels which bypassed the electoral route. The presence of military officers who condemned both Peronism and the party game *in toto*, and also responded to nationalist, statist, and anti-big capital slogans was seen by the Peronist unionists as the possible catalyst of a nonparliamentary political regime which might cement an alliance between the armed forces and the unions which they considered to have been frustrated in 1955.

Military Predominance and the Deepening of Authoritarianism

As pointed out in the introduction, the political formulae tried out from 1966 onwards had a markedly more comprehensive character than those applied by the military and constitutional governments of the 1955–66 period. In the decade following Perón's overthrow, each institutional break contributed to the establishment of a mode of political activity in permanent crisis within the relatively modest bounds set by the politicians and the military. The former wanted to consolidate a democracy but were unable to incorporate Peronism fully, and the latter tried to reserve powers of veto and tutelage but did not advocate a stable authoritarian regime dominated by the armed forces.

After 1966 the pattern of alternating military and civilian governments continued; however, its resemblance to the previous decade was superficial. In spite of the collapse of the projects of 1966, 1973, and 1976, each change of government introduced significant innovations and was associated with a break in previous modes of political activity. Thus, the return to relative balance occurred through the unfolding and exhaustion of the respective political formulae; in each case the balance brought substantial redefinitions of the political scene. The social mobilizations of 1969–73, the militarization of politics and the massive, illegal state repression begun in 1974 and accentuated in 1976, and the profound economic crisis unleashed after 1981 are all examples of the process.

Since 1966, then, there has been no common mode of political activity, as in the previous period. Despite a certain continuity from 1966 to the present, the political resources of the central actors have been redefined drastically with each institutional break. To clarify this point, the remainder of this chapter will analyze each period of government separately, after which I will underline central characteristics of current Argentine politics, focusing on possible courses of action confronting central players in the future.

The 1966 Coup: Administration Supplants Politics

The "professionalization" of the armed forces undertaken by General Onganía culminated in the military coup of June 1966, in implicit alliance with the liberals and the labor movement. The objectives of the "Revolución Argentina" were twofold: on the one hand, the suspension *sine die* of the activities of political parties and of parliamentary institutions; on the other, the express divorce of the armed forces from government, whereby the armed forces "would neither govern nor co-govern."[7] The attempt to eradicate democracy by party rule (*partidocracia*) was accompanied by the hope that the leader of the armed forces, Onganía, would be a sort of autocratic monarch in a regime whose sole political actor would be the government. Thus, with (military and social) unity achieved, politics would give way to administration; technicians, situated above sectoral interest, would predominate. The institutional formula of the Revolución Argentina was also colored by a corporativist rhetoric emphasizing the gradual articulation of "community councils," which would channel social activities and serve as advisory bodies for the authorities.

The central theme in Onganía's program was the renovation (and simplification) of Argentine politics. It responded to the conviction that Argentina's problem was fundamentally a political one, and proposed to accelerate economic growth by dispensing with the inefficient and potentially dangerous intermediation of party, parliamentary, and corporate circuits. On the economic front, the Onganía government's formula contained little that was new, consisting mainly of a reworking, with some modifications, of the developmentalist prescriptions which had prevailed until 1962.

For a couple of years the regime achieved important economic successes: stabilization without excessively high social costs; increased investment; decreased inflation; and improvement in the balance of payments. It also notched up a series of political triumphs: the parties became irrelevant and inactive; the unions were forced to accept the abolition of the right to strike (as a result of the August 1966 law of mandatory arbitration). In addition, the government took over the most important industrial unions, owing to the failure of the 1967 "Plan of Action," and Perón was apparently stripped of all the resources which he had employed so effectively between 1955 and 1966 to destabilize civilian and military governments. For a time it seemed that a harmonious decision-making system was being created, whose central protagonists were economic policy-makers from senior posts in state institutions and managers of the large companies.

Nevertheless, between late 1966 and mid-1969 relatively novel phenomena appeared, the repercussions of which would become manifest only after May 1969. The first was the growth of internal divisions within the armed forces—paternalists, nationalists, and liberals.[8] The underlying causes of such divisions were not new, but what did change radically after 1966 was the fact that dissent within the forces acquired an institutional framework, which excluded the kind of conspiratorial gymnastics they had used between 1955 and 1966 in opposition to constitutional regimes and within temporary de facto governments. In addition, the armed forces were prohibited from participating directly in governmental tasks. The combined effect was that both the military's internal conflicts and its contacts with key outsiders were disauthorized, and increasingly took place underground. The predictable consequence was that the military *caudillo* of the three previous years became progressively isolated from his comrades-in-arms. Moreover, Onganía's rigid personality limited his ability to compromise or negotiate in response to pressures from comrades.

The second area of significant modification occurred in spheres of civil society that had been controlled before 1966 by restrained but extrainstitutional pressures, whereby civil organizations such as the unions and employers' associations moved outside the government's institutional channels while trying to control the mobilization of their own members. Once this aim had been generally attained, workers' and employers' mobilizations and collective actions were generally subjected to top-level negotiations in which the respective corporate organizations aimed to reinforce their stability and the authority of their leaders. Within this scheme, the leaders tended to use the threat of mobilization as a form of pressure against other actors and against the state.

The antiunion measures taken from late 1966 on aimed not to eradicate the unions or their leaders, but to force them to accept government policies. The success of the official strategy of intransigence dealt a further blow to the union leadership's faltering control over rank-and-file workers, a process which had been underway since before the June 1966 coup. This was partly a result of the policy of large companies of promoting "one-company unions," which undermined the possibility of national wage agreements, and partly because of the Popular Radical government's strategy of deliberately favoring union pluralism in order to weaken the Peronist unions. In 1968, cracks began to appear in a union movement that had since the late 1950s been relatively united behind Vandor. Between 1959 and 1966, Vandorismo had maintained power in the CGT by subordinating Peronist and non-Peronist unions to a common strategy. In 1968–69, Vandorismo lost that ability as it was out-flanked by the Right and bypassed by the Left. In March 1968, the devaluation of the unions' negotiating strategy made way for the appointment of Raimundo Ongaro, a printworker, as secretary general of the CGT, in a "nor-malizing" congress called without government recognition. Vandor's forces were defeated by a heterogeneous mix of hardline Peronists (influenced by "Christian Left" ideology), progressive independents, and Marxists hostile to Communist party lines. Vandor immediately convoked a second congress which elected a new executive committee; thus, two rival CGTs came into being. Partly because of state repression and partly because of its own erratic tactics, Ongaro's "CGT de los Argentinos" rapidly lost the support of the majority of its original members. Nevertheless, its frontal opposition to the Onganía regime and its condemnation of the tactics of soft-liners and Van-doristas emphasized its anticapitalist stance. Thus it retained appeal at the plant level and in some regional federations in the country's interior. The discourse of the CGT de los Argentinos became, in short, an ideological and "practical" tool which could be appropriated by other protagonists in massive collective actions.

The popular insurrection of 1969, which culminated in the *Cordobazo*, fused together blue- and white-collar workers, students, and the urban poor. As O'Donnell points out, their actions "in part expressed, and in part released the tensions which had been mounting up since the installation of the [mili-tary government]."[9]

Onganía had attempted to close down the institutional and extrainstitu-tional social and political mechanisms through which compromise had been possible and had sought instead to control the various interests via a suppos-edly omniscient and hierarchical state. This program brought about the very outcome it had hoped to avoid. On the one hand, the spontaneous popular explosion illustrated the government's isolation from society. On the other, the armed forces were unwilling to use greater repression against those explo-sions in spite of Onganía's pressures. The nobility of Onganía's government was irremediably undermined. Thus, 1969 initiated a period unprecedented in Argentine history, in which the authority of many leaders in civil society was profoundly questioned. Union leaders most inclined to negotiation and most dependent upon state tutelage, teachers and university and school authorities who had been promoted by the traditionalist and hierarchical orientations of the Onganía government, the conservative hierarchy of the Catholic church, and managers and employers in the business sector all fell within this category.

From the *Cordobazo* until the fall of Onganía's ephemeral successor, General Levingston, the sharpening crisis of the military regime strengthened the threats posed to the foundations of social domination. First, Onganía's stubbornness in salvaging his scheme and then Levingston's attempt to "deepen" the Revolución Argentina in a nationalist direction alienated the majority of their comrades and accentuated the social crisis. Antiauthoritarian discourse was increasingly fused with the discourse of three other groups: (1) those who had questioned the "liberal" economic policies which had harmed the interests of public and private employees; small and medium employers; workers in more traditional industries and services who had been hurt by the military governments' modernizing programs; and the population of regions like Tucumán, affected by economic rationalization programs; (2) those who had called for the political liberalization of the military regime, and now demanded full democratization and elections without proscriptions of any kind; (3) those, concentrated around the incipient Peronist guerrillas, who promoted an armed popular insurrection, advocating a nonparliamentary and "national socialist" social and political structure.

The sharpening of the crisis accelerated the breakdown in the system of political practices built up after 1966. When the fear and political passivity imposed by the three-year dictatorship had been shaken off, the regime suddenly lost its momentum, although alternative government projects were blocked. This impasse became increasingly dangerous. The bourgeoisie were alarmed by proposals which increasingly diverged from the Krieger Vasena stabilization scheme, while radical watchwords reached their peak in early 1971, at the second *Cordobazo*, which was more classist and insurrectionist than the first. In fact, it became clear that the military government had to withdraw, admitting its failure and recognizing that the social balance had to be restored through a political liberalization (*abertura*) that would address the demands of the opposition forces. During the last year of Onganía's government, a sort of liberalization around the figure of ex-president Aramburu had been proposed. However, Aramburu's assassination by Peronist guerrillas in May 1970 precipitated the fall of Onganía. After Aramburu's disappearance and the "time wasted" by Levingston's government, the military had to promise a democratization process in which it would transfer power to an elected government.

The operation implemented by the third military president, General Lanusse, recognized from the outset the government's limited margin of initiative and transferred the axis of policy from the social and economic crisis to formulating the characteristics of the regime which would replace the military dictatorship. Although Lanusse and the military were to suffer a series of defeats in this effort, the political fabric was in some ways repaired during those crucial months, thus lessening the unpredictability and indeterminacy that had begun in May 1969. From the point of view of reestablishing a balance in social domination, this process helped redirect the social crisis (and challenges to authority in the spheres of civil society) toward a struggle around the nature of the future political regime.

Lanusse's assumption of the presidency allowed the government to recover in part the ability to determine the ground on which the political battles of Argentine society would be fought. This did not mean, however, that the government or the military were assured victory in those battles; in fact, their limited success had its costs. The unceremonious replacement of the second president of the Revolución Argentina—less than a year after Onganía's equally abrupt exit—could only be justified by Lanusse's commitment to the liquidation of the military regime. The armed forces concentrated mainly on the conditions of their own withdrawal, thus depriving their policies of effectiveness and credibility. Even though the government recovered some of its ability to determine parameters for political action, in numerous arenas it ceded the initiative to the opposition.

The Lanusse years were substantially different from those of the two previous governments, not so much because of any reduction in political turbulence (which grew, if anything, as social conflicts increased and guerrilla actions became more spectacular), but rather because of the increasing organization of politics. That is, the government was no longer bypassed, nor were social actions left without definite channels. Rather, actions were organized around initiatives generated by fairly well-defined political actors. Although the opposition groups—Perón, the non-Peronist parties, unions and business leaders, and the radicalized young with guerrilla tendencies—all held distinct objectives, they shared a common perception of the social crisis which began in 1969 as suitable ground to work toward their respective objectives. Thus Perón maneuvered to become the axis in any new political definition; the parties billed themselves as mechanisms which could contain the crisis; union and business leaders defended their corporate privileges and sought to maximize their influence in the future constitutional government; and the guerrillas called for an authoritarian political leadership which would lead Argentina toward the goal of "national socialism."

Between 1971 and 1973 the various groups confronted one another on two different levels: first, there were struggles between the military government and the opposition groups, most often resolved in favor of the opposition; secondly, radical proposals emerged within the opposition camp, but usually did not extend beyond ideological confrontations. In general, analyses of the period have concentrated almost exclusively on these two levels of the political struggle, correctly pointing out that they occurred in the context of an unusual political liberalization and of fevered ideological discussion. Similarly, the consequences of these struggles on events after May 1973 have been highlighted: on the one hand, that the defeat of the military determined its hostile withdrawal during the first stages of the Peronist government and, on the other, that the alternative proposals of the period prefigured the savage confrontations within the winning front in 1973, especially within the Peronist movement, when the unifying objective of displacing the military government disappeared.

The aim of this discussion, however, is to underline the point that the political crisis of 1971–73 helped to weaken the challenges to the authority patterns in civil society. This was due partly to the fact that established political actors responded to proposals for social change only when those proposals clearly held the possibility of strengthening their own political power. This phenomenon would become even more accentuated between 1973 and 1975. Similarly, the traditional political loyalties of the Peronists, and to a lesser extent of the Radicals, turned out to be fundamental in determining the course of the crisis that began in 1969. In effect, Perón's return to center stage (and the reemergence of Balbín, president of the Unión Cívica Radical, through his co-leadership of the Hora del Pueblo grouping and his historic reconciliation with Perón) had two important effects: it assured the failure of the controlled transition to which Lanusse and the military aspired, and it demonstrated the impossibility for opposition forces in civil society to disseminate new, more radical, social discourses. These new discourses were not, in any case, those of the guerrilla organizations. These organizations, in their haste to attribute to social practices meanings which reflected their ideology, also contributed to the process by which the Argentine political elites reformulated the social crisis and contained the popular mobilizations.

Perón's Return and the Failure of His Project of Political Institutionalization

Despite all the differences which separated Perón in 1973 from Onganía in 1966, Perón did share one essential idea with the Revolución Argentina—that Argentina's problem was a political one. The two leaders' cures, however, were radically opposed: Onganía tried to abolish politics, while Perón tried to institutionalize it. Perón's formula aimed to create a dual system of aggregation for social and political actors. The first, not entirely new for Peronism, consisted of rearticulating the accords between workers' and employers' organizations which had been initiated during the last years of the previous Peronist government. The two confederations—the CGT and the employers' Confederación General Económica (CGE)—were again asked to agree on general levels of wage increases, and then to respect the conditions of the agreements while also submitting any disagreements to final arbitration by the state. The situation was more propitious than that of twenty years before in two respects: first, Argentine exports were enjoying good prices on the international market, and the margin of idle capacity in the industrial sectors was considerable; and second, the CGE was more extensive and representative than the organization originally created by the same José Gelbard, who led it in the early 1970s. To its unification of vast segments of small and medium-sized businesses, the CGE added big companies wholly owned by Argentines (of which the group led by Gelbard was a good example) and, just before Perón took office, the chambers of more powerful firms grouped in the traditionally anti-Peronist Unión Industrial Argentina.

In the CGT, the Vandorista leadership had lost ground since 1968 to opposition activist groups, varying from militant Peronists to independent and revolutionary Marxist currents, who attacked the leadership for submitting to the state and employers. The election of the Cámpora–Solano Lima ticket reaffirmed the decline of the Vandoristas and the apogee of the Peronist Left, within which the Montoneros insisted on the physical extermination of the union leaders. The first months of the Peronist government were characterized by increased mobilizations of workers, often directed against the Vandorista wing.

Perón's project also aimed at establishing a second arena of articulation, unprecedented in its history. It aimed to turn Parliament into a sphere of real negotiations between the parties, thus reversing Peronism's tendency to delegitimize the projects, activities, and criticisms of opponents. The restitution of Parliament as a sphere of negotiation and the implicit intention to create a representative party system went counter to the stress on mobilization given in previous Peronist politics. This authoritarian component—apparently abandoned by Perón on his return to power—was nevertheless kept alive by important sectors within his party. The positions of these sectors were diametrically opposed: from the revolutionary Jacobinism of the guerrillas to the right-wing authoritarianism of segments of the union movement, and the neo-Fascist groups which surrounded Perón's private secretary, López Rega. They all agreed, however, in their condemnation of democracy by party rule (*partidocracia*) and of the "formalism" of liberal democracy. Thus, Perón encountered the main sources of support for the revitalization of Parliament and the parties outside Peronist ranks. Major support came from the Radicals, with whose leader, Balbín, Perón celebrated an historic reconciliation in late 1972, and from the most important groups of the parliamentary Right (the Alianza Popular Federalista) and Left (the Alianza Popular Revolucionaria).

The reconciliation between Peronists and Radicals was not merely a result of Perón's ideological about-face, but also of the change in attitudes of the Radicals, who understood that democracy could be attained only through Peronism's full integration into political life. Thus, the Radicals abandoned their (lukewarm) support for the proscription imposed by the military since 1957.

Finally, Perón's proposal also redefined the role of the armed forces. In trying to break the pattern of their repeated intervention in political life, he proposed, on the one hand, to preserve for them a sphere of corporate autonomy, and on the other, to subordinate the military to the authority of the state, the control of which rested in Perón's hands. These moves, in turn, dictated changes in the project of creating a Peronist armed forces, which had been attempted in the period 1946–55, and had been accompanied by purges, loyalty oaths, and the like. Perón also took advantage of the inertia generated by the political defeat of the military, during the short *camporista* interlude which preceded his return to power. On his return he favored political participation directed through *natural* channels over spontaneous popular mobilizations, and reaffirmed the traditional precepts of *justicialista* doctrine over the watchwords of "national socialism" and revolutionary war that he himself had often echoed during the last years of his exile.

The complex politico-institutional network Perón conceived was backed by some minor sectors of political and unionist Peronism, by the majority of the allies of Peronism in the Frente Justicialista de Liberación (FREJULI), and by the main opposition party, the Unión Cívica Radical. However, the scheme never got off the ground. From the political point of view, the consolidation of Perón's project would have required a considerable reduction in the levels of tension and drama prevalent in Argentine politics. Political players would have had to believe in the long-term efficiency of their reinstitutionalization rather than the short-term impact of spectacular actions against their foes. The consequent triumphs and defeats eroded the precarious legitimacy of democratic and parliamentary institutions. Furthermore, the successive confrontations between the different rivals within Peronism itself brought the dissolution "from within" of the corporate and parliamentary mechanisms, thereby neutralizing their power to arbitrate conflicts.

Nearly three years of Peronist government witnessed a constant acceleration of the political tempo, determined mainly by the single-minded haste of all players to consolidate their immediate gains and dislodge adversaries at any cost. Against a backdrop of intensified paragovernmental and guerrilla terrorism, various episodes undermined the viability of the constitutional government and the democratic regime.

The union bosses, and especially those in control of the "62 Organizations," played a decisive role in the orientation toward short-term considerations and disregard for institutional consolidation. With the partial exception of the months when Perón was president, the union leaders made no significant move away from the defensive and oppositionist tactics they had employed since 1956 against governments which proscribed Peronism. Faced with the threat to their predominance posed by the union opposition, the leaders of the CGT and related union organizations reacted not just by promoting a greater centralization of their power, but also by undermining attempts (like those by Gelbard and Cafiero) to link incomes policy to the other fundamental variables of the economy.

By mid-1975, the Peronist Left and the employers and political sectors linked with Gelbard had been politically pulverized. At that stage, the clique grouped round López Rega tried to eliminate their only serious rival within Peronist ranks—the union leadership. The operation, both economically and politically, was unprecedented in the history of Peronism. On the one hand, López Rega's clique attempted to contain the unbridled race between prices and wages which had started in 1974. On the other hand, they sought to involve the armed forces in a scheme whereby the military would become the main support for a political regime which would eliminate parliamentary institutions and public liberties. The result was a disaster, culminating in the jettisoning of López Rega and his closest associates and the irreparable deterioration of President Isabel Perón. At this point the armed forces, and those sectors of the bourgeoisie that had been on the defensive since 1973, fully regained the political initiative. In the third quarter of 1975, the military, which had gained considerable ground when given the task of putting down the guerrillas in Tucumán province, began to liquidate the democratic regime.

Meanwhile, the problems of a badly governed society multiplied. The most visible manifestation was the collapse of Isabel Perón's government: it lost contact with society and was ultimately unable to govern social processes amidst a series of episodes that included presidential hysteria, palace intrigue, and paralysis at the helms of Parliament and the parties. On a deeper level, this collapse also affected the general political environment; politics was reduced to savage confrontations between armed groups and the hunting of defenseless victims; violence became an everyday occurrence. Most sectors mobilized since 1969 were caught in a parabola of deactivation and withdrawal from fear of and disappointment in Peronism. The economic conduct of the main social classes mirrored politics: bargaining efforts stopped almost completely; workers and employers lived from hand to mouth. Workers tried to ensure that wages did not fall too far behind, while union leaders demanded ever more frequent increases. Employers openly defied any price controls the government tried to impose; they likewise effected a complete investment strike. A pattern of "plunder" economy emerged, rounding off the image of chaos which characterized Argentina in late 1975 and early 1976. The government lost the last vestiges of its authority.

The image of chaos and misgovernment was not, however, simply the result of the government's ineffectiveness or the paralysis of those actors associated with it. From mid-1975 this impression was further promoted by two groups who severely criticized not just the government but the organization of Argentine society as a whole. These two groups were the armed forces and the leadership of the liberal employers' organization, the APEGE (the Permanent Assembly of Business Associations). They both issued increasingly damning political and economic critiques and condemned the government for its ineffective tactic of repression and its inability to control the various social sectors opposed to and allied with it. Their criticism of Argentine society as a whole went even further: populism—*qua* political regime and *qua* behavioral style of the fundamental social classes—was seen as promoting bad habits (the most extreme of which was subversion) among "subjects" used to the tutelage of a protective state.

The armed forces' refusal to get mixed up in a decaying regime prolonged the pattern of unprecedented levels of misgovernment and economic chaos until 1976, and served two major purposes: first, it reflected the deep anti-

Peronism of the majority of the officers' corps and their social allies; secondly, it taught the people a "lesson" and paved the way for the military to introduce an alternative order to the populist society of "the last thirty years." Thus, the order of the day included not just the tidying up of previous modes of political organization, but also the creation of a new society.

The 1976 Coup

Successive military interventions from 1955 to 1976 marked a progressive multiplication of the areas of civil society that gave concern to the armed forces and, similarly, an increase in the level of military involvement which was thought necessary to correct the alleged vices.

The guerrilla challenge and the accompanying social crisis were interpreted by the military as symptoms of a sick society. It traced the "illness" back to 1945, or even 1930, and judged Argentina too weak to resist the "virus" of subversion. In this interpretation, populism and modernizing developmentalism figured as two sides of the same coin. Populism had predominated between 1946 and 1955, and between 1973 and 1976, spearheading opposition to successive developmentalist projects attempted between 1955 and 1973. But the developmentalists had never proposed any real change in the basic Argentine social equation. In 1976, the military linked one of the basic premises of the populist platform—that industrial growth must be the axis of the Argentine economy—to a central weakness in the developmentalist position. In fact, the developmentalists had always favored a pact with the Peronist unions: although they demanded sacrifices from them, the developmentalists simultaneously helped to expand the unions' formidable organizational power. The most notable moves in this direction occurred in 1958–62, when Frondizi sanctioned the law of professional associations that returned the CGT to the Peronist unionists, reaffirming the notion of a single union for each trade and a single confederation, and in 1969–70, when Onganía applied that law and significantly expanded the unions' control of resources. Thus, the simultaneous condemnation of developmentalism and populism by the military in 1976 left the field clear for the liberals.

How did liberalism manage to assert itself so decisively? First, the liberals could claim that they had no responsibility for the economic policies implemented since 1943. Although some leading liberal figures—Verrier, Alsogaray, Krieger Vasena, Martínez de Hoz, and Pinedo—had reached senior positions in economic management after Perón's fall, they could argue that they had never been free to implement the liberals' "true" policies. During the 1960s, the policies of the liberal ministers were often sabotaged by sectors within their administration, making implementation difficult if not impossible. Hence, when Martínez de Hoz became minister of the economy in 1976, he made the credible claim that those who had been denied power for more than thirty years were finally being given their turn.

By the mid-1970s liberalism had another advantage. For the first time in contemporary Argentine history, the old liberal ideology secured sympathetic audiences within the armed forces, particularly its insistence that the market should be the sole mechanism of resource allocation and its criticism of "artificial" industries and "excessive" state intervention. Since the late 1950s, when the military's doctrine of national security first emerged in discussions of "ideological frontiers," liberal themes had simultaneously attracted and repelled the hegemonic sectors within the armed forces. Liberalism had been the only consistently anti-Peronist current, but liberal doctrines implied consequences which the military had traditionally opposed: the restructuring of industry, the revitalization of the capital market, and the criticism of nationalist and statist practices. Finally, in 1975–76, the liberals focused on three threats in Argentine society whose eradication was called for: (1) all forms of subversion—including guerrilla activity, popular agitation, challenging behavior in schools, factories, and within the family, artistic and cultural nonconformism, and questioning of authority in general; (2) populist political society—Peronism, the unions, the "obliging" opposition composed of Radicals and the parliamentary Left, and the tutelary state; and (3) the "inefficient" industrial sector, which formed the base of the urban economy, together with its "undisciplined" working class.

Contrary to some opinions, the liberal prescription of 1976 emphasized a strong state. Starting from a critique of the populist-developmentalist democratic state as a weak state, subject to the swings of excessive sectorial demands and totally unable to put an end to chaos and subversion, the liberals proclaimed the state's need to subordinate sectorial privileges—"social rights," to use a terminology that would be abolished—and individual rights to the "logic of the war" against subversion. On the one hand, the liberal program gave priority to Argentina's status as a society at war against subversion. To this end, the armed forces were presented as the "principal guardians of the national destiny." Three corollaries underscored the implication of such a role: the absolute (and often explicit) disrespect for the law; the supplanting of the government's constitutional powers by the three branches of the armed forces, who divided the control of the country down to the remotest villages; and the exercise of supreme state power by the junta of commanders in chief, not by a semimonarchical despot in the style of Onganía or Pinochet.[10] Similarly, the military was charged with the detection and punishment of all forms of challenging behavior in civilian society. All criticisms of the regime were considered aberrations in this reactionary utopia of a strictly stratified society. However, things did not stop there. The state also subverted the populist "old order," actively intervening to "destroy the mode of accumulation toward which the economy tended naturally." For more than forty years, this model had presupposed the existence of a tutelary state, controlled prices, a semiclosed economy, and the regulation of the capital market, among other things.

The real "liberal" revolution required, first, that the state should discipline itself, by disposing of public enterprises and "superfluous" jobs, by dismantling the systems of subsidies, and by refraining from fixing subsidized prices for its services. In addition it proposed to destroy the "old habits" of workers and employers and to generate new ones. This generic scheme was never intended to benefit all subjects equally. In the case of the workers, the appeal to the market idea (a society composed of isolated individuals) aimed to destroy the unions and the plant-level structures of worker representation which mediated blue- and white-collar workers' interests both with employers and the state. The military government hailed the dissolution of confederations and the takeover of individual unions as a step toward purging the populist corporate state, to the benefit of all. The effects on the labor movement were spectacular: the Videla years marked the longest period of labor protest inactivity since 1943.

The more general aim of the liberals was to modify the whole system of social relations, which required the reformation of employers as well. To this end, the government set up a free market economic system mainly through the opening of the domestic market to foreign competition. Another decisive "novelty" was the financial reform of June 1977, which implied paying "exclusive attention to the problem of inflation, [taking] decisions expressly aimed at cutting the process of economic expansion [without hesitating] to damage the immediate interest of members of those social classes who made up the political base" of the military government.[11]

But even more important was the adopting of the *tablita* policy in December 1978 (a preannounced schedule of devaluations). That policy, which seemed to be the *desideratum* of anti-inflation in practice plunged the Argentine economy into the deepest crisis in its history.

While Onganía's utopia, governed by omniscient administrators, was ultimately destroyed by those social classes and sectors who were its victims, the liberal project of 1976—to return to the market's "natural" modes of discipline—was never realized: even its direct beneficiaries failed to conform to the expectations of the liberal technocrats and their military partners. Almost simultaneously the crisis into which this experiment entered was greatly accelerated by the Falklands/Malvinas fiasco.

Postscript

Against the background of regime collapse at the end of the summer of 1983, there was a major political change in Argentina. This was linked with the process of party affiliation, the primaries, and, finally, the electoral campaign. The central character in this change was Raúl Alfonsín. In little more than six months, Alfonsín displaced the Balbinist leadership that had controlled the Radical party since 1957, took the political initiative in the face of the military government and of Peronism, and, finally, defeated the Peronist candidate, Luder, in the presidential elections of October 1983. These results marked Peronism's first electoral defeat at a national level since its birth in 1946. I do not intend to discuss here the reasons for the Radicals' victory. Instead, focusing on the historic moment that culminated in the elections, I will analyze new elements that could permit an outcome for this "process of institutionalization" different from those of the three earlier attempts.

The most striking feature of the process begun in 1983 was the transformation of the Radical party into serious electoral competition for the Peronists. Between 1955 and 1976, the party system in Argentina suffered from constant instability, making the reconstruction of a democratic system almost impossible. In the first decade (1955–65), Peronism was outlawed, and all attempts at establishing an institutional democracy were doomed at the start. In the second decade, increased authoritarianism and militarism culminated in 1973 in a virtual electoral monopoly for the Peronists. Their wide margin of victory in that election brought negative consequences in that it left the rest of the parties without real possibilities for disputing power. Even more critical was the fact that Peronism proved incapable of transforming itself into an arena for institutional competition among the different sectors and forces that existed within it. This may be seen in contrast to other parties that have held comparably predominant positions for long periods, such as the Italian Christian Democrats and the Liberal Democrats of Japan.

The qualitative transformation of the Radical party in 1983, then, introduced several new ingredients to Argentine politics. It represented the appearance of a second party capable of appealing to a wide spectrum of different social classes (although the areas of emphasis varied in comparison with Peronism) and thus offered the Argentine citizenry a new alternative. Citizens may now express their opposition or distaste for proposals, orientations, styles, and leaders of the party that may temporarily be supported by the majority without challenging the limits of the institutional system. As of 1983, both the Peronists and the Radicals must take into account that the logical consequences of a loss in popular support will be electoral defeat. Diversification of the electoral alternatives, then, constitutes a factor that will probably reinforce the likelihood of democracy in Argentina.

A greater parity between the two major parties also favors the stabilization of an institutional system that regulates political conflict. On the one hand, Peronists are faced, for the first time in their history, with a legitimately elected government; the old argument that Peronism is the majority party has been drastically refuted. On the other hand, the Radicals must adjust to the fact that the electoral results still permit the opposition significant room to maneuver within the government structures; the Peronists won the majority of the provincial governorships, as well as the first minority in the Senate. In addition, the relative balance between the two main parties provides new opportunities in the institutional set-up for smaller parties. Should these opportunities be seized, and should the minority parties begin to exercise their capacity for negotiation and pressure, new incentives for change may be provided within what have been the Right and Left wings of the Argentine political spectrum for the last thirty years. The rightist parties have been characterized, with few and insignificant exceptions, by their antidemocratic actions and orientations. The Left, which may also be criticized for frequent lack of democratic convictions, has been unable to develop strategies that, admitting the position of electoral minority, nevertheless set forth ideological and cultural alternatives.

The reorganization of the parties after seven years of being banned from political activity and the subsequent electoral campaign have also brought the idea of constitutional democracy and the stability of institutions to the forefront. These themes, as we have seen, had been conspicuously absent from Argentine politics in recent decades. In 1983, however, the two principal presidential candidates centered their campaigns on the necessity for the construction of a stable democracy based on popular sovereignty and constitutional legality.

Despite the similar emphasis chosen by both candidates, the two encountered dramatically different results. Among the Peronists, Luder's accent on such themes appeared flagrantly to contradict the incitement to violence presented by such figures as Herminio Iglesias, the candidate for the governorship of Buenos Aires. In addition, possibilities for revitalizing the party through reorganization with full participation of the affiliates were frustrated. Instead, particularly in the large electoral districts such as the province of Buenos Aires, the Federal Capital, and Santa Fe, the old practices of nominating party authorities and candidates held strong. This not only discouraged many leaders and sectors of the party's grass-roots support; it also seriously weakened the credibility of Peronism's proclaimed advocacy of institutional democracy.

The Radicals, in contrast, focusing their slogans on "return to the constitution" and denunciations of a "military-union pact," had more success. With such banners as the *leitmotifs* of the campaign, they were able to widen significantly their traditional base of support, inject a level of popular mobilization unprecedented in contemporary Radical history, and, finally, make the question of democracy the crucial issue. Alfonsín himself embodied the party message much more effectively than did Luder. While the Peronist candidate was immersed in a fragmented, even hostile party, and publicly surrounded by union leaders whose reputation did not help his electoral chances, the Radical leader was able to exploit two strengths: in personal terms, his attractive style, his emphasis on honesty and firmness, and the changes he had achieved in the workings of the old Radical party; and in political terms, his clear record of opposition to the military regime, his focus on human rights, his purpose of restructuring the state, and his condemnation of the military adventure in the South Atlantic War.

In conclusion, despite the magnitude of Argentina's current economic crisis, the combination of factors that surrounded the December 1983 change in government provides a glimpse of potential changes in the parameters of contemporary Argentine politics. In this sense, the question of the role of the parties and the national Parliament is of vital importance. Despite the negative legacies that still weigh on the two principal parties and other sectors of the political spectrum, all of the parties, not simply the governing party, have won a new space—but this space can be used with different degrees of political wisdom. The significance of the Parliament lies in the fact that, in the intervals between elections, it seems the only arena in which tensions, conflicts, and agreements between the two main parties may be processed. In order to obtain satisfactory results, however, it will be necessary for the Peronists and the Radicals to develop new modes of interaction. Both parties will be faced with serious challenges. The Peronists will have to strike a balance between their role as effective opposition and their loyalty to the institutional system. The governing party, on the other hand, will have to learn to recognize the legitimacy of the opposition's criticisms, in order to avoid automatically attributing to them an eagerness to destroy democracy. The challenge, then, looms as large for the Radicals as for the Peronists. Both must place proper emphasis on the negative (but necessary) checks on the presidential power, and seek the positive resolution of conflicts and negotiations between various social actors through institutional channels. In addition, the increased role of Parliament will help to make the president's role less critical in each political decision, thereby reducing the probability of a premature deterioration of his image.

3 ·

Bolivia's Failed Democratization, 1977–1980

Laurence Whitehead

Introduction

On 17 July 1980 the Bolivian military seized power. Congress was closed, civilian leaders were detained with a great show of violence, and hopes for a civilian constitutional government were dashed. An implacable and unsavory military dictatorship was established, another in a long series that has marked Bolivia's history as an independent nation. However, this dictatorship has acquired a worse reputation than many of its predecessors, in part because of the major effort at democratization that it thwarted, in part for the "Southern Cone" ruthlessness of its methods of repression, and in part because of its close involvement with the flourishing and gangster-ridden trade in illegal exports of cocaine.

This chapter considers the failed attempt to democratize Bolivia between late 1977 and July 1980. Applauding the military takeover, nine Bolivian banks took out an advertisement in the *Wall Street Journal* of 3 October 1980, which characterized the attempted democratization as follows:

> Towards the end of 1977, much to the surprise of many people both inside and outside Bolivia, it was decided to put the country on a democratic course, and to hold general elections in May 1978. Since then the question of why has often been raised. There were several reasons: partly the genuine belief that the years of political stability and socio-economic progress could only be consolidated under a democracy; partly because it was felt that the final steps of important economic readjustment could only be taken with the kind of political support that a democracy supposedly creates; last, but not least, it was undoubtedly the result of international political pressure. Thereafter managing the economy gave way to political considerations, electioneering and demagoguery. A short period of two years brought about not less than three different interim governments, eighty political parties for an electorate of less than one and a half million; to say nothing of countless strikes, inflationary . . . increases. . . . In summary, the nation was immersed in a climate of political frustration, social upheaval, a dangerous economic disequilibrium and at the same time stagnation in the economy.

Readers of the *Wall Street Journal* were being told, in short, that no doubt well-intentioned efforts from abroad to promote "democracy" in the unfavorable setting of Bolivia had created an intolerable situation. Adopting the language of economic determinism, the bankers portrayed an authoritarian government (supposedly wedded to financial responsibility) as the necessary antidote to the excesses accompanying attempted democratization.

A Bolivian case study must therefore address the following three issues: What was the character of the authoritarian state in the Bolivian context (whence did it derive its strength, what interests did it serve, and how indispensable was it for the dominant groups in society)? Why, then, was a process of democratization set in motion (what were the motives, calculations, and miscalculations of the major participants)? Once underway, what determined the direction taken by the democratization effort, and was the final outcome (in this case the abortion of the process) inevitable? In order to explain the recent past effectively it has proved necessary to introduce a long historical perspective, and so to address a prior question that is specific to this chapter. What could be the social meaning of traditional "democracy" (constitutional government, rule of law, a competitive electoral system) for the people of Bolivia, with their distinctive history, traditions, and socioeconomic problems?

One Hundred Years of . . . Democratic Experimentation

In a formal sense, constitutional democracy is far from new in Bolivia. Separation of power, the rule of law, rights of association, and periodic competitive elections between nationally organized civilian parties have been the rule rather than the exception over the past hundred years. Such were the officially accepted norms in operation more or less continuously from 1880 to 1936, from 1938 to 1951, and from 1956 until 1964, or more arguably until 1968. The military authoritarianism of 1964–78 (or more precisely, of 1971–78) represented a sharper and more complete break with the norms of constitutional government than had been the case for a century. That said, it must also be recognized that such norms were quite frequently honored in the breach. The reality of political, and above all of social, life was generally far harsher and more authoritarian than the formal provisions would suggest. Thus we must go beyond juridical definitions of democracy to ask what such political arrangements meant in practice for the main groups in society.

What for Bolivians has been the actual social content and meaning of "democracy"? It will become apparent from the rest of this section that the social content has varied markedly. Oligarchic democracy meant almost nothing outside a very restricted circle of educated property-owners. Somewhat more extended democracy meant a desperate struggle for ascendancy between still rather limited groups in the small "modern" sector of the economy. Mass democracy meant social transformation of an overwhelming and unpredictable character. It is this third connotation of "democracy" that was uppermost in the national consciousness when the most recent attempt at democratization got underway. It is because that connotation excited such widespread hopes and such deep-seated fears that the 1978–80 process became so convoluted, and ultimately led to tragedy.

Bolivia had made three serious attempts to establish relatively open and impersonal forms of constitutional government before the 1978–80 attempt. Such attempts occurred in the 1880s, the 1940s, and following the revolution of 1952. The three were quite distinctive forms of constitutionalism, ranging from oligarchic rule to restricted to mass democracy. The differences can be explained partly in terms of the international economic context prevailing at each point and partly in terms of internal social development. But considerable weight should also be given to more transient factors, such as the short-term geopolitical balance in the region, and such subjective but powerful influences as those deriving from traditions, memories, and alignments.

After half a century of arbitrary and chaotic military-based forms of government, Bolivia (like many other South American countries) embarked on a prolonged period of fairly open and constitutional government, running roughly from 1880 to 1930. Elections generally occurred more or less on schedule; opposition parties and newspapers experienced only intermittent and relatively ineffective harassment; there was a fairly genuine division of power and some effort to maintain a neutral rule of law. Why? If we look first at the internal social development of the country, we find that the conditions for genuine modern democracy were absent. But that was probably an advantage, rather than an obstacle, to the establishment of a façade of constitutional government. The property qualifications ensured a very restrictive franchise, and all political actors had some stake in the maintenance of social peace. Constitutional government meant security and guarantees for the haves and an institutional framework to contain the have-nots. It also offered a prospect of long-term gradual incorporation. Bolivia was a latecomer to nineteenth-century liberal formulas of political development, but for quite a long time those formulas seemed adaptable to internal social conditions. If one analyzes *how* this system became adopted, the pressure from the international economy seems clearcut and forceful. Essentially, foreign investors (British and Anglo-Chilean) would not risk capital to develop Bolivian mines and railways unless an impersonal framework of constitutional guarantees could be provided and enforced. These powerful facilitating conditions lasted until the slump of 1930, when Bolivia and other Latin American governments were forced to choose between upholding the external guarantees they had given to foreign investors and meeting a minimum of their domestic political commitments. But a favorable international environment for limited democratization after 1870 was not enough on its own. Domestic resistance of various kinds (military parasitism, regional insubordination, the habits of caudillos) had to be overcome, and this required committed local leadership and the spur of geopolitical necessity. The geopolitical necessity came from Bolivia's defeat in the War of the Pacific in 1879, which left her landlocked (until foreigners built the missing railways) and visibly on the decline relative to her more advanced constitutional neighbors, Chile and Argentina. The committed local leadership was provided by a new class of mine-owners and bankers who had learned some liberal political ideology as an extension of their liberal economic ideology, whose interest in stable impersonal government was obvious, and who had suffered arbitrary taxation and exactions under the pre-1880 caudillos.

The breakdown of the liberal international economy was accompanied by a breakdown in liberal political institutions that culminated in World War II. During the war, powerful groups and interests in Bolivia (and elsewhere in Latin America) that had lost ground during the liberal hegemony were attracted by the prospects of an Axis victory and by the example of economic *dirigisme* and political authoritarianism offered by the Axis powers. The worldwide Allied victory of 1945 brought with it a new wave of "democratization" and "de-Nazification," which shaped Bolivia's second transition from authoritarianism. At least in Bolivia, perhaps more than in Argentina and Brazil, it was overwhelming pressure from the international context that determined the process and character of the transition, and that overwhelmed some powerful internal forces tending toward a different outcome. Bolivia's vulnerability to international pressure derived from the distinctive character of her export sector. Because the country was a leading producer of strategic minerals which were owned by U.S.- and European-registered mining houses, its political affairs were undoubtedly of direct interest to the governments of the victorious Allied powers. There was at this point no clear distinction between the geopolitical and the more narrowly economic aspects of the international pressure, which aimed to eliminate a redoubt of pro-Axis sentiment and to consolidate a constitutional form of government that could guarantee the smooth supply of essential industrial and military raw materials.

Turning to domestic factors, the most striking feature of this democratization pact was that it rested on an alliance between the conservative and mine-owning interests linked with Britain and the United States and the Marxist political groups that had acquired a substantial following among Bolivia's increasingly active popular movement. How could such a pact come about? In fact it mirrored on the internal front the heterogeneous character of the anti-Axis alliance internationally. And like the international alliance, it rested on such a fragile base that within a year of "de-Nazifying" Bolivia, the cold war had shattered the democratic front, leaving the conservative and mine-owning interests as sole inheritors of the "democratic" legacy. This type of formal democracy was quite incapable of meeting even a minimum of popular aspirations, or indeed of serving the true interests of even the narrow social group whose patrimony it had become. The basic process leading to its collapse derived from Bolivia's internal social development—generating a mining proletariat, an incipient urban organized labor force, and an awakening peasantry, all of whom had been victims, rather than beneficiaries, of Bolivia's restricted and class-oriented forms of constitutional rule. The franchise, although enlarged to include much of the urban and mining proletariat, still excluded some four-fifths of the country's households. Thus, far too few social groups had a voice in the system, and yet from the standpoint of the dominant elites even this narrow franchise gave political expression to social forces far too radical and demanding to be accommodated by peaceful compromise.

It was these internal social forces, frustrated during the democratization process of 1946, that prevailed over adverse international economic and geopolitical realities in 1952 (notably the physical isolation of the Bolivian Revolution at the time of the Korean War–induced paranoia) and accomplished a much more radical and transforming kind of democratization. The 1952 revolution may look tame compared with later developments in Cuba and Nicaragua, but it was extremely bold and far-reaching for its time. It was also a democratizing, as well as a socially redistributive, revolution. The type of democracy was, of course, quite different from that envisioned in the 1880s or 1940s—with more emphasis on mass mobilization, direct action, local and workplace assemblies, and transformed property relations—and less concerned with division of powers, and alternation in power of competitive parties, or even with the formal structure upholding the rule of law. Nevertheless, the 1952 revolution did give rise to a twelve-year period of civilian rule, with universal suffrage extending the vote to women and illiterates. Elections were held regularly, opposition parties secured some representation, the presidency rotated every four years, and freedom of the press was for the most part sustained. Perhaps the best way to convey the character and limitations of the "democracy" envisaged by the Movimiento Nacionalista Revolucionario (MNR) leaders is that they were largely imitating the Mexican PRI. A newly enfranchised peasant population benefitting from massive land reform was expected to give the governing party a virtually captive electorate and a built-in majority that would make formal democracy "safe" for the revolution.

Note how radical this was at the time. It was before the Cuban Revolution, in the middle of the Korean War. Geopolitical realities were as unfavorable as during the anti-Somoza revolution in Nicaragua. Almost all neighboring governments felt potentially threatened by an uncontrolled revolution in Bolivia, and international unease was compounded by the sensitivities of the United States. Note also the ambiguity that the revolution was in the name *both* of democracy (the thwarted 1951 election victory) and of a profound transformation of property relations.

Military Authoritarianism since 1964

The 1952 revolution nearly destroyed the armed forces. It temporarily armed the workers and the peasantry. It also granted universal suffrage, thus making peasant beneficiaries of the land reform the numerical majority in future elections. Organized labor was deprived of electoral strength by this move but initially received compensation in the form of other privileged lines of access to the party and state apparatuses, including cabinet representation and a certain degree of worker control in the management of state enterprises. The result was an internal distribution of forces very threatening to the middle and upper classes and unpropitious for private investment. But after a couple of years, the United States used the leverage of economic aid to restore private incentives and to encourage the reestablishment of the conventional hierarchies. Faced with this prospect, the post-1952 coalition proceeded to fragment, with organized labor soon occupying a strategic role in the opposition, and with the purged military apparatus reestablished with the help of U.S. aid and playing an increasingly assertive role on the Right. Also, after 1957 the government worked to turn the peasant *sindicatos*, or labor unions, against the opposition-minded labor movement.

Since 1964, Bolivian politics have been dominated by an authoritarianism whose central pillar has been the military. Bolivia's authoritarianism has taken a distinctive form, shaped by the legacy of the 1952 revolution. For example, the military-peasant pact was an essential ingredient of the ruling formula from the early 1960s to its disintegration in 1978. When local garrisons disarmed the peasant militias in the closing years of the second Paz Estenssoro administration, the officer corps acquired a vast clientele of rural dependants, whose vote could be manipulated in accordance with military policy. However, Bolivia's new officer corps was as socially mixed and as politically factionalized as was the revolutionary party it succeeded. Hence the military authoritarianism of post-1964 failed to establish its internal stability, either through institutional means or through personalisms. Within the officer corps, alliances had to be continuously renegotiated, and the armed forces always remained permeable and unpredictable in their relations with the other organized groups in society.[1] Military ideology was correspondingly confused, yielding episodes of socialist rhetoric, as well as bursts of probusiness activism, and swaying to the influence of models projected respectively from Peru, Chile, Brazil, and Argentina. Even constitutional democracy had a fleeting appeal. This invertebrate appearance did not extend to all aspects of Bolivia's military authoritarianism, however. Uncertain what they were for, the officer corps could nevertheless agree most definitely on some things they were against. Prime among these was any repetition of the 1952 events that had come so close to destroying their institution. One constant has therefore been their hostility to the political organization of the mineworkers, for whom 1952 was a frustrated dawn. In fact, all sources of opposition to the remilitarization of society and the reimposition of social hierarchy would elicit hostility from the armed forces. In this respect, their ascendancy shared the general characteristics of authoritarian rule throughout the continent, even though some specific traits were shaped by the legacy of 1952.

Banzer's Authoritarianism

Although military rule assumed many forms between 1964 and 1978, the Banzer dictatorship proved the most successful and durable. Consideration of the 1971–77 regime indicates the essential character of military authoritarianism in contemporary Bolivia and helps to explain how the most recent democratic transition came about. Where did General Banzer's government derive its strength? Was such a regime inevitable? Why did it peter out?

Banzer's government was always a precarious balancing act.[2] The initial pact on which it rested was inherently unstable. Ministries were parcelled out between two rival political parties (the Falangistas and the Paz Estenssoro wing of the MNR), each of which tried to use its positions in the public administration to bolster its mass support and enhance its leverage within the armed forces. The organized private sector, which had helped to finance the coup of August 1971, was also given formal representation in the cabinet, and claims for power were also made by regional lobbies (such as the commercial interests of the eastern lowlands) and personalist factions (such as the extreme anti-Communists around Interior Minister Selich). It seemed unlikely at first that President Banzer, encumbered with all these commitments, could marshall the independent authority to consolidate his rule. It is important to remember that the various garrison commanders assented to his assumption of office in the name of the armed forces only on the understanding that he would work toward an eventual constitutionalization of the regime, and that in the meantime he would submit his mandate to their periodic approval.

Despite this apparent fragility, the Banzer presidency achieved a degree of consolidation and longevity exceptional by the standards of Bolivian history. He was the longest-serving president since 1871, and unlike the great majority of his predecessors, he exercised significant control over the manner of his relinquishment of office. This is the more remarkable since General Hugo Banzer lacked either the demagogic appeal of General Barrientos or the administrative talents of General Ovando, his main predecessor in office. A man of limited vision and no great natural authority, his success must be attributed not only to luck but to the substantial economic interests he served and the shrewd advisers he attracted, and to his intermittent bursts of bold and unpredictable assertiveness. For the middle period of his government (from the *autogolpe* of November 1974 until sometime in 1977) power was pretty effectively concentrated in the presidency and in the leader's immediate circle of technocrats and business associates. In the pattern established during his seizure of power, popular protest was forcefully suppressed (La Paz factory workers in October 1972, Cochabamba peasants in January 1974, highland miners in June 1976), although none of these apparent successes enabled the regime to enlist new social bases or lastingly block off the subterranean currents of opposition. At any rate, the regime proved resilient enough to ride out a series of internal shocks and to accommodate to such external shifts as Geisel's liberalization in Brazil, the rise and fall of Perón, the fall of Nixon, and even a period of acute international tension, involving Chile, Peru, and Bolivia, over Bolivia's outlet to the sea. Perhaps the best way to highlight the Banzer administration's record of survival is to recall that his anti-Left coup anticipated by two years the outcome in Chile and Uruguay, while his move toward democracy began over a year after the similar steps in Peru and Ecuador.

Clearly, division among the regime's opponents (of which more below) provided an important opportunity for its consolidation. Reviewing the record of botched intrigues against the dictatorship, it is beyond doubt that *fortuna*—indeed sheer luck—played a not inconsiderable role in explaining its longevity. A period of remarkable economic opportunity greatly enhanced the advantages of incumbency (for a couple of years) although it is arguable that the windfall gains accruing to Bolivia after 1974 as a minor oil exporter were in fact sadly wasted. However, such factors are the traditional staples of Bolivian politics. The regime's relative strength and effectiveness compared to its predecessors' also rested on some more structural characteristics. By 1971 the "militarization" of the government apparatus, and particularly of the state enterprises, had created a substantial nexus of economic interests and clientele groups that required the shelter of conservative military rule. A succession of failures and defeats had taken its toll of the civilian and popular organizations that would be essential for any more democratic alternative. The once dominant populist revolutionary party, the MNR, was so badly split that one-half, or more, initially supported Banzer (the Paz Estenssoristas), while a very substantial minority, including most of the younger elements and many lower-class groupings, remained opposed. Conservative economic restoration had already gone far enough to create relatively powerful new social forces of the Right (the so-called "medium miners," who had escaped nationalization, and the sugar and cotton bourgeoisie of the Santa Cruz area, who had escaped land reform). With the nationalization of American oil companies in the late 1960s, a major source of discord weakening the Right had been removed. All these developments favored Banzer's government. It could also draw inspiration from the example of apparently successful "modernized authoritarianism" in neighboring Brazil. Finally, there was the catalyst of fear which did much to crystallize right-wing unity. In quick succession conservative interests had been threatened by the 1968 guerrilla campaign of "Che," by the example of Allende's 1970 election victory, and by the undisciplined radicalism that accompanied General Torres's government and found its chief expression in the proclamation of the People's Assembly (mid-1971), seemingly promising a return to the experiments of 1952. Thus, by Bolivian standards, the Banzer government rested on a relatively solid basis of interest, ideology, and class sentiment. The power seizure of August 1971 was accompanied by a significant display of military ruthlessness which left several hundred dead.

For all that, Banzer's variant of authoritarianism was not solid if compared with other Latin American cases. Although arbitrary and repressive, it was not efficient and systematic in the Southern Cone style. In fact, miscalculation and overreaction contributed substantially to some of the worst excesses of the regime (the killing of Cochabamba peasants in 1974 and the confrontation with the miners in 1976). For the most part, it was little more oppressive than several earlier Bolivian dictatorships, and a great deal milder than the dictatorship established in July 1980. Institutionally it required continuous improvisation, lacking either the agreed process of decision-making and promotion that has characterized the Brazilian military rule, or the forceful personalism of Franco, Somoza, or Pinochet. In addition to the general reasons for the typical impermanence of military rule, the lesson of Bolivian history had been that no such government ever lasted very long, and this tradition encouraged personal ambition and insubordination throughout the officer corps. The spread of corruption throughout the armed forces was apparently tolerated by the Banzer government (itself corrupt) as a suitable way to contain these disciplinary problems.

The regime's basis of ideological legitimation was also unclear. Initial promises of democratization were mixed with the rhetoric of an anti-Communist national security state, followed by more emphasis on national unity to secure economic development. Even the *autogolpe* of November 1974, through which Banzer consolidated his personal power, contained flagrant contradictions.

On the one hand, the Banzer government outlawed representative organizations, sending the political parties into recess, replacing elected labor leaders with government-appointed "coordinators," and even providing for the conscription of civilians whose occupations were deemed strategic by the state. On the other hand, preexisting constitutional conventions were not completely forsworn. Thus, Banzer still acknowledged the limitation of a six-year term, simply changing the starting date from August 1971 to November 1974. He again pledged elections at the end of his term, now postponed to 1980. Between 1974 and 1976, even this degree of dictatorship seemed relatively benign compared with the political and economic disasters befalling neighboring countries, but from 1976 onwards economic performance waned and the contrast between Bolivia and her neighbors lost its power to impress. By the end of Banzer's government, anti-Chilean nationalist sentiment had been awakened by his unsuccessful attempts to reach a compromise with Pinochet, and in the absence of any persuasive account of the higher objectives necessitating an authoritarian form of government, the original commitment to democratization resurfaced as a plausible theme. Such ideological and institutional improvisation faithfully reflected the limited social basis for Bolivian conservativism. Most propertied interests are limited in scale and divided among themselves by rivalries of region and sectoral conflicts (e.g., between mine owners, tropical agriculturalists, bankers, and importers). The catalyst of a Marxist menace lost some of its power to unify these groups as other types of danger became more visible (such as the risk of Chilean- or Argentine-style state terrorism, or the unbridled corruption and gangsterism associated with government-protected cocaine trafficking). In these conditions, external influences could play a part of some significance. Andean Pact pressure for democracy was reinforced when the Carter administration took up the same issue. Even a British government decision to withhold aid from the Bolivian mining company until there was an improvement in workers' rights may have had some impact.

An Ill-Fated Transition

In November 1977, when President Banzer embarked on a process of electoral transition, he had no sense of being defeated. This was one more improvisation, no more dangerous than many of his successful earlier moves. Certainly popular demands for change had mounted, and the international setting had also changed in ways that required adaptation. Probably the decisive impetus came from Banzer's soundings of opinion within the leading army garrisons, the only real form of political consultation allowed at that time. The ostensible focus of concern was Bolivia's claim to an outlet to the Pacific. Banzer had for a while benefitted from this issue when he reestablished diplomatic relations with Santiago and opened negotiations with Pinochet for a territorial exchange, but the Chileans had maneuvered skillfully, trying to shift blame onto Peru for any failure to resolve the question before the hundredth anniversary of the War of the Pacific (1979). With this symbolic deadline approaching, and no demonstrable gains from his policy in prospect, Banzer seemed somewhat vulnerable before his military and civilian critics. A democratic opening that could be arranged on Banzer's own terms would deprive these dissidents of the excuse to conspire, and might enable the government to deflect possible disappointment over the Pacific coast issue from the executive to an array of squabbling and ineffective political parties.

A calculation such as this seemed plausible enough at the time, even to leading strategists of the opposition. With the military-peasant pact still in operation, the Ministry of Labor more or less in control of organized labor, and the political parties demoralized by three years of compulsory recess, only the church and the incipient human rights movement (neither of which seemed very formidable opponents) retained a capacity for autonomous organization. This suggested that Banzer could conduct an election on very favorable terms, and might well succeed in prolonging his personal ascendancy by "constitutionalizing" his rule. This was, after all, the course adopted by General Barrientos in 1966, transforming a junta in which Banzer himself had initially served as minister of education. The president's confidence in his strategy probably rested on an underestimation of the grievances of the opposition, a misperception rulers often suffer from when they deny their rivals any open means of expression.

The 1966 precedent seemed encouraging, but contained one major source of embarrassment. General Barrientos had surrendered his claim to military command during the six months preceding his election as president. A military candidate for public office must not be on active duty during the campaign, it was said, for that would contaminate the supposed institutional purity of the armed forces. So, if Banzer wished to win the election, he would have to pass control of the military apparatus to some rival. On reflection, his advisers seemed to have concluded that this course was too risky. The alternative was to delegate presidential office to a trusted nominee, whose definition of the role would be constrained by the knowledge that Banzer retained command over the troops. This was the alternative adopted, and it explains why, according to the most complete official returns of the presidential election held on 9 July 1978, General Pereda Asbún (formerly minister of interior of the Banzer dictatorship) received an absolute majority—a suspiciously exact 50 percent of votes cast, achieved through massive fraud.

This panorama was transformed by the twenty-day hunger strike in demand of a political amnesty, begun by four miners' wives on 28 December 1977. One week earlier, the government had responded to church lobbying by decreeing a partial Christmas amnesty that would supposedly create a suitable climate for the electoral campaign. However, only thirty-three prisoners were released; the army was not withdrawn from the mining zones; workers who had been dismissed in earlier strikes were not reinstated; many exiles would still not be allowed to return to the country; and the labor unions remained under government control. In protest against this "mockery" of an amnesty, and disregarding warnings of the political parties, who said the time was not yet ripe, the four women and their fourteen children took refuge in the archbishopric of La Paz, declaring that they would fast until their husbands were released and a full political amnesty was granted. With tacit support from the church and active encouragement from the budding human rights movement, the hunger strike soon gathered momentum. By 18 January, over a thousand protesters were on strike in churches and public places all over the republic. Later in the day, Banzer realized the seriousness of the challenge, and some violent police assaults took place, but the public discredit was too visible. If the election campaign was to proceed, and if international sanctions were to be averted, it would be necessary to concede the hunger strikers' demands in full. From the government's point of view, the worst aspect of this challenge was that it destroyed the Ministry of Labor apparatus of labor control. When progovernment labor "coordinators" called for a protest against the hunger strikers, the rank and file responded with demands for free trade unions. By the end of January 1978, unrestricted amnesty was established, the independent labor movement had resurfaced and gained legal recognition, and the Banzer regime was thrown onto the defensive.

Thereafter, as the electoral process gathered momentum, the basis of authoritarian control crumbled away. As with similar upsets elsewhere (such as the Uruguayan plebiscite of November 1980), it is easier to list contributory factors than to arrive at an agreed explanation. The opposition viewpoint is that years of clandestine organization and internal resistance were what really drove the regime to seek an electoral outcome. Such efforts also provided the groundwork for civilian forces to seize the initiative and campaign aggressively the moment competitive politics were authorized. Exponents of this view can point to a series of conflicts and protest movements that preceded the announcement of an electoral timetable. But it is doubtful whether the Banzer administration perceived these as irresistible pressures against the status quo. More probably the dictatorship calculated (wrongly as it turned out) that the opposition was sufficiently cowed and divided that an electoral solution would prove manageable for those in power. Such miscalculations easily occur when all channels of expression have been controlled for too long, but another factor also seems to have complicated the picture.

Those sharing power under Banzer's regime could envisage more than one strategy for managing the electoral process. The political ambitions of many generals had been frustrated during Banzer's almost unprecedentedly long six-year ascendancy. Some, with more enthusiasm than subtlety, rallied to General Pereda's electoral bandwagon, hoping for a crushing victory that might free the elected president from dependence on the commander-in-chief. Others, fearing that their careers or their economic prospects might be sacrificed in the event of an overwhelming triumph by the Pereda faction, sought a variety of strategies to weaken the *oficialista* candidate. Thus, for example, the Paz Estenssoro wing of the MNR (with 10.8 percent of the official vote) and the Christian Democrats each enjoyed a certain degree of influence within the officer corps and could muster significant regional and sectional support.

However, the candidate with least influence among the military emerged most strengthened from the contest. This fact lends some weight to opposition claims for the effectiveness of their resistance work, if not during the dictatorship, then more probably during the run up to the election. Hernán Siles Suazo (president, 1956–60) had, from the outset, opposed the Banzer coup of August 1971. His 1978 campaign rallied student, worker, and peasant support around a coalition that ranged from progressive churchmen to Communist trade unionists, endorsing a platform that was unmistakably antimilitarist. Perhaps the most dynamic element in the coalition was provided by the MIR (Movimiento Izquierdista Revolucionario), a new party with particular appeal among students and youth. It claimed the heritage of the 1952 revolution and condemned those older civilian leaders (like Paz Estenssoro) who had compromised with the military in exchange for a fragment of patronage. This party used militant language and provided enthusiastic activists, but its leaders were in practice rather pragmatic and capable of appealing to some significant military and business interests. Despite the electoral fraud, Siles officially obtained 24.6 percent of the vote, registering particular strength in the *altiplano*, especially in La Paz and the mining zones. This was largely an expression of the strong hostility toward the dictatorship felt in those areas and a consequence of effective organizing by the UDP (Unión Democrática y Popular) coalition, both in the urban areas and among the surrounding *aymará*-speaking peasant population. Nevertheless, for such a public display of dissent to be recognized also required some lack of vigilance or even some connivance from the higher reaches of the administration. The human rights movement and international observers certainly played an important part in drawing attention to the scale of officially tolerated fraud. But it should be recalled that President Banzer remained directly responsible for the conduct of the electoral campaign and may have had his own reasons for undercutting Pereda's victory. His political interests would not necessarily be ill-served by a strong showing from the antimilitarist opposition. The Siles coalition could hardly rest content with a "constitutional" Pereda government based on military and conservative support. Consequently, a strong showing by Siles would keep the Pereda government weak and dependent upon the most highly organized nucleus of conservative leadership, which was still centered on President Banzer's military and financial associates.

It would be misleading, however, to overstate the orderly and rational basis of the behavior of Bolivian powerholders at this juncture. Disunity and distrust characterized the ruling group as their initial calculations fell apart and centrally held power devolved onto a range of semi-independent local factions. In this complex process one aspect was the most strategic. A majority of the electorate were still rural cultivators, most of whom had benefitted from the agrarian reform of the 1950s. Both Paz Estenssoro and Siles Suazo could claim credit for the land distribution of that period. But since the death of General Barrientos in 1968 there had been no military candidate who could appeal to the peasantry as a benefactor. A younger generation of better-educated peasant organizers had emerged since then and had found that the complex postreform needs of the rural sector were not being well attended by a military establishment accustomed to manipulating docile peasant leaders and contemptuous of an indigenous population known mainly for the conscripts it provided. Once independent labor unions had been reestablished in the cities, the example of autonomous organizations overthrowing government-protected pseudo-leaders soon spread to the countryside, and the twenty-year-old rift between worker and peasant organizations began to close. Thus, in 1978, military control over the rural vote was far more tenuous than it had been in the previous electoral contest of 1966. So the electoral campaign caused a crisis for the military-peasant pact, already partially discredited by a previous history of misuse. The crisis was first felt at the garrison level, where local commanders customarily maintained a clientele of dependent peasant leaders. Any garrison commander had to fear that the regime would measure his loyalty by the electoral returns secured in his region. But as the election campaign gathered momentum, the task of delivering an acceptable result became increasingly onerous. In a region like Tarija, where Paz Estenssoro had a traditional ascendancy, the solution might be for the garrison commander to renegotiate his relationship with relatively manageable local peasant organizations. In parts of the northern *altiplano* where rural activists were most assertive and Siles did best, the mechanisms of the military-peasant pact quite simply failed to operate. But in much of the eastern lowlands, where conservative and landlord influence remained entrenched, blatant fraud and intimidation became the norm. With such a diversity of strategies employed at the local level, officers were forced into decisions for which there was no institutional consensus. In short, the election campaign undermined military discipline, disintegrated the military-peasant pact, and created a climate of uncertainty in which radical mobilization might be rewarded by political success. What began as a "controlled" liberalization slipped out of control, as long-repressed social demands surfaced, and the authoritarian regime split into warring factions.

As the election results were announced, denunciations of fraud came pouring in. Here, international pressures may have played their most important part. The electoral process had been launched to promote national unity against Chile and to head off complaints by the human rights lobby. Instead it had aggravated internal disunity and confirmed some of the worst fears of the regime's international critics. Generals Banzer and Pereda each sought to shift blame for this disaster onto the other. Pereda called for an annulment of his own election, hoping to try again with less tainted results.[3] Banzer declared that when his term ended on 6 August power would devolve on the armed forces, given the absence of a clear electoral mandate. On 21 July, with support from Banzer's traditional stronghold of Santa Cruz, Pereda seized power, promising new elections within six months.

In the ensuing two-year interregnum, rival civilian factions intensified their bids for military support, successive generals attempted to hold the reins of power, and fresh elections were alternately approved and then postponed. An intricate sequence of developments occurred, worthy of reconstruction but beyond the scope of this chapter. A series of simplifying assertions must substitute for a full account. The military found themselves unable to resolve their internal problems by once again suppressing civilian political life. Civilian political groups were unable to construct a united front against the military, at least in part because they lacked an electoral verdict which measured the true weight of each party against its rivals. A series of precarious interim governments faced a cascade of social demands that had been pent up during the dictatorship. These were not only economic demands from the independent peasant, worker, and student organizations, but also political demands for freedom, justice, and the investigation of past crimes and abuses, pressed by the church and human rights movement. Conventional businessmen found this absence of governmental authority inimical to any orderly economic management. The narcotics mafia, already well entrenched during the Banzer government, stepped up its political and criminal activities, and added to its paramilitary capabilities. Outsiders reacted to the turmoil in Bolivia's internal affairs by increased meddling. The result of these competing tendencies was eventually to create the possibility of an "unmanaged" and genuine electoral transition to constitutional government, but only in a climate of great confusion, high tension, and severe risk.

Relatively unmanaged elections were held in July 1979, but they produced inconclusive and disputed results. In the presidential contest, Siles officially led Paz, but only by 1,500 votes, with Banzer running a respectable third (Siles, 528,700; Paz, 527,200; Banzer, 218,600). This time the Socialist candidate, Marcelo Quiroga, who had gathered support by denouncing the Banzer regime's crimes, jumped to fourth place with over 100,000 votes and five deputies, a significant force to the left of Siles. (In 1968 Quiroga had made similar charges in Congress against the recently deceased president, General Barrientos.) According to the 1967 Constitution, since no one candidate had over 50 percent of the popular vote, the issue had to pass to the newly elected Congress. But there Paz had 64 votes to only 46 for Siles, with 73 required for ratification as president. Each of the two front-runners denounced the electoral fraud practiced by his rival, but Siles probably had more grounds for complaint.[4] In any event, Congress failed to elect either, and after nine days of humiliating deadlock, the two leading candidates had to compromise, throwing their joint support behind the president of the Senate, who was elected on an interim basis for one year.

The failure of Bolivia's second presidential election to produce a broad-based civilian coalition or an indisputable victory for one party left the process of democratization in jeopardy. The Socialist candidate, Marcelo Quiroga, announced ten days after the election that the armed forces had presented a sixteen-point set of demands to the various civilian candidates. These alleged demands included involvement of the high command in all cabinet discussions and decisions; preservation of the purchasing power of all military salaries, with pay raises for the officer corps; and a guarantee of adequate resources for COFADENA, the military institution that operated various strategic public enterprises. Although the military denied making these demands, Quiroga's sources of information generally proved well informed, and his party proceeded to use its reputation in Congress to introduce a series of well-documented indictments against the Banzer administration, charging corruption, human rights violations, and even treason (the latter concerning the negotiations with Chile). On 3 September 1979, the army high command responded with the following warning:

> Instead of promoting a united effort to settle differences which are an obstacle to the consolidation of democracy, some elements have decided to promote actions intended to involve the armed forces. . . . [They are following] a path which is dangerous for the institutionalization of the country, even inciting a confrontation between the branches of government. . . . Let no one be deceived, because the consequences of a policy of provocation will be entirely shouldered by those who intend to plunge the country into an unbearable situation.

Two months later the army briefly and bloodily seized power and closed Congress, but in the face of determined popular resistance it backed off after sixteen days, allowing democratization to proceed.

Nevertheless, while Congress was functioning, the Socialist party proceeded with its documented denunciations, and the other parties were unable to restrain this initiative (which had considerable popular support) ahead of the next round of elections. It was in such a climate that, in July 1980, a third and final attempt was made to complete the formal democratization process.

At least there was general agreement on the procedures for holding genuine presidential and legislative elections. However, following the open election of 29 June 1980 the experiment definitely collapsed.

Within the military leadership there were those who favored a Peruvian-style return to barracks. As usual their most persuasive argument was that this would restore the prestige and unity of the armed forces, which would, of course, retain the possibility of returning to power in the event of civilian mismanagement. This argument prevailed, however, only for rather short periods of time, when the evidence of military unpopularity and disunity was most unmistakable. As the July 1980 election drew closer, counterarguments became more persuasive. According to one senior officer,

> Bringing off a successful coup in Bolivia presupposes bringing one off in the army first. García Meza and Arce Gómez utilized the campaign that the left-wing parties were waging against the armed forces at that time [accusations levelled against General Banzer, slashing the defense budget] to reverse the majority trend in the high command, which favored respecting the democratic process. They pointed out that the military institution could not tolerate such attacks on its prestige any longer and cleverly played on the fears that troop strength and salaries might be cut.[5]

Here we have a recurring problem of political strategy for aspiring democratizers. On the one hand they must demonstrate that democracy offers the opportunity to correct past abuses and ensure against their repetition. Too much restraint on this score will demoralize their followers and be viewed by the authoritarian Right as evidence of weakness. On the other hand any reference to military excesses may trigger an institutional backlash that jeopardizes the whole process of transition. There is probably no safe and reliable strategy that escapes this dilemma. In Bolivia there was quite pervasive criminality in the officer corps, so that the temptation to denounce military excesses was hard to resist, especially in a closely fought election. My own guess is that however skillfully the civilian democratizers had handled military susceptibilities, they faced an unavoidable risk of failure, since the military and economic factions involved in the narcotics traffic would be under no illusion that their privileges could survive a democratic government, no matter how tactfully the civilians behaved.

There can be no precise reconstruction of the rival political strategies that led up to the coup of 17 July 1980, for too many disparate forces competed for allegiance, too many incompatible perceptions were in play, and the scene shifted too quickly to permit the operation of stable and well-informed calculations. As in other episodes of attempted democratization under study, the margin of unpredictability can for a brief period become extremely wide, with unsettling effects on the outlook of all participants in the political process. There were ample reasons for such uncertainty in Bolivia. In November 1979 there had been a coup to thwart the electoral process. This coup, which had the evident support of some fifty congressmen, lasted sixteen days and cost over two hundred lives. The following month another fragile civilian government, under pressure from the IMF to confront a rapidly deteriorating economy, discovered that the result of raising gasoline prices was an impressive nationwide movement of peasant protest which blocked roads across the country until farm prices were raised. Throughout the ensuing seven months of electoral campaigning there were repeated incidents of threats and violence, expressing the military's discontent with the democratization process. The murder by paramilitary forces of a leading Jesuit advocate of the human rights cause brought out a 70,000-strong funeral procession, but not long thereafter a plane carrying UDP leaders crashed in circumstances that pointed to sabotage. Siles was deterred by violence from setting foot in the lowland city of Santa Cruz, despite its importance for the election campaign. On the other side, the civilian political groupings were too uncertain of their relative strengths, and too riven by historical rivalries and memories of betrayal, to construct a firm "democratizing alliance" among themselves. Although they shared a common awareness of the dangers from the Right, they differed profoundly in their reactions to that threat, and differed also in the behavior they anticipated from each other, given a common danger. In brief outline, Paz Estenssoro responded to the threat by strengthening his ties with the "less extreme" Right; Siles Suazo redoubled his efforts to secure international protection and support (especially from the Carter administration); Lechín concentrated on reviving the labor movement, in the process flirting with some unsavory right-wing associations; and Quiroga Santa Cruz focused on the past misdeeds of the military. While difficult interpersonal relations undoubtedly contributed to their differences (Paz Estenssoro, Siles Suazo, and Lechín had for almost forty years campaigned together and maneuvered against each other in the merry-go-round of Bolivian populist politics), the obstacles to more effective collaboration lay deeper. There were profound underlying disagreements about what kind of democracy was possible or desirable in Bolivian conditions, which may be summed up as disagreements over what should be the correct relationship between the machinery of the state and the mass organizations. The electoral process was only seen as one step toward resolving these long-standing issues of political controversy. It might temporarily determine who became president, and under what formal or implicit understandings, but that was only a proximate, rather than the ultimate, objective of civilian political action. The deeper issue remaining to be resolved concerned which parts of the legacy of the 1952 revolution could be revitalized or adapted to provide mass support and direction for future popularly based governments. Both the character and the durability of any "democratization" process would depend upon how that question was answered.

The campaign to produce a constitutionally elected government was touch-and-go to the very end. Just as the military contained an uncertain current of prodemocratic opinion, the civilian sector included various groups that might compensate for a poor electoral showing by defecting from the "prodemocratic" alliance (as some close associates of Paz Estenssoro had done in November 1979). In his efforts to avert a preelectoral coup, U.S. Ambassador Weissman unavoidably became a controversial figure.[6] The fragility of the democratizing effort is best illustrated by the contrast between the three successive electoral tests that were held. The 1978 results appeared to favor the Right, those of 1979 gave considerable strength to the Center, whereas the results of 1980 gave a clear margin (though not quite an absolute majority) to the two candidates of the Left.[7] My own guess is that on a true count the 1978 and 1979 results would have resembled those of 1980 (i.e., those in control of the count inflated the strength of first one anti-Siles candidate, and then another), but the conflicting sides will never reach agreement on this point. Their disagreements over the electoral results reflected more than just a series of differences over empirical questions. The rival candidates also had different perceptions of the distribution of real power in the society and differing conceptions of what type of more or less democratic political arrangements might be viable. It is doubtful whether a different set of constitutional or electoral provisions would have softened these differences, although the question is worth debating. It seems that the minimum conditions for a stable democratizing alliance were absent—there was disagreement over the character of the desired democracy, disagreement over the means to promote democratization, and disagreement over both the strength and the reliability of the constitutional elements that would compose the alliance—with the result that every part of the alliance had grounds for discontent with the rest, and the process of democratization itself was characterized by costly delays and unseemly recriminations, providing just the discredit for which the enemies of the process must have hoped. Although Siles Suazo finally emerged with a clear lead in the third election, he did not obtain an overwhelming victory, and even some of his supporters concede that their enthusiasm had been sapped by the length of the struggle.

Once the 29 June elections had taken place, most observers supposed that the moment of greatest danger had passed. Provided this third electoral test produced a relatively clearcut verdict, there should be, it was thought, clear sailing to the inauguration of a constitutional president on 6 August 1980. In reality, however, the postelectoral period was the most dangerous of all. The results of the popular vote were sufficiently clearcut to dispel any illusions either within Bolivia or in neighboring countries about the likely outcome of a successful democratization. As General García Meza, the army commander, told Brazilian reporters on 3 July, "In Bolivia there is an extremism disguised as democracy . . . [the Armed Forces] have always shared that desire of the people [for democratization]. What we disagree with at this time, as the neighboring countries also disagree, is that an extreme leftist government should assume power, something that could influence other nations, especially in South America, including Brazil."[8] Since Siles Suazo had not received 50 percent of the popular vote, and had only 57 supporters in the newly elected Congress (out of 157 members), it was still possible to imagine some maneuver that would deprive him of victory. On 9 July, however, Paz Estenssoro finally ended his conflict with Siles Suazo, as he had long been urged to do, telling a Lima newspaper it would be "negative for the country's democratization process" to prevent Siles Suazo from taking office or to force him into a constraining political pact.[9] Thus, after almost nine years of estrangement from the Siles wing of the MNR, Paz Estenssoro parted ways from Banzer (who had, after all, played his part in blocking Paz Estenssoro from the presidency the year before) and moved towards reconciliation with the Left. As he may well have feared, in the eyes of the Right this move clarified the need for a coup.

The military had learned from their previous unsuccessful efforts to thwart the democratization process, particularly the short-lived dictatorship of November 1979. This time great violence would be needed to break the expectations established by the election and to overcome an aroused resistance. Having waited so long to intervene, and having allowed the victims the moral support of an election victory, they had to proceed with unrestrained ferocity. What gave the impetus for this assault was not so much fear for the survival of their institution (which, if anything, is more threatened by the proliferation of paramilitary forces than by the Left), nor any deep ideological commitment. Rather, it was a condition that sets the Bolivian example apart from most of the examples of authoritarianism under study: the prospect of large-scale illicit enrichment for the officer corps through a more unfettered development of the narcotics trade.

Concluding Reflections

The issues I have indicated as impediments to a stable democratizing alliance in Bolivia were also present to varying degrees in several other Latin American countries, although not perhaps in quite the same acute form. Formal democracy may not be an entirely convincing end in itself for popular movements whose followers have urgent material needs to satisfy, and whose leaders have learned that political power can be used to redistribute income and reshape the processes of production. This is especially true in countries where mass politics is linked in the historical memory to the idea of socioeconomic transformation, and where the collapse of mass politics led both to a reconcentration of income and wealth and to a closure of political avenues of expression. In such circumstances, it is hardly surprising if subsequent generations of popular leadership come under pressure to view democratic procedures from an instrumental rather than a fundamentalist standpoint. For popular movements of this kind, democratically elected government is clearly preferable to conservative authoritarianism, but important groups within such movements inevitably demand that social redistribution accompany formal democracy. And in due course, if it is necessary to preserve the new pattern of distribution by sacrificing some of the formal liberties which accompanied democratization, Latin American history suggests that some popular movements (not just their "totalitarian" leaders) may, perhaps reluctantly, make that sacrifice to "save the revolution." We can see this as a major issue for contemporary Nicaragua, and it remains an unresolved issue for the Chilean Left, and presumably for the various fragments of Peronism. In Bolivia, the dominant interests threatened by the democratic transition did their best to create alarm about the scale of this threat, trying to show that they were not opposed to a "responsible" democracy, whereas their supposedly democratic opponents were totalitarians in disguise. This campaign had some effect, in part because it contained an inescapable grain of truth, although the front-running candidate, Siles Suazo, could lay a more plausible claim than any rival Bolivian politician to being a true democrat. He had already served as president from 1956 to 1960, showing an unusually scrupulous regard for constitutional propriety, but inevitably in the 1978–80 period his critics described him as a dupe of the totalitarian Left. (When interpreting these charges, it is as well to recall that General Banzer has bluntly described the Socialist International of Brandt and González as a form of international "extremism.") Conscious that the authoritarian Right was eager to appropriate the mantle of "democracy" for itself, the political leaders of the Center and the Left tried to avoid open disagreements among themselves about their respective views of democracy. But these political leaders were deeply divided over the issues raised by socioeconomic redistribution, and they had learned from past experience that their political rivals might adopt a purely instrumental approach to the value of formal democracy. Quiet awareness of these underlying truths did prevent Bolivia's civilian politicians from uniting around a more solid and effective "democratizing pact." Generalizing from this example, while one is always justified to inquire into the scope for promoting democracy through the conscious strategies chosen by political elites, it would be rash to underestimate the structural and historical constraints on such initiatives that now exist in various Latin American countries.

Bolivia's economic and social structure seems to resemble that of neighboring Peru and Ecuador, both of which achieved successful transitions to "democracy" at the end of the 1970s. However, Bolivian political traditions were far more radical, as indicated above in the discussion of the 1952 revolution.

It is debatable whether the Ecuadorean/Peruvian form of democracy could have generated a significant degree of support and enthusiasm in Bolivia. Indeed, Cotler (Chapter 7) and others have argued that even in Peru, "formal democracy" elicits little positive allegiance, existing more because of a temporary bankruptcy of the alternatives than because of its inherent local appeal. Although it had once had far milder connotations, "democracy" after 1952 meant for Bolivians the kind of social redistribution associated with the names of Siles Suazo, Lechín, and Paz Estenssoro. For Peruvians it still meant the more modest activities of a Belaúnde Terry. The Bolivian version of "democracy" necessarily excited more hope, and also aroused far more fear, particularly among the military, the bankers, and the major private exporting groups. These privileged groups contained elements that were exceptionally hostile to any form of democratic control because of their links to the military-controlled narcotics smuggling industry that had flourished under the shelter of the Banzer dictatorship. In addition, the international setting for a Bolivian attempt at democracy was distinctly adverse. (Note the contrast with 1945, when the international conjuncture was very different.) Argentina in particular, and the Southern Cone dictatorships in general, perceived a threat that might have internal ramifications, if the civilian form of government established in the Andean Pact region were to spread any further south. From this standpoint, any rebuff to the political ambitions of the Bolivian armed forces, however well merited, might set an unacceptable example. It would not be necessary for Siles Suazo to act recklessly in order to incur the enmity of southern governments. Indeed, no matter how much restraint his administration might show, its mere existence would be regarded by neighboring governments as intolerable. Thus, the election apparently gave rise to some degree of precautionary intervention by elements of the Argentine military.

The legacy of Bolivia's failed transition to democracy will not be an asset in any future attempt of the same kind. In the same way that a failed attempt at economic stabilization increases the difficulty of making any future stabilization policy effective, a failed democratization teaches lessons that may be harmful to future endeavors. For example, it teaches privileged minorities that they need not run the risks of a political transition, that a viable alternative exists if they resort to redoubled ruthlessness. It teaches the victims of deprivation to insist on immediate satisfaction of their needs, before the tortuous and uncertain process of democratic construction collapses around them. It teaches revolutionary minorities not to disarm and place their trust in a civilian political compact. For the democratic politicians themselves, perhaps the lessons are not so clear. To some extent the experience of failure, and the high costs it entails, may teach them to make greater efforts of adaptation and to construct more ambitious and broad-visioned arrangements to safeguard political freedom. That would be the most hopeful interpretation, and some supporting examples can be found (Venezuelan and Colombian politicians after the debacles of 1948).

However, even for the civilian politicians who have managed to survive the dispersal and attrition that followed the July 1980 coup, the lessons are at least partly discouraging and disorienting. For example, after the assassination of Quiroga Santa Cruz (which followed immediately on García Meza's coup), how many future unarmed democratic politicians will dare to speak out in Parliament denouncing the crimes of authoritarian rulers? And what kind of democracy is possible if civilian leaders dare not, for fear of their lives and their few precarious freedoms, question the arbitrary power of the security forces?

This issue arises above all in such countries as Bolivia, where illicit enrichment has become the mainstay of the authoritarian regime. But it is not confined to such cases. Spanish democrats have recently been confronted by this painful issue, for the failed democratization of their country in the 1930s still casts its long shadow over their efforts. In all of the countries under study, the same issue is likely to present itself in one guise or another. In my opinion it is a defining characteristic of authoritarianism that the security forces may commit crimes with the promise of impunity. Unless that promise is conclusively revoked, there can be no definitive transition to democracy. (By this standard we must recognize that some authoritarian tendencies may exist even in apparently well-established democracies.) Whether we analyze the social meaning of democracy in a particular country, or examine more generally the source of its appeal, or the obstacles to its attainment, a central question is always how to subject the official security forces to democratic control and to the rule of law. Although past success in this regard may feed upon itself, the process is always precarious. A history of failure to curb military excesses makes the task of democratizing far more costly and laborious.

Epilogue

Although the redemocratization efforts of 1978–80 ended in failure, that was not the end of the story. The military dictatorship lasted for two years, during which criminality flourished as never before and the illegal export of narcotics became an economic mainstay. The Bolivian government became a pariah in the international community; internally, the armed forces found themselves exceptionally isolated from their potential bases of support. Some superficial comparisons can be drawn with the isolation of the military governments of 1946 and 1952. Once again, as on these previous occasions, it proved impossible to maintain the cohesion of the armed forces. But whereas the MNR and the mineworkers had provided a source of civilian support to the Villarroel regime prior to the 1946 revolution, and the Right and the mine owners had supported General Ballivian prior to the 1952 revolution, this time it was only the paramilitary groups (organized by such figures as Klaus Barbie, the Nazi "butcher of Lyons") who propped up the García Meza dictatorship. By mid-1982 all the "respectable" political parties and social organizations of the country had rallied to the opposition. After an internal upheaval, the armed forces bowed to this reality and authorized a transfer of power to Siles Suazo, respecting the results of the 1980 election after a two-year interregnum.

Given the shortsighted, indiscriminately repressive, and parasitic nature of the outgoing military regime, the redemocratization of mid-1982 was a fairly unplanned and disorderly affair. Although the civilian parties managed to work together reasonably well until the transfer of power was accomplished, the internecine conflicts which had blighted the 1978–80 process were never far below the surface. After the repression and disarticulation of 1980–82, the political parties needed to reconstruct their links with the country's underlying social movements. These, in turn, had been demoralized and even driven to desperation, not only by the repression, but also by the disintegration of social organization caused by the narcotics traffickers. For many, the return of democracy seemed to offer an unexpected new chance to create a participatory framework for tackling the country's overwhelming social and economic problems.

Unfortunately, President Siles Suazo's second term of office has proved even more unhappy than his first. So unsuccessful was his administration in addressing the economic crisis that the only way he could head off another relapse into authoritarianism was by voluntarily foreshortening his term of office. He and his political rivals have for the most part cooperated in averting a new military dictatorship, but in little else. Elections for his successor were originally scheduled for mid-1986, but were then brought forward to mid-1985. Like Belaúnde in neighboring Peru, Siles Suazo's highest ambition became to hold on until the sash of office could be transferred to an elected successor. (Víctor Paz Estenssoro narrowly defeated Hugo Banzer in July 1985.) The economic and social situation of the country continues inexorably to deteriorate.

In summary, then, the 1978–80 redemocratization process proved more fragile in Bolivia than comparable processes in Peru and Ecuador, and ended in spectacular failure. The ensuing period of military authoritarianism was also characterized by extreme mismanagement, and also ended in humiliating failure. With these antecedents, the restoration of democracy in 1982 occurred *faute de mieux* rather than from any historical necessity. Sadly, this least bad formula of government has proved almost as fragile and unsuccessful as the regime that preceded it. The economic and social conditions of the country make Bolivia an extremely difficult country to govern well, and the inherited political traditions tend to further weaken the cohesion and credibility of almost any government, whether democratic or authoritarian.

4 ·

The "Liberalization" of Authoritarian Rule in Brazil

Luciano Martins

Analytical Approach

In my view, three main findings must be stressed from the considerable fac-
tual material gathered and the intellectual progress made in recent years on
the comparative study of the emergence and the demise of contemporary
authoritarian regimes: (1) contrary to what their apparent stability might
suggest, these regimes are subject to more or less continuous processes of
change and adaptation; (2) the transformation of authoritarian regimes is not
necessarily achieved by means of their overthrow, but may also result from
these processes of evolutionary change; (3) in any case, the (re)establishment
of "democratic forms" of government is only one of the possible outcomes of
their transformation. To this it should be added that we are still unable to
generalize concerning the circumstances in which this or that outcome will
prevail—and to explain fully *why* it prevails.

If this is correct, one must concede that there is not yet an articulated set of
propositions which could be convincingly presented as a "theory" of the transformation or the demise of authoritarian regimes. In fact, it could not be
otherwise, first, because we lack the proper time perspective needed to appre-
hend the historical trend underlying both the emergence and the decline of
contemporary authoritarian regimes; and second, because present theories of
social change seem inadequate to keep up with changes in class dynamics and
class behavior in capitalist societies, where productive systems, social and
power structures, values and lifestyles, are in permanent transformation,
when not in disruption. This dynamism is a consequence of the accelerated
pace and sometimes erratic course of economic change, and also a result of the
drastic cultural changes that follow from the existence of an authoritarian
regime. If this is so, I suspect that the question of why these regimes are
transformed (assuming that the answer to this question necessarily provides a
link between class structures, collective interests, and/or systemic trends and
power structures) will have to wait until we have acquired a better knowledge
of what changes and how it changes when an authoritarian regime enters a
process of political transition.

In line with this view, I will confine myself in this chapter, first, to characterizing what appears to be a self-promoted "liberalization" of authoritarian

rule in Brazil and, second, to making a few speculations on what the regime's ability to initiate and control its own change may suggest concerning its internal dynamics and its articulation with society. This first part will be carried out through a contrapuntal analysis by means of which I will relate some characteristic features of the Brazilian authoritarian regime and the way in which crisis situations may evolve from these characteristics, with the dynamics of the political process (i.e., impulses for change and for conservation) which give form and content to the "liberalization" of authoritarian rule. These orientations will be explained in the next section.

To set the parameters for the analysis and to demarcate the field where the phenomena we are interested in may occur I have adopted a simplified descriptive "model" to represent the logical or analytically distinguishable sequences of a political transition process, and the alternative developments that these sequences may produce. This model assumes: (1) that after its emergence and consolidation, an authoritarian regime acquires some defined characteristics and tends to reach a certain state of equilibrium; (2) that this state of equilibrium can be *stable* or *unstable*, according to the degree of institutionalization reached by the regime;[1] and (3) that crisis situations which may trigger a regime's transformation tend to occur when the regime's ability to deal with "internal" or systemic problems diminishes, ushering in a state of unstable equilibrium.

The two initial tasks of the analysis would then be to identify the main characteristics of the regime in order to set the parameters for the evaluation of subsequent changes, and to identify the origin and the nature of the critical situation(s) which may trigger the regime's transformation. Because changes can be introduced in the regime without transforming it into a different one, or because its effective transformation could take a long time, there is a state of *transition*. Thus, it is considered here that transition differs from transformation in the sense that the former is marked by the introduction of a certain number of changes *in* the regime, and the latter implies a change *of* regime. Two modes of transition may be proposed: *continuous* and *discontinuous* transitions. At this level of generality one can only say that what distinguishes one mode from the other is the ruling elite's greater or lesser ability to deal with critical situations. This is of course a tautology, but such a formulation may serve to isolate the intervening variables (statesmanship, internal cleavages or fractures that may affect the regime's operational capabilities, foreign pressures, economic crisis, and the like) which could speed up, delay, or even redirect developments more or less independently of the correlation of forces between the regime's protagonists and their opponents. In the case of a discontinuous transition we have two possible developments: either the regime manages to meet the crisis through different forms of compromise or through the deployment of a higher degree of coercion (in which case it reconsolidates itself); or it does not meet these requirements (in which case it collapses). In the case of a continuous transition, we will probably have a series of limited political coalitions and of successive and contradictory balances between impulses for change and impulses for conservation. Their interaction will produce a sequence of slow incremental changes *in* the existing regime, until it is eventually transformed. The third task of the analysis is, therefore, to identify the mode of transition.

Next, we must consider the possible outcomes when an effective transformation of an existing authoritarian regime occurs. At this level of generality, we can make use of the conventional paradigms concerning political regimes. Therefore, three hypotheses can be proposed: transformation into another "authoritarian" regime; transformation into a "democratic" regime; or, finally, transformation into a "totalitarian" regime. Needless to say, the concept of *outcome* could be a misleading one when used in situations where it is still difficult to distinguish the end of one historical cycle from the beginning of another. This is why I use "outcome" here to mean the emergence of a regime which differs from the previous one, regardless of its subsequent success or otherwise at consolidation. Thus, the first and last task of the analysis would be either to characterize the passage from transition to transformation and to identify the resulting outcome (if that is the case), or to speculate on the possible outcomes (if the transition is still in process).

As in any attempt to formalize social processes, this simplified representation of possible sequences and developments raises a series of conceptual and practical difficulties. Since my intention is only to define a strategy for the analysis of transitions from authoritarianism, we can deal with these difficulties in the course of the analysis. However, some clarifications must be made right now concerning the way I have approached what I have called the four main tasks of analysis. The first of these deals with the characteristics assumed by the existing regime after its consolidation. The orientation adopted here is to emphasize what is more specific to the case in question (Brazil) and, at the same time, to emphasize those features which are more directly linked to the dynamics of the process of transition. In this connection the main dimensions which will be considered are values and ideology, structure of authority, norms and rules of the game, and public policies. Attention will be focused much more on practices than on institutional forms, for the former tend to prevail over the latter whenever arbitrary power is the rule.

The second task consists in identifying the points of crisis which are supposed to trigger the process of change. Here it seems important to make a difficult analytical distinction between crises which originate within the regime ("internal" crises) and those engendered at the level of society ("external" crises). By the former I mean those crises linked to the resolution (or nonresolution) of the problems related to the "internal economy" of the regime.[2] The second type of crisis may originate in (1) the growth and/or diversification of societal demands (social unrest, appearance of new collective actors, a new capacity of groups and classes to express themselves politically, etc.); (2) the erosion of the regime's support caused by the diversification of strategic groups' interests or by new coalitions among them; (3) incongruence between societal requirements and the ideological stand or the operational performance of the regime (obsolescence of values, inefficiency or corruption of the bureaucracy, etc.); (4) the emergence of economic crisis which could affect the regime's ability to control the economy and/or to allocate financial rewards to its supporters; (5) the emergence of alternative political projects able to mobilize the support needed for a redefinition of political coalitions; (6) foreign pressures or intervention, and so forth.

To what extent a crisis may originate in any one or more of these dimensions and spread to or reinforce others is a matter for empirical investigation, just as the relationship between political developments inside the regime and social developments in the larger society is a matter for historical analysis. The main practical difficulty of an investigation into the genesis and development of a crisis under an authoritarian regime comes from the lack of visible or reliable indicators. One has to deal with situations where, on the one hand, the standard channels of expression of political aspirations and interests in the society are inhibited and so are usually rechannelled into (and refracted by) substitute arenas (the church, professional associations, etc.) rather than through whatever political parties or political associations may be tolerated by the regime. On the other hand, developments taking place inside the regime are usually difficult to evaluate, thanks to the opaque curtain separating regime from society. Therefore, the differentiation of interests, internal fractures, the emergence of political coalitions, and the birth of new leaderships, both within the ruling elite and at the level of society, all have a sort of clandestine gestation. As a consequence, the evaluation of critical situations must rely heavily upon the analyst's intuitive perceptions and procedures, which substantially increases the margin of error in the analysis of a transition process—so much so that transition under authoritarian regimes often produces "surprising" developments: regimes which suddenly fall apart or, conversely, regimes which show an undetected ability for reconsolidation.

As has been said, the third task of analysis consists in defining the mode of transition. The alternatives proposed are only indicative and are difficult to formalize, first, because the political process is marked by rather contradictory moves, in which actions and reactions take the form of limited advances from and partial relapses back into authoritarian rule; and second, because what appears as a continuous mode of transition can suddenly be transformed into a discontinuous one. Accordingly, it is not always easy to distinguish one mode from another, except *a posteriori*. In spite of all these difficulties, the characterization of the mode of transition is essential to the definition of the concept of "liberalization." In this connection, the practical problems one has to face relate, first, to the nature and the scope of changes introduced *in* the regime (the degree of liberalization), and, second, to the dynamic of the political process during the transition (a dynamic based on the relationship between the intensity of the crisis and the regime's ability to face it). The first problem could be solved through a comparison of the regime's characteristics at a certain point (say, the moment of its consolidation) and its characteristics at subsequent $t + 1$. Tackling the second problem requires an analysis of who has the initiative in, and control over, the transition process (the regime's protagonists, or its opponents), of how political coalitions are redefined, and of what alternative political projects are in contention. Both questions are intimately linked to the modal types of transformation of authoritarian regimes. Here I would tentatively adopt the four alternatives proposed by Philippe Schmitter: seizure of power, transfer of power, surrender of power, and overthrow of power.

The final task relates to the identification (or forecast) of outcomes. This seems to present two practical problems: first, how to determine the degree of change which converts a transition into a transformation; second, what new type of regime results. Both problems are easier to solve when the demise of the authoritarian regime takes the form of a collapse *and* when the new regime conforms to either a "democratic" or a "totalitarian" paradigm (the latter being at least a logically possible outcome, although not necessarily a likely one). Difficulties appear, however, when one deals with a continuous mode of transition (probably slow and nonviolent) and/or when the newly emerging regime is a subtype of one of the above-mentioned paradigms—or indeed a new form of authoritarianism. The reason is that in such a case transition follows a more or less protracted evolution, produces developments that include some "transfer of power," and gives birth to hybrid forms of domination.

These are the general orientations I have adopted in search of a framework for the analysis of what changes and how it changes when an authoritarian regime passes through a process of transition. Needless to say, it will not always be possible (for lack of information or other reasons) to exploit all the paths suggested by this framework. *Per contra*, I will not sacrifice the intuitive perception of situations and elements of a still difficult apprehension on the altar of formalizations which, besides being naively premature, empty the analysis of what could be its main interest: to register and express the ambiguities of a process which still may be underway.

Characteristics of the Brazilian Regime and of Its Crisis

As is well known, political authoritarianism and economic "modernization" have been present, in one form or another, throughout Brazil's political and economic evolution. However, the regime which was established after the overthrow of the constitutional government in 1964 acquired characteristics which make it different from the typical forms assumed by the previous mode of domination, in relation to (1) the organization of the state, the exercise of power, and the structure of authority, and to (2) the content of public policies adopted to make the society conform to a given "model" of capitalist expansion. These two features justify inclusion of post-1964 Brazil in the category of the bureaucratic-authoritarian regimes and also reveal what is probably its historical function, namely the "revolutionary" task of promoting and generalizing a mode of capitalist expansion based on strong state intervention, oligopolistic organization of production, and the internationalization of the economy. The relationship between these two dimensions requires consideration beyond the bounds of this chapter. However, both are needed in order to identify the characteristics of the regime in its consolidated state (i.e., after 1968). The purposes of this identification are to establish a basis for evaluating the regime's subsequent evolution and to locate internal sources of crisis. The characteristics I identify are as follows:

Values and ideology. The regime adopted as official doctrine a certain vision of the Brazilian society which could be summarized thus: (1) that Brazilian society had not yet reached the stage of economic and social development where it could afford the practice of a "true democracy"; (2) that the consolidation and extension of capitalist relations ("promotion of economic development," in the official lexicon) constituted preconditions for the establishment of social structures out of which "stable" and "democratic" institutions would evolve in the future. It is important to note that this was officially perceived and presented as the long-term strategic goal to be attained.[3]

It was in the framework of these assumptions—a rationale which has been elaborated by the Escola Superior de Guerra, but which has deep roots in the Brazilian elitist tradition—that authoritarian practices could be reconciled with the "democratic ideals" of the 1964 revolution, according to military thinking.

Institutional organization of the state. The regime abrogated constitutional, civil, and political rights; suppressed or controlled channels for the representation of interests; and established a virtual dictatorship of the federal executive over the other powers of the republic (legislative, judiciary) and of the federation (state administrations). This was accomplished mainly through the Institutional Act No. 5 (1968) and its successors.

Structure of authority. For the first time since the proclamation of the republic (1889), the armed forces, acting as an institution, took direct control over the major functions of government; there was partial abolition of corporatist-type practices through which nonbureaucratic actors had obtained controlled inclusion in the decision-making system; and there was the build-up of an extensive "intelligence apparatus" for ideological screening and control of loyalties within the state apparatus, in an attempt to produce a standardized outlook both among top officials and among intermediary administrative personnel.

Norms and rules of the game. The principle of political legitimation through direct and secret voting for the executive was abandoned, as was the practice (which in the Brazilian political tradition preceded or substituted for secret voting) of choosing rulers through intraelite consensus. Instead, there was a search for legitimation through economic performance and the exclusive attribution of government roles to the bureaucratic elite or to those sanctioned by it. There was also a succession of arbitrary modifications to the rules of the electoral game and those governing party organizations in order to diminish political competition, to guarantee predictable electoral outcomes, and to keep party alternation in government under strict control.

Political practices. Opponents were neutralized through negative sanctions of various kinds (dismissal from public service, economic pressure, suspension of political rights, police harassment, and even physical elimination). Large financial rewards (subsidies, tax exemptions, etc.) were distributed as a means of acquiring support from strategic groups. Populist-type practices of mobilization were replaced by partially redistributive policies (upwards) and limited welfare measures (downwards).

Public policies. There was a considerable expansion of the normative and entrepreneurial roles of the state in the economy; a dramatic increase of the state's extractive capability (through tax revenues, etc.);[4] and decision-making was increasingly centralized. These developments were considered functional requirements for the promotion and "management" of an economic development project aimed at rapidly diversifying the productive structure and at achieving high rates of growth. The social implications of such a project (in terms of those who pay for it and those who benefit from it) are sufficiently well known to obviate discussion here.

These six characteristics and constitutive features of the regime have already been sufficiently studied, which is why I have merely summarized them here. Less attention, however, has been paid to the sources of crisis that they might engender. Three aspects are particularly worth noting: the regime's ideology, the regime's methods of generating support, and the nature of the relationship between the military and the structure of authority.

Ideology. Although there is nothing new about the ideological rationalization which consists in justifying authoritarian practices and capitalist expansion as "instrumental" to the promotion of democracy in the future, it has important practical consequences concerning the political values and the immediate behavior of actors. It means that in the regime's hierarchy of values, guarantees for the social hegemony of capitalism must take precedence over any search for the regime's own political legitimacy. This hierarchy of values, and the order of practical priorities derived from it, explains how a political and an economic order which was historically quite congruent has subsequently become dissociated. The notions of hegemony and legitimation have their origins in different conceptual frameworks. Hegemony, in the Gramsci tradition, refers to the ideological subordination of exploited classes to dominant classes which allows the latter to exercise their dominance by "consent"; legitimation refers to a political-judicial formula through which consensus for the exercise of authority is obtained. Perhaps because in the historical experience of modern Western capitalist democracies the social (hegemony) and the political (legitimation) phenomena tend to overlap, a confusion between them has resulted. In fact, not infrequently they have been approached as if they were similar in content, as if they were interchangeable, and/or as if the first were a necessary condition for the second and as if both were a condition for the stable maintenance of any given capitalist system. These assumptions have left clear prints in Latin American studies. I am referring, for instance, to those studies which view the "instability" of the region as a consequence of the "hegemonic crisis" brought forth by the disruption of the "oligarchical system" in the absence of a class (say, a "national bourgeoisie") able to impose its hegemony and legitimate itself as a dominant class.

My view differs from this sort of interpretation on two main points. First, and as Gramsci suggested, hegemony is not necessarily linked to the existence of a particular "hegemonic" class (or fraction of a class), but to the social hegemony of capitalism as a mode of production. Secondly, the search for (or the need of) political legitimacy seems only to occur in societies where (1) democratic values are deeply rooted, generally because they have been instrumental for the rise of a bourgeoisie; (2) strong political competition exists; and (3) conflictive social interests are well structured, can be voiced, and take the form of a criticism of capitalism. In societies where these conditions are not present (as is the case for Brazil), social class dominance and political legitimacy do not have a necessary relationship; accordingly, actors may attribute to each of them different values and priorities. If one accepts the existence (with the qualifications I make elsewhere in this chapter) of an elective affinity between delayed-dependent development and authoritarianism, there is no reason not to accept as well the specific implications of such a pattern concerning social behavior. What in my view is interesting about the Brazilian case is how this split between social hegemony of capitalism and political legitimation appears at the ideological level and is, at the same time, used to reinforce both capitalist expansion and political authoritarianism.[5]

It throws some light on the *problématique* of interest representation. If the priority given to capitalist expansion develops "naturally" from the military doctrine which has been used to justify the regime's existence, then the classes and strategic groups in civil society which should organize themselves politically to impose the same goal (if they are to compete with noncapitalist ideologies) tend to undergo continuous political demobilization. That entrepreneurial groups, for instance, are the main beneficiaries of public policies and simultaneously have very limited access to economic policy-making is generally explained only from the perspective of the instrumental role played by the bureaucracy in carrying out the interests of a "weak bourgeoisie." Historically, this may well be true (as I believe it is), but currently it creates a very ambiguous political situation. In fact, this "elective affinity" between the regime's ideology and entrepreneurial interests guarantees a broad passive support for the authoritarian regime and allows the regime's bureaucracy a considerable degree of freedom and a growing margin of maneuver in policy-making. This is particularly true when the society is passing through a period of economic bonanza. However, in periods of economic slowdown or of a perceived potential economic crisis, when resource allocation and the setting of new economic priorities become crucial, the absence of institutionalized mechanisms of representation of interests, as well as the "autonomy" previously acquired by the bureaucracy, tends to be perceived as a serious political handicap by the very beneficiaries of the regime's developmental policies. It is then that the criticism of *estatismo* (meaning "excessive" bureaucratic expansion) begins to take shape, and the argument of political legitimation is raised by strategic groups to justify their demands for some sort of "liberalization."[6] At the same time, these same strategic groups become receptive to criticism of the economic model as a way of undermining the prestige of the bureaucracy and of searching for new alliances in the society at large. This seems, in the Brazilian case, to account for the subsequent transformation of protagonists into dissidents. The result has been that the previously strong entrepreneurial-bureaucratic coalition came under stress, the social basis of the regime began to erode, and a situation of unstable equilibrium arose.

However, the ability of the regime's protagonists to adapt (specifically the military) tends to be hampered by a second political effect derived from the ideological dissociation mentioned above. Since the ideological hierarchization of values gives top priority to economic achievement, any real or perceived risk to the fulfillment of this goal will tend to weigh more heavily than equivalent risks derived from the regime's lack of political legitimacy. Demands for redemocratization or denunciation of the regime's illegitimacy are not acknowledged as a *value* by the regime's protagonists, least of all by the military.[7] On the contrary, such demands and criticisms are viewed as obstacles to attainment of the regime's strategic goals and, as a consequence, dismissed as demagoguery, or more dangerously, as a front for subversion. It is not (as is often supposed) the lack of political legitimacy *per se* that makes the authoritarian regime vulnerable to political criticism, but rather the criticism emanating from those strategic groups who have been turned into dissidents in the absence of mechanisms for representing their interests. The main problem, both for the regime and for its dissidents, is, of course, how to restore such mechanisms without opening the door to opponents who are rightly or wrongly perceived as capable of jeopardizing the strategic goal of accelerating economic development. And this is precisely the dilemma of the politics of "liberalization" (*abertura*): how to "liberalize" and at the same time block an opposition which proposes immediate distributive and social policies.

Methods of generating support. Some of the regime's characteristics suggest that one of its most important methods for making strategic groups acquiesce to bureaucratic authoritarianism is the offer of economic benefits as a substitute for political freedoms. In fact, the irrational scale of the regime's "subsidies" indicates, in my view, that these acquired a very precise political function that extended beyond their supposed economic rationale: that of buying support for the bureaucracy.[8] This makes the "autonomy" enjoyed by the bureaucracy (and to a certain extent the very maintenance of the regime) highly dependent on two complementary factors: (1) continuous high rates of economic expansion, as a condition for (2) growing fiscal revenues (since a substantial part of them is used to substitute for political freedoms). It is no coincidence that these are also the main targets of the post-1968 "model" of economic development at any cost. In other words, an economic crisis, or a slowdown of economic development, acquires for the regime a significance that goes far beyond its objective importance for the productive system—a political significance. It is thus that the regime "legitimizes" itself through its economic performance.

Relations between the military and the structure of authority. The takeover of government by the military as an institution, along with the fact that the general-president has a mandate from the armed forces, to whom alone he is accountable, have engendered the notion of a "fusion" between the military and power. This has to be qualified. First, the accountability of the general-president in fact applied only to the areas covered by "national security" doctrine, not to ordinary decision-making or to the regime's public policies—except, of course, when the military perceived these as in conflict with national security doctrine.[9] Second, the accountability of the government to the armed forces was to some extent offset by the military's commitment to the principles of hierarchical discipline under their commander-in-chief (the general-president). Third, the power resources at the disposal of the general-president (along with his possible qualities of statesmanship) tended to increase his personal autonomy from the only institution to which he was accountable. This had two important political consequences. First, although the military, as an institution, were *historically* responsible for the regime, they did not feel, as individuals, *politically* responsible for the acts of government. (The same could also be said of the middle echelons of civil bureaucracy.) Second, the "autonomy" of the general-president tended to signify not only a strong personalization of power (within an essentially bureaucratic power structure), but also a considerable freedom of maneuver for his entourage (known in Brazilian political slang as a *grupo palaciano*). This gave rise to a sort of personal dictatorship within the authoritarian regime, and thus increased the space for choice. Both features also created a permanent space for "internal" military crisis to the extent that they favored the emergence of cleavages within the armed forces (between *duros*, or hard-liners, and *blandos*, or soft-liners, for instance), cleavages which could take the form of "internal" opposition to the government (in the name of the defense of the regime) but which at the same time were established along lines of clique interests that only distantly coincide or overlap with the cleavages or social interests existing in society. Thus, the military world was more or less permanently exposed to infights between rival factions and cliques (as seen in succession crises experienced by the general-presidents) and was simultaneously segregated from the civil world, making the establishment of political alliances between military dissidents and civil opponents almost impossible.[10]

This *problématique* of the relationship between the military and the structure of authority, so frequent in authoritarian regimes, was aggravated in the Brazilian case by the creation of a parallel power structure within the military bureaucracy and the government, the so-called intelligence community. This was formed by the network of secret services of each of the three branches of the armed forces, generally under the control of the hard-liners, who succeeded in keeping the extensive power resources they had acquired during the 1969–73 repression (more accurately, the overkill) of guerrilla activity. By choosing their own targets for repression (irrespective of the military hierarchy or the government), by exerting pressure on the government to adopt repressive measures against the opposition, and by establishing their own system of alliances, these *réseaux* had begun to subvert the principle of hierarchical discipline to such an extent that they were transformed into quasi-political groups. In short, an apparatus created to conduct ideological screening and to control loyalties on behalf of those in charge of government reversed its functions. It began to control the loyalty of the regime's protagonists (including the military hierarchy) according to its own orthodox ideological criteria, as a sort of SS within the regime. This development contributed greatly to the unpopularity of the military and helped to transform former protagonists of the regime (the church, professional associations, etc.) into passive dissidents or even active opponents, as they sought to dissociate themselves from the regime's violence. This was the situation by the end of the Medici government (1973), and it began to unbalance the internal economy of the regime.

The reestablishment of order within the military establishment and the restoration to the armed forces of their prestige as an institution became a major preoccupation of the military faction which regained control of government through General Geisel in 1974. To accomplish these tasks two things were needed. First, it was necessary to curb the activities of the intelligence community and to expel politics from the barracks—something attempted through the gradual disengagement of the military from national politics and through a strong personalization of power. This, in turn, closed some channels of interest representation (mainly for industrialists), thus raising opposition to the government. Second, it was also necessary to restructure the basis of military prestige and of support for the regime through a political détente and the restoration of some sort of political life. These were precisely the priority goals set by the government of General Geisel (1974–78). They were partially achieved through the politics of "liberalization."

The Dynamics of the "Liberalization" Process

The basic assumption of this chapter, as must be clear by now, is that the Brazilian "liberalization" was originally triggered by the regime's difficulties in solving problems of its "internal economy," and did not originate from any substantive change in the correlation of forces between the regime's protagonists and its opponents—although the opposition largely benefitted, subsequently, from the political space opened up by the liberalization process. It must be added that if the economic difficulties of the post-1968 development model, aggravated by successive oil shocks, later contributed to the new political course, this was mediated through the sources of crisis discussed above. In this connection, the liberalization of authoritarian rule in Brazil may also be viewed as the regime's response to a cumulative "crisis of policy adaptation," to use Philippe Schmitter's concept.

These internal origins of the regime's difficulties explain why liberalization followed a pattern of contradictory moves, on simultaneous fronts, and why every concession by the regime or conquest of the opposition was immediately qualified in its political significance by the imposition of alternative authoritarian controls. And this explains why the regime retained both the initiative and the control of the liberalization process for so long. The succession of unilateral modifications to the rules of the political game made from 1974 onwards, in order to contain any advance of the opposition within the limits of liberalization set by the regime, provides a good indication of the contradictory pattern which marked the political process.

The suspension of press censorship and the November 1974 legislative elections, held eight months after the inauguration of the Geisel government, initiated the new political course. In spite of the fact that state governors were elected by indirect vote, that there was no political amnesty, and that Institutional Act No. 5 was still in force, the 1974 elections were the "freest" since 1966. Enjoying free access to radio and television, the parliamentary opposition succeeded in undertaking a substantial campaign of political mobilization, in consolidating itself as a political party (the Movimento Democrático Brasileiro, or MDB), and even in "discovering" its popularity in the country. Not only did the percentage of blank votes considerably diminish; the MDB also elected sixteen senators (out of twenty-two elected in 1974) and 160 federal deputies (34 percent of the House) and increased its total by 16 percent in the overall national vote (from 21.3 percent to 37.8 percent). The 1974 elections also showed that the opposition stronghold was in urban centers and in the more industrialized regions (to the south of the country). The government's reaction to this setback demonstrated the dynamics of the political process—and the regime's control over it.

The government reaction was aimed, first, at guaranteeing its control over the legislative process and, second, at avoiding a new opposition advance in the municipal elections to be held two years later (1976). The first objective was attained through maintenance of the institutional controls over the legislature and the use of the Institutional Acts to administer exemplary "punishment" to five congressmen from the opposition. The second goal was reached by the establishment of rigid controls over the dissemination of electoral propaganda on radio and television (the Falcao Law of 1976). Falcao was the minister of the interior who proposed that electoral broadcasts be restricted to the presentation of the name, the number, the photo (on TV), and the *curriculum vitae* of each candidate (Law 6.399, 7 July 1976). As a result, the government party (ARENA) comfortably won the 1976 municipal elections (3,176 mayors to 614) and therefore guaranteed the government a majority in the electoral college which would "elect" the president in 1978. In other words, the rules of the game were changed to curb the opposition's progress.

The third election under the Geisel government was to be held in 1978, for the entire House of Representatives, two-thirds of the Senate, and, for the first time since 1966, the governors of the states by direct voting. This was what the Constitution of 1969 had stipulated. But again the rules of the game were changed. There was a renewal of torture, the beginning of terrorist acts against personalities and associations linked to the opposition, and, on the other side, a reinforcement of the oppositional tendencies. The church, the press, and professional organizations voiced protests against these regressive acts. Thus in 1976–77 the Geisel government was under a double threat: that of losing its "authority" over the military bureaucracy and that of losing its political control over the "liberalization" process. The first threat was curbed through the partial (or temporary) disarticulation of the hard-liners and their repressive apparatus; the second threat was curbed by using the Institutional Act No. 5 to introduce new rules for the electoral and political games (for the second time in two years). Congress was put in recess and a package of political changes which became known as the "Pacote de Abril" (April 1977) was promulgated by decree. The main innovations were as follows:

1. The government would appoint one-third of the Senate (the "bionic senators") in order to guarantee its control of the upper house, irrespective of electoral outcomes, thereby attempting to make any change in the regime by legislative procedures impossible.

2. State governors would once more be chosen by indirect election.

3. The criteria regulating the number of federal deputies and the choice of municipal delegates to the electoral college would be changed in order to diminish the political weight of the more industrialized regions. Seats would be allocated in proportion to total population rather than to registered voters.

4. Under the second Falcao Law the same rigid restrictions on propaganda already adopted for the municipal elections were extended to all elections involving a popular vote.

By the end of 1977, the Geisel government had succeeded in restoring its control over the military bureaucracy and in creating rules that would obstruct political mobilization and the electoral progress of the opposition. This was followed by the institutionalization of alternative controls to compensate for the abrogation of Institutional Act No. 5: incorporation into current legislation of the regime's so-called safeguards (national security, labor strikes, and press laws), and introduction into the constitution of a provision barring from judicial review any act of the regime since 1964 covered by the laws of exception, such as the *Atos Institucionais*. Through these measures the Geisel government set the course of liberalization. The president also succeeded in imposing his successor, General Figueiredo, in spite of the military unrest this decision provoked—a clear indicator that the problems derived from the ambiguous relationship between the military bureaucracy and the structure of governmental authority had been only temporarily solved.

The Figueiredo government was inaugurated in March 1979 with a six-year mandate. In his inaugural speech, the new president solemnly pledged to "make of this country a democracy." In fact, the pattern of limited and calculated concessions was continued, with the purpose of controlling liberalization. For the first time since the regime's consolidation (1968) some (informal) channels of communication with sectors of the parliamentary and extraparliamentary opposition were opened up by the new government. At the same time, the Figueiredo administration adopted what was perceived as a more tolerant attitude toward the first major workers' strikes for a decade, which took place in São Paulo's industrial periphery. This tolerance was in fact more apparent than real. It consisted in letting the strikes break out without any preemptive or immediate repression. This was a good way to measure their social impact and at the same time to make dissident business representatives understand what a nonauthoritarian regime might mean. After the demonstration was over, the leadership of the labor movement was to be broken.[11] Notwithstanding this, the opposition began to be optimistic about the authenticity of the president's commitment to democratization. The political strategy conceived by General Golbery (kept on by Figueiredo from Geisel's administration as his main political counsellor) was apparently based on the idea that any further progress in liberalization should rely on two things.[12] It would be necessary, first, to avoid any electoral dispute which could lead to a plesbiscitarian type of confrontation between supporters and opponents of the regime (such as the two-party system would almost inevitably produce). It was also necessary to stimulate the creation of a mild, or "trustworthy," opposition party, which could play the role of the government's second-best political force and could eventually become a *solution de rechange* for alternation in government in the future. Following this plan, a general political amnesty was conceded to "normalize" the political situation. It was also hoped that the return from exile of the pre-1964 populist leaders would produce fragmentation in the opposition (a hope only partially fulfilled). More important, the two-party system was abolished, and new and complex procedures were unilaterally imposed for the formation of a new multiparty structure.[13] *En passant*, the municipal elections scheduled for November 1980 were "postponed" to 1982. Thus the pattern of limited concessions combined with strict control of the political initiative and of the political process continued to prevail under Figueiredo. This was illustrated by the reestablishment of direct voting for state governors (beginning in the scheduled elections for November 1982) and, simultaneously, by the government's clear veto of two successive attempts by Congress to regain some of its lost constitutional powers. By mid-1980 the profile of the new political party system began to take shape. A "trustworthy" opposition party (named Partido Popular, PP) was created from the ribs of the ex-MDB (now renamed Partido do Movimento Democrático Brasileiro, PMDB) and joined by miscellaneous dissidents from the government party (ex-ARENA, now Partido Democrático Social, PDS). Some influential leaders of the *novo sindicalismo*, joined by intellectuals and supported by important sectors of the church, decided to create a workers' party (Partido dos Trabalhadores, PT). Ex-populist leader Leonel Brizola fought with rival populists to rebuild the Partido Trabalhista Brasileiro (PTB), which had been created by Vargas in the 1940s and had been the main populist party up to 1964. By the end of 1981 five parties (the above-mentioned and the PDT)[14] succeeded in obtaining provisional registration.

More important than any ideological cleavages (not easy to establish) either between or within the new parties was the fact that the complex procedures required for their formation (such as the holding of conventions in at least one-fifth of the *municipios* in at least nine states) considerably reactivated political party life and political competition throughout the country. This gave credit to the diffuse belief that liberalization was "irreversible," a belief by then shared by some Latin Americanists as well. As part of this optimistic view, the leadership of the two main opposition parties—PMDB and PP— became convinced, first, that they could substantially increase their parliamentary forces at the next election (November 1982), or even constitute a majority in Congress, and, secondly, that with the PP as a mediator they could then negotiate a "political solution" with the Figueiredo government over the choice of the next president in 1984. Thus, transition to civilian-democratic rule could be completed in an undefined "near future." By the end of 1981, however, this climate of optimism had been abruptly shattered. By mid-1981 it was confirmed that terrorist activities carried on against the opposition were being sponsored by military hard-liners.[15] The military hierarchy, including the president himself, decided to cover up the whole affair. This was apparently done against the advice of General Golbery. Golbery's departure from the government jeopardized the political strategy he had set in motion, which had been perceived as the strategy of the entire administration. (This shows clearly, if more evidence is needed, that individuals can play a disproportionate role in this kind of regime.) During President Figueiredo's illness in the second half of 1981, the military accepted, for the first time, the idea that a civilian vice-president might exercise the function of the presidency. Because of this the opposition was somewhat reassured of the continuity of liberalization.

That sense of reassurance, however, led the opposition parties and some government party dissidents in Congress into certain unfortunate tactical maneuvers, including the defeat of two important government-sponsored law projects. It also contributed to the formation of an alliance between the PMDB and the PP to wage the 1982 elections. These moves were interpreted by the government as a defiance of executive authority. Moreover, they threatened to deprive the governing party of governorships in an intolerable number of states. In short, the military feared losing control over the pace and timing of "liberalization."

In November 1981, the government reacted by unilaterally imposing new rules for the electoral process (the "Pacote de Novembro"). All electoral alliances among parties were forbidden; each political party was obliged to present a complete slate of candidates (councillors, mayors, federal deputies, senators, and governors); and voters who chose candidates not belonging to the same party slate (for instance, a councillor from one party and a senator from another) would have their vote invalidated. In concrete terms, these laws forced competition between the four opposition parties, to the advantage of the (sole) government party. It was also a warning that the government was not willing to lose control of the electoral college, which would choose Figueiredo's successor as president in 1985.

One of the consequences of the "Pacote de Novembro" was to make the Partido Popular nonviable. By February 1982, the majority of the members of the PP acknowledged this *fait accompli* and decided to (re)merge with the PMDB, becoming an influential moderate faction within the latter. Once more the pattern of Brazil's party structure was transformed.

All this tinkering was perceived by the opposition as a redefinition of the Geisel-Golbery strategy and as a setback to liberalization. Actually, it was nothing more than the tactical adaptation to the new circumstances of the same strategy of "liberalization": limited concessions combined with tight control over the political outcomes. In other words, in spite of its successive electoral gains, the opposition was still unable to secure fair rules for the political game and, therefore, to use its incremental growth to change the nature of the regime via Congress. One of the reasons for this is that the progressive erosion of the regime's social support was not entirely converted into a proportional increase of the opposition's political strength. This was in part due to its inability to mobilize popular support between elections, to establish military alliances, or to present an alternative and credible political project.

This sort of non-zero-sum game model was confirmed by the general elections held in November 1982 (for state governors, one-third of the Senate, the lower house, and municipal officers), although this time the opposition scored electoral gains on a scale suggesting that the liberalization pattern could no longer be maintained indefinitely at the same slow rhythm. This new factor, combined with the accelerating economic crisis, gave birth to a new situation and pushed the liberalization process to the crossroads, as we will see later.

The liberalization model adopted in Brazil under the Geisel administration and part of the Figueiredo government can be summarized as follows: (1) the progressive restoration of civil and political rights; (2) the reestablishment of channels of interest representation; (3) the adoption of forms of legal validation for the choice of rulers and for acts of government. But at the same time, authoritarian controls were institutionalized in order to contain the exercise of such rights and political functions within the limits imposed by the executive's authority. These limits could be extended or narrowed, according to the phase of the political process, the political mentality of the ruler, and the intensity of the demands voiced by strategic groups and the press. They could also become the subject of partial negotiation—if certain nonnegotiable items were accepted as such by the opposition. These nonnegotiable items seem to consist of the following: (1) the regime's protagonists must not be called to account for arbitrary acts performed in the name of the revolution; (2) the oppositional sectors that propose what could be perceived as a fundamentally different organization of society cannot be represented politically; (3) opposition forces cannot aspire to govern before the "work of the 1964 revolution" has been consolidated. This "work of the revolution" is a broad and changeable concept defined by the regime protagonists themselves.

The liberalization of authoritarian rule can therefore be defined as the adoption of formal democratic institutions and the simultaneous exclusion of the four principles which give to such institutions their true democratic content: consensus concerning the rules of the game, political accountability of the rulers, the right to ample political representation, and alternation in power.

This is the political project that the regime succeeded in carrying out from the inauguration of Geisel (1974) through most of the Figueiredo administration (to autumn 1983). This period of almost ten years is a time span which should raise some questions concerning the use of the concept of "transition." Historically, ten years may not be sufficient to constitute a "transition"; politically, it is too long.

"Liberalization" at the Crossroads

As previously stated, the general elections held in November 1982 introduced new elements in the political situation. For the first time since 1965 the governors of twenty-two states were elected by direct vote. In spite of the remaining political restrictions (prohibition of political alliances among parties, restrictions on political propaganda, etc.), the opposition parties elected ten governors (nine from the PMDB and one from the PDT) in the most politicized and industrialized states. (These ten states contain 62 percent of the national electorate and generate 75 percent of the gross domestic product.) Also, for the first time the four opposition parties (PMDB, PDT, PT, and PTB) gained a larger share of the popular vote than the government party (PDS) in the legislative elections (48.0 percent against 36.6 percent).[16] As a consequence, the government party lost its previously comfortable majority in the House. However, in spite of these electoral returns, the government party (PDS) retained its majority (by 38 votes) in the electoral college that chooses the president, owing to official tinkering with the electoral law. Moreover, the opposition parties (even if they combined in a concerted program of action) would have too slender a majority in the legislature to pass new laws affecting the electoral game (introducing direct elections for the presidency, for instance), or to change the authoritarian institutional framework and therefore the nature of the regime. Constitutional amendments require approval by two-thirds of both houses, and the government has a large majority in the Senate, thanks to the "bionic senators" introduced in 1977.

Even so, the 1982 election helped to create a new political situation, for three main reasons. First, the victory of the PMDB in the four most important states in the south (São Paulo, Minas Gerais, Rio de Janeiro, and Paraná) considerably broadened the party's political base and strengthened the voice of the opposition.[17] Second, the new opposition majority in the House, although small (only nine votes), tends to compel the government to negotiate (even with its own party) whenever a controversial bill is up for approval.[18] Finally, some of the PDS governors, elected this time by direct vote, became much more aware of and accountable to their constituencies. They consequently began to express a greater degree of independence from the military and the central government. Indeed, by 1983, seven of the twelve PDS governors had come out in favor of direct elections for Figueiredo's successor, and some of them supported the idea of convoking a constituent assembly.

These political developments would be perfectly compatible with the "logic" of the liberalization process (partial concessions, incremental growth of opposition parties, controlled political dissent) were it not for the concurrence of two intervening factors of a different nature, one "objective" and one "subjective." The first was the eruption of a severe financial and economic crisis; the second was the exposure of the Figueiredo administration's corruption and of the president's inability to exert firm political leadership. These two factors combined to trigger both internal and external sources of crisis, along the lines discussed in the first section of this chapter, placing the liberalization process at a crossroad. Let us briefly trace this new course.

Without entering into the causes of the financial and economic crisis, which are too complex to be treated here, it is sufficient to state that after a period of extraordinary expansion, during the years known as the Brazilian "miracle" (1968–74), the economy began to slow down. This coincided with and was aggravated by the first "oil shock" and the resulting world recession. Although common sense would suggest—as indeed many Brazilian economists recommended—that subsequent public policies should be directed toward the adaptation of the economy to these world trends (especially since Brazil was importing more than half of its oil needs), the Geisel administration took the opposite view. A highly ambitious economic development program (capital goods and chemical industries, huge hydroelectric projects, nuclear plants, the expansion of public expenditure and public enterprise investment, etc.) was initiated, without regard to the predictable draining of funds and economic stress this would provoke. The Figueiredo government (with Delfim Neto once more the minister of planning) followed the same irresponsible orientation, relentlessly increasing both the internal debt and the level of external borrowing at what proved to be extremely high rates of interest. The intention was artificially to sustain the hope of an economic miracle that would legitimize the regime.

By mid-1982, the cumulative effects of such a policy had become clear: domestic interest rates skyrocketed to 300 percent a year, inflation was soon above 100 percent, the national debt was twice the level of the federal budget, and the external debt rose from US$12.6 billion at the end of 1973 to $80 billion in mid-1982. On the other hand, industrial production fell by 10 percent compared with 1980. By September 1982, after the panic which followed the Mexican moratorium, Brazil, virtually in default, was obliged to go to the International Monetary Fund for help. The medicine prescribed by the IMF to deal with inflation and with the internal and external indebtedness deepened the recession, aggravated the already high rate of unemployment, and produced a drastic salary squeeze. Indeed Brazil entered one of the gravest financial and economic situations of its history.[19]

The sudden revelation of the scale of the financial and economic imbroglio, the president's obstinate refusal to replace his economic team, and the acceptance of the highly recessionary medicine prescribed by the IMF produced multiple effects on society and upon the prestige of the regime. At the most general level of ideological manipulation, the image projected by the regime—of highly inventive and competent administrators, if not miracle-makers—was abruptly discredited. This was aggravated by a succession of astonishing disclosures, through congressional investigations and press denunciations, concerning widespread corruption among the technocrats and the military in power. In short, both the legitimacy and the prestige of the military-technocratic alliance were gravely undermined.

This precipitated a crisis within the regime. Perplexity and disappointment surfaced among rank-and-file military and the middle echelons of the state apparatus; at the same time, fear that the regime might collapse triggered a new wave of illicit acts committed by the intelligence community to cover up its past activities and to intimidate critics of the regime.[20] As a consequence, new cleavages appeared within the "internal public" of the regime (as the military say, speaking of themselves). Those now favoring a rapid military disengagement separated from those afraid of the consequences of such a move in the midst of a crisis. In this process, former *duros* were converted into *blandos*, and vice versa, according to their perception of the danger of social unrest, their place in the infighting between rival factions and cliques, their personal loyalty to Figueiredo, or their allegiance to one or another military candidate to succeed him. All this illustrates the general propositions set out above on the relations between the military and the structure of authority. These developments, together with Figueiredo's erratic leadership and total lack of ability to cope with complex political situations, contributed to the creation of a sort of permanent crisis of governmental credibility superimposed upon the crisis of the regime. By the autumn of 1983 there was an almost daily stream of contradictory statements from high government officials concerning economic policies and political issues; moreover, within the ranks of the government party (PDS) divisions became more visible in view of the presidential succession and disputes over the future course of liberalization.[21] This growing political dissent and social unrest produced, on the societal level, a rapid increase and diversification of social and political demands. For the first time since 1964, influential business leaders openly and collectively voiced strong criticism, no longer only against "statism" but also against technocratic management of the economy and against the regime itself. At the same time, social unrest attained new levels of violence. Towns in the interior of the country were invaded by desperately hungry *nordestinos* in search of food and clothing; looting of supermarkets in the periphery of Rio and São Paulo took place with growing frequency; and urban criminality increased dramatically. But it was not only the regime's prestige which was affected by the social unrest. Opposition-state governors found themselves obliged to take repressive actions or to adopt economic austerity measures in their respective jurisdictions. Thus expectations were frustrated and the opposition's prestige was also tarnished—diminishing its capacity to mobilize support.

Overall, the economic crisis accelerated the erosion of the regime's social support in two different and complementary ways. On the one hand, the IMF-sponsored cuts in public expenditure and in public enterprise budgets and the heavy cutback of subsidies to private business deprived the regime of one of its most efficient means of acquiring support from strategic groups. On the other hand, for the first time unemployment and the wage squeeze reached the affluent middle classes, threatening the social ascent they made during the "miracle" years, turning them from active supporters to passive dissenters or strong critics of the regime.[22] In short, once the economic "miracle" was over, its political dividends drained away.

Although the economic dimension was not an important element in the decision to "liberalize" the regime, it will now probably become a major factor shaping the final outcome of the liberalization process. Here one may hypothesize that an economic crisis of great magnitude may play an analogous role (although not equivalent) to that played in other countries by external defeat as the catalyst of the demise of an authoritarian regime. The reason is that the economic promises of the regime, once frustrated, appear as a sort of internal defeat because they had previously performed such a legitimizing function. Certainly in the Brazilian case the economic crisis (and the disastrous mismanagement of the economy) has contributed, more than the politically organized opposition, to the unstable equilibrium in which the regime now finds itself. As a consequence, the process of liberalization, which appeared to be a classic instance of a "continuous transition," now finds itself at a crossroad. Using the framework for analysis set out earlier, this crossroad points toward three possible outcomes: (1) the collapse of the regime, (2) accelerated democratization after some variety of political compromise has been reached over the transfer of power, or (3) the imposition of a higher degree of political coercion. Because the degree and the political impact of social unrest created by the economic crisis are still unpredictable, and because it is also difficult to forecast which of the main actors of the process is best placed to turn it to advantage, it would be pure guesswork, at the present time, to predict which outcome will prevail or for how long.

Speculations on the Prospects for Democracy

Although it is still an open question how the liberalization process will evolve, there is room for a few remarks on the prospects for democracy in Brazil. Two different problems, implying two different levels of abstraction, must, in my view, be considered: (1) To what extent is capitalist development in Brazil compatible with nonauthoritarian forms of government? (2) To what extent can interests engendered or reinforced during the authoritarian regime be curbed by or absorbed in a democratic regime?

The relationship between capitalism and parliamentary democracy has been reconsidered, as we know, in the light of the historical evidence concerning the rather different processes followed, and political institutions adopted, by capitalist nations since the rise of capitalism. The relevant literature, beginning with Barrington Moore's seminal work, shows that a single mode of production can combine with specific historical circumstances to give birth to different modes of societal development, and that it is the latter which ultimately determines the social structure and the form of political organization.

Past and recent Latin American history gives evidence of a relationship between what has been called "delayed-dependent" capitalism and political authoritarianism. However, since both are broad categories encompassing a variety of different situations, this relationship is best viewed as an "elective affinity." That is to say that the exact *nature* of the relationship between both terms (meaning the degree and the conditions of their possible reciprocal determination) is not fully established. In this hazy zone causation is sometimes established by induction, based either on circumstantial evidence or on analogical reasoning, the latter with a strong Marxist/economicist flavor.[23] A typical example is the argument that prospects for democracy in countries such as Brazil are weak *because* of the requirements for capital accumulation. This sort of argument is based on a supposed relationship between two assumptions. First, it is assumed that capitalist development in countries like Brazil requires a huge concentrated effort to achieve rapid capital accumulation (carried out mainly through the state). Secondly, it is also assumed that the extremely high social cost needed for that achievement creates social tensions which, in their turn, give rise to repressive political controls. Both statements can be correct, as I believe they are, in the sense that they correspond to verified facts. However, there is no necessary or theoretically congruent relation between them. Indeed, the first refers to the structural tendencies of capitalist development; the second, to the social consequences produced by a historically specific experience of capitalist growth. The fact that capitalist expansion in Brazil had, at a certain point, taken on a specific pattern does not rule out the possibility that the same mode of capitalist development may not also be compatible with a different model of growth—one that might be less costly in social terms. If this is so, the relationship between "delayed-dependent" capitalism and authoritarianism must be investigated, not in terms of the requirements of capital accumulation, but elsewhere.

The Brazilian authoritarian regime was certainly instrumental in achieving a certain type of capitalist expansion and, more important in my view, in reinforcing the social hegemony of capitalism in Brazil. In this connection, if the 1964 "revolution" can be regarded as having performed a historical task, its achievement must be the liquidation of a previous structure of domination and its (populist) political expression. This is because populism had shown itself unable either to generate a competitive social order and a capitalist ethos or to expand the state-oligopolistic-internationalized productive system whose foundations were laid in the 1950s. My point is that this phase of capitalist expansion tends to activate social resistance and social unrest, although these are not necessarily linked to the process of capital accumulation. In this phase the maintenance of the social hegemony of capitalism (not dependent on the emergence of a particular social class, such as a "national bourgeoisie") precedes political legitimation as a priority of local dominant classes and of their foreign partners.

What I am suggesting is, first, that the consolidation of the social hegemony of capitalism is the dominant factor and, second, that the latter cannot be reduced to the form assumed by capital accumulation in a circumstantial *model* of capitalist growth. Whether or not such a consolidation has really occurred in Brazil during the last two decades of authoritarian rule can be a matter for speculation (now) and for empirical demonstration (in the proper historical perspective).[24] In any case, if a relationship between "delayed-dependent" capitalism and authoritarianism exists, it must be placed in a much broader context than that of the "requirements" for capital accumulation.

A second, more concrete and perhaps more immediately relevant problem is the one related to the vested interests that have emerged (or have reinforced their position) during the authoritarian regime. These interests are of various kinds: specific national and international business groups, sectors of the upper middle classes, the civil and the military bureaucracies, and so on. These social segments and specific corporate groups, regardless of the occasional critical stand they may assume in relation to the regime, may resist or even oppose democratization if they feel threatened in their positions and privileges. This might be caused by the emergence of a new social coalition, by growing social unrest, or by the adoption of a new model of economic growth—all three phenomena which will probably occur in the course of democratization. But if, as I believe, the economic and social interests of the majority of these actors can be accommodated in a different model of economic growth, the resistance they may oppose must be placed in the proper context: that of political competition.

As for specific corporate interests, such as those of the military bureaucracy, a different type of problem has to be considered. It seems clear that, regardless of their discourse or subjective feelings, the objective corporate interests of the military have, through acquired privileges or otherwise, been strongly linked to the authoritarian regime. Moreover, the ideology which shapes the mentality and actual behavior of the military in Brazil (the national security doctrine) is unequivocally authoritarian. The fact that liberalization was initiated by a military government and explicitly presented as a transition to democracy, without raising strong resistance at the time, is sometimes interpreted as suggesting a perfect fit between President Geisel's political project and the predominant feelings in the military bureaucracy. In the light of what has been said above concerning Geisel's motives for liberalizing the regime and how "liberalization" differs from democratization, such an inter- pretation does not seem accurate. Concretely, and regardless of the eventual predominance of hard-liners over soft-liners, or vice versa, the real question seems to be how to absorb the military bureaucracy as an institution into a democratic regime. In other words, what new role can be assigned to the military, after two decades of authoritarian rule, in order to justify the exis- tence of professional soldiers in a geopolitical context without real external enemies at whom to point their guns? Such a new role—whatever it might be—would require a complete reformulation of the present doctrine of "national security." There is no evidence that such a reformulation is under way in Brazil, either through the initiative of the military themselves or through that of the political opposition. Strangely enough, as a matter of fact, the political parties that fight for democracy in Brazil do not seem even to consider this a political necessity. For the time being, therefore, the "military question" will continue to be a latent obstacle to the establishment of a lasting democratic regime.

Consideration of these two different problems affecting the prospects for democracy in Brazil illustrates the following point: the main obstacles in establishing democratic forms of government in countries where the social hegemony of capitalism is already undergoing a process of consolidation come not from any abstract "logic" of capital, but from the concrete resistance opposed by specific social groups (not necessarily integrated in the productive process). In a broader perspective, this resistance arises from the difficulty of establishing an adequate system for the representation of interests in societies marked by what Alain Touraine calls a strong "désarticulation des rapports sociaux."[25] If the basic issue raised by the transition from authoritarianism to a lasting democracy is sociological and political, the key question becomes whether or not the civilian leadership and political parties of Brazil will be able to aggregate and represent highly fragmented and heterogeneous social inter- ests while at the same time agreeing on a new social coalition strong enough to absorb the many resistances to democratization.

5 ·

The Political Evolution of the Chilean Military Regime and Problems in the Transition to Democracy

Manuel Antonio Garretón

Introduction

From the point of view of democratic transitions, the Chilean case presents a certain paradox. From a historical perspective, Chile seems to possess the conditions necessary for the prompt restoration of the democracy lost in the 1973 military coup. One can cite, among other factors, the long tradition of democratic regimes, the relative strength of a nationwide party apparatus, and the breadth of political participation with an equally broad civil society associated with it. However, compared to similar Southern Cone regimes, the Chilean case appears to lag behind in the redemocratization stakes.

This chapter analyzes this paradox by considering the Chilean military regime's evolution as well as its prospects for transition. It examines first the general traits of the political system in force in Chile before the crisis of 1973, then the military regime's break with that system. A third section considers the main features and problems of the military regime's institutionalization process, describing both the political model presently in force and the type of political system desired by the dominant sectors, or at least by their leadership. A fourth part looks briefly at the crisis of this model, and the fifth section considers some of the more important characteristics of the opposition to the regime. The chapter concludes with some generalizations from the Chilean case which may be useful in the theory of political transition from authoritarian to democratic regimes.

The perspective chosen involves a global political analysis of the dynamics and processes of the regime; there is no systematic analysis of the economic dimension, of the structural transformations of society, or of the behavior of specific classes and actors. Those themes can only be touched on insofar as they throw light on the dynamics of the political regime.

The Chilean Political System and Its Crisis

In the Chilean case there was an historical correlation between phenomena which in other Latin American countries appeared in isolation, namely, the process of import-substituting industrialization with an increasing degree of state intervention in the economy; a process of *substantive* democratization, that is, of progressive incorporation of different social sectors into the political system and improvements in their standards of living; and the existence of a democratic political regime. It is the combination of these three elements which allows us to explain some of the characteristics peculiar to this political system.

In the Chilean case, the constitution of social actors was inextricably bound up with a political party structure whose features may be summarized as follows. In the first place, there was a relatively early establishment of a national political spectrum. This means both the existence of a complete gamut of political options expressed through organizations, and the absence of parties or movements which for regional or ethnic reasons might interfere with this aspect. A second feature of this political party structure was its overlapping with the totality of social organizations. These managed to become actors of national significance precisely to the extent that they were related to the party political structure. The overlapping of political parties and social organizations facilitated the development of a broad and diversified political class within which a range of ideological options could be offered.

In the third place, the significance of this political party system in the formation of outstanding actors went hand in hand with the relative weakness and dependence of the autonomous organizations of civil society. All social organizations had to operate through the party system in order to gain access to the instrument of ordering and redistribution—the state.[1]

Fourthly, "substantive" democratization occurred through the channels established by the formal democratic political system, not as the result of sudden upheavals. It was a highly segmented process, in which the extent of political participation did not necessarily correspond to the same degree of democracy at the societal level: social inequalities had reproductive mechanisms which the political democracy could not eliminate or overcome. Combined with segmentation and exclusion, this type of substantive democratization produced a form of popular integration without a parallel ideological cooptation. This implied the preservation of political ideologies which supported radical changes and alternatives to the capitalist system. From the sociological point of view, one can understand, then, the attraction and significance of a Marxist Left which, in Latin American terms, was unusually strong.

Finally, with regard to the legitimacy of this system of relations between state and society, I would argue that the general support for the democratic regime was fundamentally instrumental. This was a political regime, support for which rested more on its ability to satisfy interests and demands than on its intrinsic value. In critical situations, the precarious nature of such support was clear.

In brief, this was a system of articulation of social subjects and actors with reference to the state and stemming from a web of relationships between the organizations of civil society and the political party structure.[2] Its strength was rooted in the expansion of political participation. Its weakness lay in the insufficient autonomy of civil society and in the latent fragility of commitment to the political regime.

This system was developed and consolidated after a significant period of military intervention. Both this antecedent, with its implied lack of confidence by the political class in the armed forces, and the effectiveness of the systems of representation, exclusion, and conflict resolution provided by the political system, confined the military to a fundamentally professional development. This "cloistering" of the military was not hermetic, however. On one hand, there was the post–World War II involvement in a hemispheric military system led by the United States and, as a result, socialization in its predominant doctrine—the counterinsurgency or national security doctrine. On the other hand, this ideology, furnished both by military socialization and by political discourse pointed toward a potential political role for the armed forces as "bastion" of the nation and its institutions. All these elements contributed to a high level of hierarchization and discipline in the armed forces, where formal leaderships was the only basis of legitimacy, a factor of great importance in our study.

By 1970, Chilean society seemed to face a particular type of crisis. On the one hand, the economic model followed until then proved increasingly unable to satisfy the ever-greater demands of the masses and organized social sectors who exerted pressure through the political system. As a result, there was a crisis of confidence in the model of capitalist development. On the other hand, there was a crisis of the "state of compromise"[3] in terms of the isolation and discredit suffered by those political actors who had, until then, ruled the country. Mirroring this, there was a growing acceptance of socialist ideologies of change: organizations of the Left united around the Popular Unity Coalition (UP), following an erosion of the political center. This remained a partial crisis, however, to the extent that the political regime's legitimacy remained unchallenged.

From this particular perspective, the UP period 1970–73 represented a move from partial to total crisis, as political polarization increased and channels of confrontation were deinstitutionalized. In 1970, the key element which had limited the crisis of the development model and of state leadership was the legitimacy of the democratic system; by 1973 that had been lost. Legitimacy was adversely affected by a variety of factors, including the insurrectional strategy followed by the main organized groups of the Right, on the one hand, and the UP's chosen strategy of transformation, on the other. The design of this strategy was within the letter of the law, but it questioned the principles of moderation and negotiation through which the political system had achieved its legitimacy. To this should be added the growing abandonment of democratic values by the middle classes and by the political center because of their opposition to UP's substantive project. All of this made possible the military intervention of 1973. Intervention had not come about in 1970, despite calls for it. Three years later, however, the armed forces saw it as the only way out of a crisis which the political system seemed unable to resolve. It is evident that this involved an actively insurrectionist internal process in order to lend the coup hierarchical legitimacy within the armed forces.

In 1970–73, the claims and demands of different social sectors were no longer sufficiently well articulated through the political parties. These sectors turned to their corporate organizations, which frequently obliged the parties to follow their lead lest they lose all relevance.

In 1973, therefore, Chilean society faced a crisis on several levels. First, there was an accelerated and profound capitalist decomposition which was not matched by the coherent construction of an alternative system. Secondly, political polarization affected society to an extreme degree. In response to the mobilization and increased power attained by the popular sectors and the undeniable advance of substantive democratization, the middle classes, who had been cornerstones of the democratic regime, underwent a process of "fascistization." Thirdly, the legitimacy of the political regime was lost. All of this helps to explain the dual nature of the military intervention. It was, on the one hand, *reactive*, as shown by the massive levels of repression and the drastic measures taken to suppress the old political system. On the other hand, it offered an opportunity for the capitalist sectors to restore their dominance by *reorganizing* society. This required a project, which the armed forces had lacked at the time of their intervention. The military's internal consensus extended only to the purely reactive element.

The Emergence of a New Historical Project

Recent military regimes in the Southern Cone have emerged from political crises characterized by different degrees of mobilization and organization by the popular sectors around proposals for important transformations in society. These regimes are also linked with modernization, professionalization, and the ideological homogenization of the armed forces, which facilitates their hierarchical and organic intervention. Finally, such regimes are linked with a restructuring of the world and peripheral capitalist order.

All of these regimes, to varying degrees, combine a reactive dimension in the face of earlier processes of popular mobilization with a reorganizational or transformative dimension with regard to society. The first is expressed through repression and through the breakup of the previous sociopolitical system. The second achieves expression with the materialization of a historical project—that is, an economic, political, and cultural model whose general sense is the reconstitution of the capitalist order in the country and the country's reinsertion into the international capitalist system. The articulation of these two dimensions, the specific weight given to each, and the particular direction taken by the historical project vary from country to country. Different forms of repression characterize the reactive dimension, while the characteristic feature of the transformative dimension is the regime's process of institutionalization. This consists essentially of passing from a dictatorship that is without rules and seeks its legitimacy basically in terms of the requirements of an internal war, to a dictatorship that establishes its own rules and seeks new principles of legitimacy.

The success of the transformative dimension and, therefore, the resolution of the crisis of hegemony suffered by the dominant sectors depend on various factors. Most important is the formulation, at the heart of the coalition brought to power by the military coup, of a hegemonic nucleus, that is, a sector able to generalize interests within the dominant bloc and to stamp a direction or specific content on the historical project of capitalist reconstitution and reinsertion. (The term "hegemony" in this context refers to relationships within the dominant bloc, and not in society as a whole.) This transformative dimension involves not only an attempt at capitalist reconstitution and reorganization, but also the establishment of a political project. The great difficulty which military regimes experience in establishing adequate systems of mediation between state and society, and their explicit attempts to eliminate politics, frequently leads one to think that their historical project simply envisages the indefinite perpetuation of the military regime. However, these institutionalization processes, although they tend to require the maintenance of the military regime as a historical condition for their desired social transformations, also involve a particular form of "transition," not toward democratic regimes, but rather toward properly authoritarian regimes. In these regimes the military would cease monopolizing formal power. Some forms of participation mechanisms and certain political arenas would be established, but combined with state authoritarianism, institutionalized exclusion mechanisms, and the armed forces' tutelary power.[4] This would seem to be the political utopia of this historical project. Likewise, it should be noted that this political project is not unanimously shared within the dominant bloc. There are sectors in it who affirm the permanence of the existing military regime, and it is this distinction between military regime and future authoritarian regime which polarizes the tension between those sectors in these regimes calling themselves "hard-liners" (*duros*) and "soft-liners" (*blandos*).

The crisis in Chilean society around 1973 affected the course of the military regime in several ways. On the one hand, it gave the reactive phase an unusual intensity, scale, and duration even among Southern Cone regimes. At the same time, the extent to which the capitalist system had been disarticulated was such that the urgent tasks of economic "stabilization" and "normalization" partially obscured the project of capitalist reconstitution and reinsertion. Initially, there was a relative lack of definition. Prior to 1975 one can pick out several possible directions for the regime within the framework of this new historical project. At this time of repression, of the predominance of the so-called stabilizing or normalizing tasks, there emerged a hegemonic nucleus at the helm of state, clearly visible from 1975 onwards.

On the other hand, the intense degree of political polarization attained in 1973 had prompted the political center (the Christian Democrats) to give tacit or explicit approval to the military coup. Immediately after the coup, some centrist sectors lent their support to the military government in technocratic matters, while the official line of the Christian Democrats (DC) recommended (conditional) support, subject to respect for certain matters relating to human rights, something which the government rejected.[5] Subsequently, and particularly when repression affected certain of its activists and leaders, the Christian Democratic party traveled along what has been called its "Road to Damascus." It eventually joined an opposition initially composed primarily of the Left.

Finally, one of the elements relating to the original crisis which permitted the consolidation of a hegemonic nucleus was the feeling among economically dominant sectors of having lived through a definitive threat to their existence during the UP government. In the face of this threat, their main aims had been the recovery of their confiscated privileges and assets, and the establishment of political conditions capable of reversing the situation and of avoiding its repetition. Even certain productive sectors, especially those linked with import substitution, industrialization, and agriculture, which would be severely affected by the economic model implemented and consolidated from 1975, held the view that there could be nothing worse than what had happened in the UP period. Moreover, their hopes were initially confirmed when the military government authorized a wholesale return of properties which had been nationalized or taken over by the state under UP.

The hegemonic nucleus which gained control of the state remained intact until 1981. On the one hand, it consisted of the increasingly personalized hierarchical leadership of Pinochet in the armed forces; and on the other hand, of the technocratic group charged with the state's management of the economy, known as the "economic team" or the "Chicago Boys." To explain the combination of these two elements and their constitution as a hegemonic nucleus, one must first recall the armed forces' lack of any political project which went further than the mere overthrow of the UP regime. The concepts then prevalent among the military, especially the so-called national security doctrine, did not equip them for the task of the material and social reorganization of the country. Their cohesion stemmed not from consensus on a project but from their own organizational nature, in which hierarchy and discipline were the keystones. This facilitated a personalization of supreme leadership in the face of day-to-day government decisions.

This personalization of leadership, paralleled by the growing subordination of the other branches of the military to the army, occurred in several stages. At the juridico-institutional level Pinochet, remaining as commander in chief of the army, moved from chief of the government junta to head of state and then president of the republic (a move finally consummated in the referendum of September 1980).[6] There was also a growing concentration and centralization of the repressive apparatus under Pinochet's direct command, the climax of which was the creation of the National Intelligence Directorate (DINA) in June 1974 and of its successor, the Central Office of Information (CNI), in August 1977. Then there was the progressive removal from the army of those high-ranking officers who were Pinochet's peers at the time of the coup. This accentuated the hierarchical relationship between the commander in chief and those newly promoted officers and generals who "owed everything" to General Pinochet. In summary, the personalization of Pinochet's leadership has been achieved through force, control of the repressive apparatus, and juridico-institutional formulae, all based on the internal cohesion of the military, a cohesion founded more on hierarchy and internal organization than on any agreement on a common political project. This process has not been entirely smooth, however, especially when the powers of the governing military junta were undermined by Pinochet's personal decisions, decisions that were later ratified by force.[7]

As already mentioned, the military were unable to offer a project to resolve the situation inherited in September 1973, and the capitalist class was too politically immature to set out an alternative development project. It is for this reason that, after a period of relative lack of definition, during the acute crisis conditions of early 1975 (the period of economic "shock treatment") the precise definition of an economic program of capitalist reconstitution and reinsertion came, not from businessmen or their representative organizations, but from within the state apparatus by a technocratic sector partly composed by local academics and partly recruited from international financial institutions. The members of this group were unquestioning followers of the doctrines of Milton Friedman and of the Chicago School of Economics. In time, they came to occupy leading positions within major financial groups. Their discourse has an air of universality supposedly above the interests of different business sectors or factions, but all their measures directly favor national and international finance capital. They were linked to the international agencies that guaranteed the flow of external credit necessary to refloat the economy. Moreover, given the isolation in which the military government found itself after taking over, this was the regime's only positive link with the outside world. These economic advisers were also willing to supply the military with all of the resources required for repression, and to satisfy corporate demands and the military's geopolitical outlook. Moreover, discourse not restricted to the pure sphere of economic policy but capable of linking economic measures to a coherent societal model—that is, to a series of changes in every sphere of social life—had considerable ideological attractions. No other sector could offer this package to a military leadership which had power aplenty but no plan for societal organization. Hence the decisive backing that the economic team received from General Pinochet.

Thus, the hegemonic nucleus was made up of an alliance between Pinochet's personalized military leadership and a group of economic managers apparently capable of arbitrating on all the capitalist class's interests, even though also expressing the predominance of finance capital over the productive sectors. Until 1981 this was the dominant force within the authoritarian regime.

On the economic level, this grouping attempted to reverse the development model of the preceding decades (import-substituting industrialization and a dominant role of the state in economic activity), replacing that model with what has been called a "new model of outward development." Resource allocation was to be determined by the market; the state was to cut back its interventionist economic role and its role as employer. The inflow of foreign finance capital and products was encouraged, and private agencies were placed in charge of much of the economy. Just as significant as these economic innovations was the establishment of a model of societal organization. What was sought was the enthronement of market principles in all spheres of society; the cutting back of the state's regulatory and redistributive role, although preserving a vertical and authoritarian decision-making system; and the atomization and segmentation of social demands, obstructing the creation of unified social organizations, even those of a corporatist character. Behind all this was a historical critique of twentieth-century Chilean society, viewed as a story of demagoguery in contrast to the image of an earlier period, which for the military validates the idea of strong, impersonal government.[8] At the basis of this doctrine is the dogmatic assertion that economic freedom, understood as the unfettered validity of private property, is the only solid basis for political freedom. There was, then, an economic model, a model for social reorganization, and also a political model. The political model distinguished between the long period of military rule that would be necessary to achieve economic and social reorganization, and the eventual political order that would allow a limited degree of political representation and participation, but in which the established order would be guaranteed by some kind of veto mechanism. A military regime and a "restricted and conservative democracy" were viewed, therefore, as two phases of a single process. Thus, a symbiotic relationship was established between an apparently extremely liberal discourse and a profoundly authoritarian conception stemming from the military.

However, there was no unanimity within the dominant bloc in favor of this historical project. The first expressions of doubt from within concerned the economic model. Lone business voices defended the role of national production and state intervention. Some producer associations even objected to the high social cost of the economic model.[9] On top of that there was criticism by self-proclaimed nationalist political groups who favored a more active role for the state and who proposed corporatist mechanisms as an alternative both to the preceding political party system and to the atomization encouraged by the new hegemonic project. Within the dominant bloc, however, this was the only coherent project that dealt with every level of social activity. The propaganda about economic successes, reflected in official indicators until 1980, the absence of an independent business movement and of a proper military debate, together with Pinochet's absolute support for the economic model, all impeded effective criticism of the economic model within the dominant bloc. This lasted until the emergence in 1981 of a profound crisis, which produced new debates, especially among business and labor sectors, as we shall see below.

The other source of friction within the dominant bloc concerned the political model. Whereas the economic debate began at a relatively early stage, there was a delay of several years, owing to the state of emergency and the needs of the "internal war," before the debate on the political future was initiated. The completion of the most urgent tasks of that phase, the growing concern of some proregime intellectuals about the problems of succession and the future, and increasing pressure both from the international arena and from some Chilean institutions, mainly the Catholic church, eventually obliged the dominant bloc to discuss the political model, and these discussions produced factional coalitions within the majority. The hard-liners advocated perpetuation of the regime in force since 1973, or the search for a corporatist alternative.[10] The soft-liners urged further institutionalization in order to project a more respectable image to the outside world.[11] However, none of those who sought the institutionalization of Pinochet's leadership, through different legal formulae, proposed what might be termed an "opening" (*abertura*) or a liberalization, at least not before 1982. Thus, this debate took place within a context that was identical for both sectors: the institutionalization of the military regime. One point was not in question, namely the preservation of Pinochet's leadership.

None of these sectors could put forward a real alternative until the situation became critical. With the Christian Democrats clearly situated in opposition, no alliance with the soft-liners could be attempted unless the party leaders were prepared to risk a split. Nor could the latter turn to a party whose demands threatened the very basis of their project of domination and their model of socioeconomic organization—not, that is, unless a critical situation had developed.

There was also no real debate, during the 1973–80 period, between those groups independent of the state, such as business organizations or middle-class unions, which had played such an important part in Allende's fall. These still identified fully with a regime that they perceived as the only alternative to a supposedly definitive threat, or they were completely absorbed with the effort of adaptation required by the economic model. Until 1980, therefore, the debate between hard-liners and soft-liners was a debate lacking significant roots in the regime's social base or in the armed forces.

The Institutionalization Process

From a dictatorship's viewpoint, institutionalization (that is, the creation of game rules in different spheres of society which express its project or societal ideal) always has two faces. It is the expression of a power which is being consolidated, but it is also the space, however limited, in which opposition groups can reconstitute themselves and social movements can be regenerated. There is thus a permanent tension between the need for the institutional definition to be delayed for as long as possible in order to favor the greatest discretionary power and, on the other hand, the need to demonstrate to those sectors which make up the dominant bloc, and often to entities which can exert pressure (such as the church, international agencies, or foreign governments), that the situation is being regularized. This explains why institutionalization may be set in train in response to a critical conjuncture when either the debate within the regime, or external pressures, block further resort to discretionary power and impose a framework of rules that would govern any subsequent developments.

Two levels can be distinguished when dealing with the institutionalization of regimes with historical projects of the kind considered here. The first level refers to the working out of the game rules in different spheres of *social life*. These rules standardize and confirm the structural transformations which have been introduced, and establish the system of relations between individuals and social groups in a given sphere. The second refers to *political* institutionalization, that is, the process by which the rules of the game are established for the political leadership. The first basically concerns relationships within civil society. The second concerns the sphere of the state and its relations with society. The two are very closely related because they both belong to the same pattern of societal organization imposed by one sector or group within the dominant bloc.

I have pointed out that there is no exact correspondence between the time scale for definition and transformation in the economic model, the model of social organization, and the political model. I have also noted that in Chile the earliest definition occurred on the economic front, where a more or less precise model was developed from April 1975 onwards. However, at the societal level the purely reactive dimension predominated and, at the level of political organization, the increasingly personalized military leadership. The concentration and centralization of the repressive apparatus strengthened Pinochet's personalized leadership within the armed forces. Moreover, repression conditioned the type of opposition in the regime's first years, and also some of the problems that the regime faced in its later phases. There is thus a relationship which cannot be ignored between the basic features of repression and the features of the subsequent institutionalization.

If, then, we analyze the evolution of the repression overall, and not in specific spheres, it is possible to identify several stages.[12] First, there was a massive repression, without any great coherence or technical coordination, directed at all militant leaders and UP government sympathizers. Legal processes did not exist, judicial protection could not be sought, and the population was encouraged to denounce "disloyal" individuals. In some areas property-owners sought revenge on their own account. It was more a question of revenge than a series of systematic measures aimed at punishing specific actions against the regime. This was the period of murders and mass executions, of deaths from torture, and of "disappearances," which resulted from the arbitrary and discretionary nature of a repressive power unleashed by each of the various branches of the armed forces.

There thus emerged a "technical requirement" for the coordination and specialization of the repression. That stage began in June 1974 with the creation and development of DINA: responsibility for repression was progressively assumed by this centralized body, which depended directly on Pinochet and which tended to predominate over the rival intelligence and security apparatuses of the different branches of the armed forces. In this phase the repression became more selective, combining covert acts of murder or kidnapping with spectacular actions which, witnessed by the whole population, were designed to instill fear. The limitless development of DINA's activity; its penetration of different spheres of society, such as the educational system; its effects on certain well-known individuals who were, in general, supporters of the regime but who had criticized the repression; public knowledge of DINA's involvement in the assassination of General Prats, in the attempt on Bernardo Leighton's life, and in the assassination of Orlando Letelier—all of these things made an impact. In 1977 pressure from the international community and from the Catholic church (under whose protection those affected by the repression tend to shelter), and also from some sectors of the regime, led the government to dissolve DINA. It was replaced by the Central Office of Information (CNI). On paper, the CNI appeared to be an intelligence agency without executive powers, but in fact it followed DINA in almost all its methods. The only difference was that there were no more disappearances and that the government, having learned from its previous experience, attempted to legalize those measures which oiled the wheels of the repressive agency. The "legalization" of repression was thus attempted, although the bounds of even that legality were frequently overstepped.

Between 1977 and 1980, while the political model was being defined, the repression was more targeted, instilling fear and breaking morale. Massive detentions, internal deportations, expulsions, and tortures predominated, although there were also some executions, carried out on the pretext of confronting armed resistance. The constitution, submitted to referendum in 1980 and promulgated in March 1981, ruled out any resort to the type of conventional defense that had been tried, unsuccessfully, by opposition lawyers. It also conferred the widest discretionary powers on Pinochet without providing any judicial or other kind of counterweight.

This brief overview of the repression can be supplemented by reference to some specific institutional spheres. In 1977, a few months before a political institutionalization plan was announced, the official elimination of the political parties was completed. Until 1978, union organizations and professional colleges were banned from functioning and even forbidden to renew their leadership. In the universities and the education system, organizations that did not support the regime were eliminated. More generally, except for the changes wrought by the economic model, until 1978 there was no innovation, no creation of rules of the game, only a state of suspended animation, disarticulation, and repression. There was not even any decision about the mechanisms of succession within the military regime itself. Economic transformation and the reactive dimension predominated, then, in every sphere of social life, while the repressive apparatus gained strength and the hegemonic nucleus secured its position. There was an almost total silence in civil society, the only exceptions being the voices of the church and those sectors under its protection.

After 1978, an attempt was made to make up for this delay. The first "modernization" was the Labor Plan, containing legislation on union organization and collective bargaining.[13] There followed a series of "modernizations" concerning labor relations, the health, education, and social security systems, the agrarian sectors, and changes in the administration of the state and of the legal system. Both in form and content these modernizations have features worth highlighting.

On the question of form, usually after some sectoral crisis, the government created a commission, charged with preparing legislation on the matter in hand, and composed of predominantly civilian supporters of the regime. It became a regular pattern that the work of these commissions would be shelved until a new conflict prompted the government to reexamine the problem; the recommendations of the original commission would then be ignored, and a whole body of legislation would be dictated in a very short space of time, on the basis of recommendations made by those closest to Pinochet. In this way an extremely personalized model of norm creation was established, without consulting the interests of the affected sectors.

On the question of content, the dominant approach was to apply the principles of market competition to the area in question, together with some norms derived from a specifically military outlook. The market approach sought to relieve the state of its responsibility in the social services; to enhance the primacy of those private groups with the greatest resources; and to weaken the role of representative organizations in the resolution of conflicts. The military approach sought to ensure the exclusion of "dangerous" political or ideological sectors and to maintain the state's repressive capacity.

Thus, this process of institutionalization involved both a response to temporary crises in particular sectors and the will to transform the situation and to establish a permanent regime structure. In this process, strictly capitalist visions were combined with concessions to the military mentality. This explains a degree of ambivalence in the design of these transformations and an even greater ambivalence in their implementation, when the "chemically pure" original content tended to be distorted or modified by different pressures, sometimes deriving from the military sectors, sometimes from the interest groups most affected or even from nationalist sectors within the regime whose general advice was normally disregarded. From 1981 onwards these distortions acquired greater importance as the directive capacity of the hegemonic nucleus weakened.

It is evident that both the development model and the institutionalization process described have produced important changes in Chilean society: its profile differs significantly from that of 1973. Independent of its degree of reversibility, this establishes a new conditioning factor in the constitution of social actors and in political activity itself.

With regard to the development model, the major changes are as follows: the reorientation of the productive apparatus with a relative reduction in the importance of productive sectors, particularly industry, and strong expansion of the tertiary sector; the reduction of the state's role as economic agent; the growing concentration of wealth in a small number of large conglomerates; capitalist penetration of agriculture; and the predominance of the financial sector and increasing dependence on international finance capital.

With regard to different social sectors, there are also important effects. These include the ever-present reality of high unemployment; the reduction and impoverishment of the working class and of the main groups on which, historically, the labor movement was based; the disarticulation and pauperization of the peasantry; the transformation and diversification of the middle classes, who have lost important reference points for their identity, such as links with the state and the expansion of education; and the reconstitution of the dominant classes with the financial sector predominant. In turn, all the preceding elements have had repercussions on social, especially working-class, organizations, which now face atomization with a significant reduction in their size and affiliation and, consequently, in their ability to mobilize and exert pressure.

Thus, rather than definite consolidation of new social subjects and new, coherent modes of conduct and ideologies, what characterizes Chilean society under the military regime is the disarticulation of previous modes and ideologies and attempts at their reconstitution and combination with new elements.

This provides the social context for the regime's attempts at political institutionalization, by which I mean the establishment of the rules of the game with regard to the political leadership, to management of the state, and to the state's relations with society.

In March 1974, just six months after taking power, the military government published a manifesto,[14] which affirmed that the regime would not be just a parenthesis between the destruction of one democracy and the restoration of another. However, references to the creation of a "democracy purged of vices" were restricted to vague hints and imprecise formulations taken from Catholic corporativism. There was no significant political debate about the political future within the regime until 1976. From 1974 to 1976, the main political trends were the personalization of Pinochet's leadership and an emphasis on the repressive dimension of the regime's relations with society. This was justified by references to the "internal war" and the "international blockade."

When the military government was three years old, and DINA at its most active, an attempt was made to entrench a permanent military regime. In September 1976, provisional constitutional guidelines ("Actas Constitucionales") were promulgated which in many ways contradicted the work of the Ortuzar Commission (a body appointed in December 1973 to prepare a new constitution). In 1976 the ideology of national security predominated; official discourse argued that liberal democracy had failed to such an extent that a military regime was the only answer to the Marxist aggression confronting Latin America. The "Actas Constitucionales" attempted to give the military junta constitutional status and to legalize the repressive operations of those years.

However, this attempt to institutionalize military rule at a time when international and church pressure was becoming acute precipitated internal discussion about the future political model. In fact, the advent of the Carter administration in the United States and the announcement by several Latin American military governments of some form of return to civilian rule put democratization back on the Chilean agenda. A debate began among the regime's supporters which led Pinochet to announce a political plan in July 1977, known as the Chacarillas Plan, in which several phases of institutional development were proposed, culminating in 1985 with the transfer of power to civilians through an extremely restrictive and exclusionary form of "democracy," combining systems of representation with appointments by the military authorities.

Given the vagueness of its specific political mechanisms and the fact that the proposed time scale would depend on the progress of the regime's socioeconomic transformations, the Chacarillas Plan was a typical device to sidestep a crisis, deflecting debate within the regime and countering pressure from international agencies, foreign governments, and the church. The plan reaffirmed the transitory nature of the military regime, even though it offered a new institutional base for Pinochet's rule. The 1976 project of establishing a permanent military regime was set aside. The plan was a means of gaining time, of postponing specific commitments on transition, but announcing the advent of a particular type of democracy within a "prudent" time scale. The Chacarillas announcement reopened debate within the regime while at the same time limiting that debate. As I have indicated, this was accompanied by a change in the instruments of repression, as CNI replaced DINA in August 1977.

Pinochet's response both to international pressure and to internal debate was to intensify his personalist line. This marks the whole process of political institutionalization. For example, the National Consultation of January 1978 was an attempt, under Pinochet's control, to legitimize the transition to a "new institutional basis" using the pretext of international isolation. The consultation went ahead in spite of open disagreement by the other members of the governing junta. As a confirmation of Pinochet's personal ascendancy,

General Leigh was removed from the junta and the greater part of the corps of air force generals were sent into early retirement.

The Ortuzar Commission's report of October 1978 proposed a constitution project to be revised by Pinochet and the governing junta. This report sharpened the disagreements between those who wanted to put off any constitutional-type political institutionalization in favor of an indefinite extension of the military regime and those who, while accepting the military regime's prolonged extension, wanted a long-term constitutional definition that would reintroduce some democratic elements and overcome the political and economic problems caused by international isolation. There was no challenge to Pinochet's leadership in this disagreement, and therefore the debate was limited to the necessity or the disadvantages of institutionalizing his presidency and setting a time limit on it.

Pinochet resisted the fixing of time scales, but in 1980 there was an imminent need for a decision. In July 1980 the (advisory) Council of State presented its observations on the Ortuzar report, and the internal debate about the political future became more polarized. This coincided with some important symptoms of decomposition in the repressive apparatus which created a generalized climate of insecurity. Even the press and communications media, which supported the military regime, criticized certain political murders. Faced with this situation, Pinochet reacted in a characteristic fashion: he revised the constitutional project, taking elements from the reports of the Ortuzar Commission and from the Council of State, and at one month's notice called a referendum to approve it. This forceful initiative gave him the ascendancy in the internal debate and exposed the lack of alternatives within the regime. Thus, some were satisfied that the military regime would continue until 1989 at least, and possibly until 1997, maintaining a discretionary repressive capacity during this period, and that the governing junta would be relegated to a purely legislative role.[15] Others, however, were satisfied with the fixing of time limits for the military regime and with the creation of mechanisms which limited the range of political options when military rule came to an end and precluded fundamental changes in future political and economic institutions.

The significance of the 1980 referendum for the regime should, then, be analyzed on three levels.

First, it temporarily resolved the internal crisis and fixed a framework within which the different internal sectors must operate lest they open a Pandora's box implying the repoliticization of the armed forces. Although such a framework does not definitively resolve internal disagreements, it limits them in a way that different sectors of the dominant bloc consider legitimate.

A second level concerns the political model embodied in the constitution. In fact, it contains two political models. There is what is officially called the "transition" model, signifying only the maintenance of the status quo established by the 1973 military coup, that is, a military regime with highly person-alized features. Although the constitution regulates the power of the authori-ties, it grants Pinochet the greatest personal discretion over the management of repression and eliminates any surviving elements of legal protection. This is a military regime in which no spaces or mechanisms of representation are created at the properly political level, and whose decentralization mecha-nisms, such as the so-called municipalization provisions, cover up the strengthening of a strictly vertical authority. However, this constitutionally established political model is presented as transitory and there is, therefore, place for a second political model that would be the definitive one after the transition process. This second political model would supposedly constitute the restoration of a full democracy, although, in fact, it enshrines what in strict terms must be called an authoritarian regime. This regime makes available spaces for restricted representation. Decision-making mechanisms are seg-mented by various constitutional provisions of incompatibility and exclu-sion. No possibilities for change in the model are envisaged and, thus, political activity is rendered almost irrelevant. All of this is underwritten by the formal recognition of the tutelary role of the armed forces. To sum up this political model, the terms "authoritarian democracy" or "limited democracy," al-though contradictory, are officially used.

What we would have, then, is the institutionalization of a personalized politico-military leadership, which in turn aims at the future institutionaliza-tion no longer just of a military regime but of an authoritarian regime. This authoritarian regime recognizes the military regime as its historical basis, but would present itself as an expression of democratic values, combining the vision of society as a market and "national security" principles which reassert the underlying authoritarian view of society.

Although in some ways the 1980 Constitution represented a triumph for Pinochet and those sectors closest to him, it also posed problems for personal-ized leadership. In effect, limits have now been put on his discretionary powers, and in critical situations, solutions such as the untimely calls for National Consultation in 1978 or for the 1980 referendum or the dismissal of the majority of the air force generals in 1978 are now subject to rules. To break these rules (something which could occur at any time) would mean a back-ward step in institutionalization itself and would reopen the debate within the regime, more especially within the armed forces. However, with regard to the management of repressive activity, Pinochet's discretionary power has been maintained intact. When the regime encounters difficulties in implementing its transformative project, it can compensate by intensifying its repressive operations.

The third level on which it is worth analyzing the referendum is in terms of its significance for society as a whole and for the opposition. Here, an analysis of electoral results is not possible owing to the enormous abnormalities and irregularities which characterized both the prepoll period and the holding of the referendum itself.[16] Nevertheless, the referendum was a success for the military government—not because it demonstrated great active support for the regime, but because it confirmed the government's capacity for social dislocation and the effectiveness of its propaganda concerning the terrors and traumas of the past, its continuing ability to raise doubts about the existence of any viable alternatives, and its skill in manipulating passive conformism. The tight control of certain mass media and the physical and psychological intimidation of opposition groups played a major part in all of this.

As far as the political opposition was concerned, the referendum marked a high point in its unification and mobilization. But it also revealed the difficulties involved in penetrating those sectors of society which did not support the regime but merely passively conformed to it.

The Collapse of the Project

There is no necessary linear progression from repression to institutionalization, and thereafter to transition to an authoritarian (or some other) type of regime. Crises may well interrupt or divert any regime from such a progression. Such crises could be caused by external factors, by the regime's internal problems, or by the dynamic of confrontation with the opposition. It is essential to distinguish between a crisis *within* the regime, even including a change of ruler; and a crisis *of* the regime, or terminal crisis. A regime can stumble from crisis to crisis, making defensive or reactive adjustments and shuffling its short-term alliances. In the absence of an alternative which effectively articulates opposition discontent, such tactics may avert a terminal crisis.

A regime which lapses into mere crisis administration will display a weakened capacity for effecting transformations. Its sole aim will be to ensure its own survival, its "hegemonic nucleus" will break up as it turns to partial solutions, and its policy management will become erratic. The sectors which previously supported it will fragment and split away. A regime which becomes a crisis administrator may in time survive; it may undergo changes which lead it to redefine the direction of its original historical project; or it may break up to such an extent that it quickly terminates.[17] The last outcome may or may not be promoted, encouraged, set in train, or intensified by opposition forces.

The September 1980 referendum and the March 1981 promulgation of the constitution marked a high point in the Pinochet regime's political institutionalization. Previously visible tensions within the dominant bloc seemed to have been resolved in favor of Pinochet. At this point, moreover, the regime could still demonstrate, on the basis of official indicators, a degree of economic success, and the new Reagan administration appeared to be a plus sign for the military regimes of Latin America. In this climate of triumph, the regime pressed ahead with its project for transforming society, introducing far-reaching social security and university reforms. For their part, after the September 1980 plebiscite, opposition parties seemed impotent and disoriented.

Some months later, however, one of the important economic groups specializing in speculative activities collapsed, and leading officials of the CNI in

Calama murdered some bank employees in the course of a robbery. These two events demonstrated the extreme fragility of the regime's economic base and also the lack of social controls over the repressive apparatus, a point reinforced in the wake of further CNI crimes. The collapse of one economic group proved no more than a foretaste of what was to come. By 1982 the government itself was speaking of economic recession and crisis. What was revealed was an increasing concentration of capital, unfettered speculation, massive external indebtedness, the destruction of the national productive apparatus, irresponsible pillaging by the large economic groups, and an absence of soundly conceived investment projects. All these factors showed up the profound weaknesses that had been concealed behind the triumphalist discourse, weaknesses which had until then been obscured and attenuated by an international economic situation that permitted a large influx of foreign capital in search of pure financial speculation.

Starting in 1981, the crisis of the economic model, and the generalized perception that it was failing to resolve the country's problems, caused the military regime to move into a new phase. Several characteristics of this phase can be noted.

First, the regime's loss of capacity to transform society and the progressive abandonment of its initial vision led to the adoption of a series of contradictory and incomplete policies. Compared with the model established in the previous phase, there was now a notable lack of coherence, state intervention was on the increase, socioeconomic crises intensified, and rather than offering a medium- or long-term solution, the regime's actions seemed directed to nothing more than simple survival. This new tendency was apparent not only in the realm of economics, but also in all fields of state action.

Secondly, the dominant bloc disintegrated into several factions, each of which began to exert autonomous pressure for its corporate interests, abandoning its unconditional loyalty to the regime, and even distancing itself, albeit without necessarily offering a political alternative. The emergence of independent actors from the capitalist class and from sectors of the middle classes undermined the apparent unity of the dominant bloc. Disagreements no longer arose only within the political elite (as had been the case, for example, in the debates between hard-liners and soft-liners up to 1980), but now encompassed broad social groups with a capacity to exert pressure.[18] This development is extremely significant for democratization because such forces are capable, through their impact on the armed forces, of provoking important crises and changes, even if they cannot ensure that all transformations will be democratic. The political ideology of these groups contains contradictory elements, combining a sense of trauma still persisting from the time of the UP government, and therefore a broad sympathy toward military rule, with growing discontent over specific policies, and very little clarity about what might constitute a future political model. Thus we have newly emerging social actors whose confusions impede their development and make it difficult to predict their political behavior.

Third, the regime's weakened capacity for leadership was reflected in a fragmentation within the state apparatus and in the progressive disappearance of one dominant current, namely the "economic team" that had been consolidated after 1975. On the one hand, some of the large conglomerates built up by state policy now entered into conflict with the economic team because of the crisis in the financial sector. This conflict culminated in state intervention in the banking sector. On the other hand, pressure from various sectors who blamed the economic team for causing a generalized crisis induced Pinochet to dismiss certain leading members of the group and to destroy its coherence by appointing other figures who advocated alternative approaches. But this took place without the substitution of a coherent alternative to the original economic team and without a consistent response to those business groups who were demanding an economic reactivation. Some key elements of the original team were preserved in order to present an image of continuity to the international financial community.

Fourth, these various developments implied a progressive isolation of Pinochet from the dominant bloc, even though in their eyes he preserved a leadership authority derived from the 1981 Constitution. Forced to respond to contradictory demands and to the fragmentation of his support groups, he vacillated between the temptations of a belated populism without any real social base, the possibility of conferring real political power on the armed forces, the option of lending state power to the business community, and the final option, which would be to adopt a nationalist posture. Each of these options contains such risks and poses such threats to the president's personal room for maneuver that Pinochet has attempted to borrow elements from all of them without pursuing any one course in a coherent manner. Attempting to preserve his own discretionary power, he has appointed representatives of each tendency to positions of authority, thereby prolonging the crisis and fueling the discontent.

A particularly acute phase in this recurrent crisis took place in 1983, with no sign of any solution to the economic crisis associated with the hugely increased foreign debt. The financial crisis produced such an impact on important sectors of the middle classes that it shook their support for the military regime. Although their disengagement was only passive, it created a new climate in which the discontent felt by the popular classes could be expressed in a massive and prolonged form. Organizations which had survived or reappeared sponsored a series of "national protests" which achieved a huge following, particularly among what has been called "popular youth" (juveniles from the low-income *poblaciones* or shanty towns), joined by some more politically organized groups. It was the beginning of the "emergence of a mass movement," a radicalization more visceral than ideological which produced a major impact on the political system. After ten years of suppressing such movements by purely military means, Pinochet responded to the rapid erosion of his support bloc, and also probably to symptoms of unrest within the armed forces, by attempting a political solution. He thus appointed a cabinet whose objective was to rally support around a traditional rightist politician, a step which implied conceding some informal room for maneuver to the political opposition.[19] This political shift went hand in hand with severe repression directed against the popular sectors. Officially defined as an "opening," the true meaning of this operation was the very opposite of what we have termed a "transition." It was, in reality, an attempt to give new life to a collapsing regime in order to keep the existing structure intact at least until 1989. The authorities would make whatever concessions necessary, even legalizing political parties and convening a Congress. In the background, Pinochet always kept open the possibility of returning to his former intransigence, as is indicated by the persistence of high levels of repression.

The military regime's political project of institutionalizing Pinochet's government in order to guarantee the capitalist transformations that would provide long-term underpinnings to the authoritarian system ended in a failure rooted in its material base. This left the regime with no project or purpose other than pure survival. But a military regime can fail to achieve its historical project and yet remain in control. The absence of a project or even the intensification of a national crisis generated by the regime is not a sufficient condition to bring about its downfall. There are several factors internal to the regime which prevent its progression from recurrent crisis to total and final collapse.

First of all, within the dominant bloc Pinochet benefits from a degree of legitimacy conferred by the 1981 Constitution, which is a rallying point for that bloc. There are unpredictable risks for those within the regime who break ranks. To this one must add Pinochet's personal will to retain power, his determination to hold onto it at any price. In a crisis situation, that disposition could cause him to initiate changes in some of the dates and mechanisms laid down in the 1981 Constitution, without changing its essential features. The purpose would be to enmesh the opposition in this process.

The second source blocking regime collapse arises from the complicity of the armed forces. Isolated from the rest of the country by privilege and by their repeated acts of repression against the population, with an ever-declining prestige, separated by Pinochet from the direct exercise of political power, and with the army subordinated to him, and the other services subordinated to it, the military has yet to feel the social crisis or any internalized sense of failure. Although during 1983 it seemed possible that the armed forces might shift from unconditional loyalty to Pinochet toward some more qualified relation, as it turned out, they retained their unity and remained solidly identified with the regime.

The third factor upholding the regime is the ambivalence toward redemocratization felt by most sectors of the political Right. In other words, there was no political class capable of expressing the discontent of disillusioned former supporters of the regime, and therefore pressing for the regime's termination. Since 1983 the political Right has been reestablishing itself, after having been disbanded, voluntarily, for ten years. It now faces the alternatives of acting as a political support to the regime, in order to become its natural heir, or proposing an autonomous political project, which would imply distancing itself from the existing order. Those who form the natural social base of the regime—businessmen and upper-income groups—have yet to break away from a corporatist vision and seem lacking in any more long-term or overall view, thinking only of how to confront their immediate problems.

To move from a stage of transformations *within* the regime to a transition *from* authoritarianism will require changes in these three above-mentioned factors and also changes in the orientation of the opposition, a topic to be developed in the next section.

Political Opposition to the Military Regime

The crisis confronting the regime since 1981 did not originate in the actions of the opposition, although these came to play a role in its subsequent development. Rather, the contradictions and problems created by the actions of the regime gave rise to the crisis. This is not to ignore the existence or the significance of the opposition.

There is a certain paradox in the opposition to this type of regime and others of the same type,[20] where the opposition's aim would seem to be the elimination of the regime itself and not just the substitution of a government by an opposition as occurs in democracies. Nevertheless, changes of a regime like that under consideration here are frequently related to factors external to society, for example, wars, or to problems of internal decomposition rather than to the opposition's struggle.

The fact is that under these regimes opposition action has several goals. The first, elemental goal is the survival, maintenance, and reproduction of organizational structures. The second, and most obvious, is the struggle to overthrow the regime. The third is the elaboration and preparation of an alternative to the military regime. The fourth is the work of introducing democracy into society. Under the military regime this fourth goal has at least three dimensions. First, there is the constitution and organization of social actors expressing civil society's own dynamic and independence. The second is the resistance to the transformations which the regime's project attempts to impose on society, the barriers and obstacles put in the way of state policies. The third refers to partial democratic victories and to progress in the creation of democratic spaces.

What the history of these regimes and of the opposition to them seems to demonstrate is that the dynamic of each of these processes is dissociated from the rest; the resolution of problems and the achievement of one goal do not necessarily correspond to the resolution of problems and achievement of others. The opposition may fail in its task of overthrowing the dictatorship while successfully preserving its political organization structures. It may work out a political alternative to the regime without having the means to push through the transition process. It may progress in introducing democracy into civilian society while failing in its attempts to change the regime. It may achieve the overthrow or fall of the regime without having obtained any degree of democratization in those aspects I have indicated. It is also possible that different sectors of the opposition will emphasize one goal rather than another, or that in the evolution of the opposition, the emphasis will shift. Thus, to sum up, analysis of the opposition's role under a given military regime is never a simple matter, even though the opposition's rhetoric has a tendency to highlight exclusively the aim of overthrowing the regime.

Until about 1980, the Chilean opposition gave priority to the survival, maintenance, and reproduction of its organizational apparatus and to the creation of a front which could present itself as an alternative to the military regime; with the exception of a very minor opposition sector (the MIR), the goal of overthrowing the regime was played down. The establishment and organization of social movements were also neglected. On the other hand, under church protection, a significant effort was made to defend victims of regime persecution.

From 1980 on, after the referendum, the theme of the military regime's overthrow or termination began to figure prominently in opposition thinking. Moreover, this happened precisely at the time of visible social dislocation caused by both the repression and the regime's social transformations. The traditional reference points of political activity and organization seemed to have lost their significance, and as a result, the task of organizing new sociopolitical actors emerged as a top priority. Without such a shift in priorities, surviving party organizations ran the risk of becoming irrelevant, with debates about regime termination remaining academic.

Initial opposition to the military regime came from those social and political sectors identified with UP, i.e. from those who were really defeated by the military coup. The magnitude of the repression—expressed in deaths, arrests, disappearances, intimidation, the exile of leaders and activists, and in a systematic attack on left-wing political organizations and on popular and student social organizations—ensured that the opposition was almost solely concerned with the physical survival of its leaders and activists and the preservation of a minimal organizational structure. In the early days of the repression there emerged an actor whose political importance would be fundamental under the military regime: the Catholic church. Following its initial calls for "reconciliation," the church emerged as the place in society where information on the regime's repressive nature could be accumulated, abuses could be condemned, minimal demands for survival could be channeled, and the forms of legal defense could be spelt out in the face of a government that imposed itself by force of arms. The church was the only actor able to speak for the collectivity, for the people, for the nation. As a result, it could pitch its discourse on the same level as the government and appeal to the legitimacy of those Christian principles which the government invoked in its ideology. On top of this, the church became the only space within which social organizations could regroup and opposition be expressed. This is not the place for an analysis of the historical reasons behind this phenomenon. It should be emphasized, however, that there is a tension between the church as an organizational actor with its own rationality and the church as the meeting point of different ideological and cultural currents. This tension highlights the church's potential and its limitations as a substitute forum for the political arena suppressed by the military regime. In fact, the church, subject to its own internal tensions, has its own self-image and dynamic which prevent it from taking on all the consequences of opposition activity. As an institution defining its own mission as above both governors and governed, the church can never conceive of itself as leading the opposition, even though it may be providing the opposition with the only available space and functioning as the only actor capable of expressing many of the opposition's demands.[21]

After a time, the repression touched sectors of the Christian Democrat political center. The blocking of their initial attempts at conditional collaboration with the military regime, together with a growing awareness of the government's true nature, gradually pushed the Christian Democrats into the opposition camp. This move made the task of unifying the oppositions a top priority. At the beginning some left-wing sectors, mainly in the Socialist party, refused to collaborate in any way with the Christian Democrats; others, like the Communist party, while asserting their independence, wanted to work with them. This gave rise to a debate about broad or antifascist fronts and the type of alternatives to the military regime.

This process of unifying the opposition culminated at the time of the 1980 referendum. The public predominance of the political center became evident at that time, but the greater part of the opposition's social backing was provided by the left-wing sectors. At that point the opposition put forward an alternative to the government's constitutional proposals which, although basically Christian Democrat–inspired, managed to attract the support of some left-wing sectors. The degree of mobilization achieved, especially among those popular sectors traditionally linked with the Left, was the highest of the whole postcoup period.

Yet, the period of the referendum also marked the exhaustion of a type of political activity which consisted mainly of the revitalization and coordination of party structures dating from the democratic era. The subsequent problem was how to approach the question of regime termination and how to reconstitute social forces that had been profoundly disorganized. The exiled Communist party leader proposed the violent overthrow of the regime through a popular insurrection, causing a split with the Christian Democrats and realignments within the organizationally fragmented Left.[22]

After the referendum, the Christian Democratic party faced up to the fact that although it was an organization with resources and public presence, its capacity for representation nevertheless appeared to be seriously weakened. This realization prompted a lengthy internal restructuring and debate about the party's leadership. The normal tendency of a centrist party—to seek out a political space which would allow it to survive and grow in any regime—was offset by the lessons drawn from the Christian Democratic party's recent history. Chile's Christian Democrats have direct experience of the regime's repressive character and are linked to a long ideological tradition which is critical of capitalism. However, while these are tendencies working against the temptations of accommodation with the soft-liners (blandos) within the regime, at the same time old ideological and organizational obstacles stand in the way of solid, stable agreements with the Left. For all these reasons, until 1982 the Christian Democratic party appeared more of an onlooker than a lucid agent engaged in a historic task. That said, however, a large body of party activists became a driving force within the social movements of opposition.

The Left, in turn, was also embroiled in its own organizational problems, and deeply divided. The Communist party failed to unite the Left around itself—except sporadically, when it proposed concrete tasks to specific sectors, especially youth groups. This failure was due to the party's international position, its ideological-theoretical rigidity, and its organizational structure. The Socialist party was divided (although a reunification is under way). Those parties which split from the Christian Democratic party in the late 1960s and joined the UP in the early 1970s may have influence in some areas, but they lack the necessary roots in broad social sectors. More generally, on the Left there has been a complex process in which the classic (basically Leninist) mold of political action has tended to break apart and attempts at renovation have begun, although as yet without finding an organizational expression.[23]

Behind all these difficulties for the opposition lie some common explanatory factors. The first of these is the dislocation of the way in which sociopolitical actors and subjects are organized. In this regard, the elimination of the party political arena and of the political system was not simply the elimination of a channel for demands, as in other Latin American societies. In the Chilean case, it meant the destruction of the principal mode by which social actors and subjects were constituted. Thus, in breaking up the political system the military took a step which was both "reactive" and "transformative." Social organizations like the union or student movements, for example, were national actors precisely because of their overlap with the political class and because of their relations with the state. Under the military regime, such organizations were deprived of those elements which made them nationally important political subjects and were reduced to their corporate dimension.

At the same time, however, the party political structure that arose during the democratic regime has been able, despite its fragmentation, to survive under the military regime. There is, therefore, a political opposition whose organizations derive from historical conditions very different from the present. Hence the slowness of political reconstruction by the opposition. If we examine the development of what we might term the social opposition (expressed through student and popular—mainly labor or neighborhood—organizations) and of the political organizations, it becomes clear that there was an extremely complex process of organizational redefinition involved, which may only with great difficulty crystallize into an act of political reconstruction.

The year 1983 marked a watershed in the history of the regime. The economic crisis struck with great force just as the slow and uneven process of adaptation and development of civil society reached maturity and took a publicly visible form. For the first time since 1973, government and opposition were operating in the same arena, so that the activities of the latter could affect the former and force it to respond. The seizure of this political space and the necessity of confronting the government at this level obliged the opposition to reorganize itself from the bottom up and to establish large blocs.[24] The public appearance of the opposition; its new, more deeply rooted groupings; the eruption of a massive movement of discontent and protest; and the regime's adoption of a political strategy to counteract these trends—all were new challenges for the opposition.

First of all, it is clear that the opposition is composed of heterogeneous political forces, whose distinct styles and projects compete among themselves. However natural this may be, it creates problems in the achievement of cohesion and unity of action. Such problems arise both in relation to the military regime and in relation to the opposition's social base, which resists the efforts of any particular sector to make political capital on its own account, rather than on behalf of the opposition as a whole. Quite apart from its ideological aspects, this heterogeneity reflects a tension between two strategic orientations which are in principle complementary but in practice hard to combine. The first orientation emphasizes political struggle against the dictatorship, with all that that implies in terms of tactics, organizational alliances, selection of precise political objectives for social mobilization, and so on. The underlying assumption here is of a transition without a military defeat for the armed forces. The second orientation emphasizes mobilization of the social base, in the hope that the regime will fairly automatically fall apart. Without precisely specifying how the regime is expected to end, the implication is that there will be some sort of insurrection in which the fall of the dictatorship will create the possibility of a social revolution. The difficulties of achieving unity within the opposition are also closely connected with long-standing tendencies in the Chilean party system. We have already noted how hard it is for the Christian Democrats to establish stable alliances without attempting to subordinate their supposed allies, owing to their emphasis on their own programmatic or tactical alternatives. In particular, they have sought to isolate the Communist party, excluding it from their antidictatorial fronts. The absence of a highly representative political force with a considerable capacity for political mobilization leaves these fronts weakened. It also reinforces Communist ambiguity about the appropriate methods of struggle against the dictatorship, and pushes the Communist party to control social movements on its own. On the other hand, the hoped-for dividend from excluding the Communists— namely, the recruitment of new forces from the Right—has failed to materialize. Finally, the reunification of the Socialist Left has progressed so slowly that it has deprived the opposition of a balancing force which could have provided greater flexibility in the construction of political alliances.

Secondly, the opposition still seems to lack a precise definition of the process of transition it hopes to bring about. Apart from demanding the departure of Pinochet, there is no institutional proposal with any appeal within the armed forces that could permit the realignments necessary for a transition. Although necessary, the social mobilization is not sufficient to set in train all the dynamic readjustments required for regime termination. We will return to this point.

Thirdly, the opposition as a whole faces the problem of how to relate to a diversified social base, confronting enormous problems of daily life, and full of pent-up demands but lacking clarity about how its discontent with the regime and its wish for political participation can achieve political expression. The disarticulation between the "political world" and the "social world" will oblige the opposition to diversify its political and cultural appeals and to accept a greater autonomy of popular consciousness and of social organization.

To sum up, the evolution of the opposition will be defined in relation to that of the regime. In the current phase, the regime is driven by the urge to survive and will therefore make whatever concessions are required in order to do so. The problem facing the opposition is how to promote advances and transformations within the regime and at the same time achieve the necessary external strength to bring that regime to an end, given the tendency for each of these developments to impede the other.

The Chilean Case and the Transition to Democracy

Let us reexamine some of the themes which have been developed, placing them in the more general context of transitions from authoritarian to democratic regimes. In so doing we must keep in mind the distinction between those transformations within a military regime which lead the regime to open up spaces for restricted political competition and representation—that is, to institutionalize an authoritarian model—and those processes which lead to a properly democratic regime. It is evident that there may be overlap between the two processes and that institutionalization may unleash a process of transition, but it is important that we neither confuse the two nor regard every form of opening as a transition to a democratic regime. Likewise we should remember that we are dealing with regimes which do not consider themselves to be merely regimes, but rather view themselves as the bearers of a historical project (even if the project has failed), a particular project of domination. Hence, opposition to these regimes is not just about substituting one government for another or reinstating a previous regime, but also about resisting a given project of domination. In other words, the struggle for political democracy is only one of the struggles taking place under these regimes, not *the* struggle. In order to analyze the significance and exact priority of such struggles in any given society, we have to shift the focus from the dynamics of the regime itself to the conduct of social actors at large, and from the "alternatives" proclaimed in politico-ideological discourse to the "demands" which grow up in society. Thus, democratization of society and transition to political democracy are processes whose rhythms, dynamics, requirements, and social agents may or may not coincide.

At the beginning of the chapter I pointed to the paradox that Chile, a society with a long democratic tradition, had faced greater difficulties in reestablishing a democratic political regime than other countries with less experience of democracy. Throughout this chapter I have tried to identify the reasons for this. To the particularly deep crisis that was in the origins of the military intervention and to the ever-present repression, we must add the nature of the regime's project of transformation. These transformations have not, as in other cases, such as Brazil, aimed at consolidating a mass society by means of industrialization and the expansion of the state, with all the associated implications for the consolidation of new social forces. On the contrary, what has predominated has been marginalization, segmentation, and atomization in both rural and urban contexts; a shrinking of the state's role as point of reference for collective action; a reduction in the industrial productive apparatus and in public-sector employment, with a permanently high level of unemployment; and the expansion of sectors precariously linked to the productive system. Rather than promoting policies that would create new social classes or sources of social dynamism, Pinochet's policies have promoted disintegration and dislocation, which must be placed in the repressive context I have indicated.

The historical solidity of the party political structure and the consequent weakness of the independent organizations of civil society have a negative side here. Changes in the state's role have disrupted the old basis of political activity, disorganizing the social bases of political representation and the links between those social bases and the party structure. In fact, the party structure has been frozen and left in suspension, making the processes of renovation and party reconstruction lengthy, difficult, and complicated. For their part, most social movements also face a difficult process of reconstruction in the absence of facilitating conditions at the formal political level. The labor movement, for example, despite its growing, and indeed decisive, role in recent social mobilizations, is experiencing problems similar to those confronting the political parties.

In the absence of a terminal regime crisis, democratization progresses much more in terms of social organization than it does at the political level. There is, then, a kind of invisible transition to democracy which cannot be measured in terms of mechanisms and stages of the political regime but only in terms of the democratization of society and in terms of political reconstruction by the opposition. We should not, however, underestimate the hidden potential of such a situation, in which the survival of a political class, a collective democratic memory, and a political party structure may facilitate the rapid reconstruction of political leadership during a period of severe crisis or in extraordinary circumstances.

Looking beyond the marked progress toward an "invisible transition" in 1983, we have to explore the possibility that these recurrent crises may end in a regime termination and an effective transition to democracy. I have already indicated the obstacles to this both on the side of the regime and on that of the opposition. Despite the failure of its project of transformation, the regime may combine repression with a limited opening that leaves it still in political and military command at least until 1989. This seems to be its dominant intention. Since there is little room for maneuver for the opposition, that possibility must not be discounted.

From the standpoint of the opposition, what are the relevant factors in order to promote a process of transition? The existence of modern and relatively unified armed forces, and of a diversified and politically autonomous middle class, makes it unlikely that an insurrection that defeats the military could terminate the regime. The theory of an insurrection which ends the dictatorship and paves the way to a social revolution must be considered rather unrealistic. If so, a decision by the armed forces to withdraw is needed. But, as indicated above, the armed forces are isolated and relatively well insulated from the social crisis. Since they will obviously not withdraw voluntarily, the opposition will need a two-edged approach. First, it must promote social mobilization which persuades the military that the society is ungovernable and forces their recognition of their failure. Second, the opposition must create a political front capable of aggregating social demands around a proposed alternative to the military regime. This proposed alternative must exist at two inseparable but distinct levels. One level involves an agreement on the termination of the dictatorship and the institutions which will replace it, i.e. a political pact embracing all sectors opposed to the dictatorship. The other requires the establishment of a sociopolitical bloc in favor of a prospect of social transformation. Clearly the social and political forces that make up this bloc will derive from those sectors which in previous decades clashed among themselves because of their conflicting projects of transformation, and which failed because of their isolation. In short, the Center and the Left will have to create this sociopolitical bloc. These are the challenges facing the opposition if it is to speed the downfall of the dictatorship and thereafter ensure a stable democracy.[25]

6 ·

Political Liberalization in an Authoritarian Regime: The Case of Mexico

Kevin J. Middlebrook

Mexico's recent political history in many ways contrasts sharply with the abrupt regime transformations that some Latin American countries underwent in the 1960s and 1970s. Mexico has experienced basic political stability and institutional continuity since the formation of its "official" single-dominant party in 1929. The last major military revolt against civilian rule occurred in that same year, and since 1940 the armed forces' political role generally has been limited to symbolic representation in certain public offices and regular private consultations on issues of national importance. There has not been a significant challenge to the official party's presidential candidate since 1952. The early consolidation of centralized political power following Mexico's 1910–17 social revolution and state controls over organized labor and peasant movements contributed substantially to rapid economic growth in the period after 1940. The "Mexican economic miracle" came under increasing criticism in the 1970s as the rate of economic growth slowed and diverse socioeconomic problems (income and regional inequalities, unemployment and underemployment, inflation, and foreign indebtedness) worsened. The severity of these problems and the emergence of urban and rural guerrilla movements in the early 1970s led some observers to conclude that the Mexican authoritarian regime was in crisis. The sudden collapse of a petroleum-led economic boom in 1982 produced a sharp reversal in popular expectations and raised new concerns regarding Mexico's political stability. Yet none of these challenges led to a breakdown of the established regime.

Despite these contrasts, Mexico's contemporary process of political liberalization parallels political transitions in other countries in Latin America and Southern Europe. The liberalization initiated by the López Portillo administration's 1977 political reform increased the number and ideological diversity of officially registered political parties participating in the electoral process. It also altered the rules governing elections, augmented opposition parties' representation in the federal Chamber of Deputies and in state and local governments, and expanded opposition parties' access to mass communications. (A more detailed summary of the major provisions of the 1977 reform law appears below.) Political liberalization in Mexico has been more gradual and less conflictual than many other political transitions examined in this volume, in part because the well-institutionalized and broadly inclusive Mexican regime is a less severe form of authoritarian rule. As a result of its revolutionary origins and a long-standing commitment to balance diverse interests in a governing "revolutionary coalition," the Mexican regime has historically offered a number of opportunities for the expression of interests within the established system. Yet Mexico's liberalization experience is interesting from a comparative perspective precisely because it involves an authoritarian regime whose historical origins and evolution are distinctive. The Mexican case offers an opportunity to examine both the general characteristics of political change in an authoritarian regime and the specific factors that shape the process of political liberalization.

Political liberalization in the Mexican case thus involves the expansion of alternative mobilization channels through legalizing additional opposition parties and creating new opportunities for political competition and representation in the electoral and legislative arenas. This chapter examines four aspects of Mexico's liberalization experience. The first section analyzes the origins of the contemporary liberalization, considering both the broad challenges that the established regime faced in the late 1960s and early 1970s and the particular factors that motivated the regime-sponsored political reform. Second, the chapter evaluates the formulation of the 1977 political reform law and the impact of the regime's sociopolitical bases and institutional structure on the characteristics of the reform process, drawing attention to efforts by conservative elements in the governing "revolutionary coalition" to limit the reform measure's scope. The third section examines the consequences of the 1977 political reform for the registration of new political parties, election results, opposition party representation in the federal Chamber of Deputies, and the problems of voter abstention and electoral fraud. Finally, the broader implications of the liberalization process for future regime change in Mexico are considered. The López Portillo administration's political reform opened significant new opportunities for opposition forces and altered the national political map in important ways. However, the federal government has retained close control over the liberalization process. The challenges posed by Mexico's economic crisis and the continuing resistance on the part of conservative elements in the established regime constitute important obstacles to more extensive political liberalization. For these reasons, the future prospects for regime change in Mexico remain uncertain.

Origins of the Contemporary Liberalization Process

Characterizing the Mexican system as an authoritarian regime underlines the importance of the state's active intervention to regulate and limit sociopolitical pluralism, mass political mobilization, and socioeconomic and political demand articulation.[1] The governing "revolutionary coalition" is a heterogeneous grouping of sociopolitical actors and competing interests that, despite considerable internal competition and frequent conflict over policy issues, has been linked over a relatively long period by an overarching consensus on broad norms regarding political action and by the shared goal of national economic development. As part of the heritage of Mexico's 1910–17 social revolution, organized labor and peasant movements constitute the regime's principal mass base. Their inclusion in the government-affiliated Institutional Revolutionary Party (Partido Revolucionario Institucional, PRI) is an important source of political legitimacy. (Organized business has never formed part of the party, although business interests and the military are both important elements in the broader revolutionary coalition.) However, broad state controls on labor and peasant organizations substantially restrict their actions and significantly limit opposition leaders' opportunities to mobilize mass groups competitively. Thus the Mexican authoritarian regime is both elite dominated and mass based.

Several other elements are also important in characterizing the Mexican regime. Elections play a significant legitimating role as a formal validation of popular consent and as a means of periodically mobilizing public support for government activities, the party system, and "official" party candidates. The electoral process represents a continuing elite commitment to regular leadership succession, and it offers some opportunity for the presentation of citizen demands to future officeholders. The "official" PRI provides a major institutional forum for intraelite competition and serves as a mechanism for leadership selection. In addition, a reliable system of office rotation (including a constitutional prohibition against presidential reelection) creates opportunities for the expression of a comparatively wide range of sociopolitical tendencies. The formal guarantee of liberal political rights (such as a relatively free national press) in a civilian-ruled system and the presence of legally recognized opposition political parties also contribute to the comparative openness of the regime. Nonetheless, the dominant position of the PRI and its close ties to the state have traditionally insulated the governing political elite from effective electoral competition and the possibility of major electoral defeat. The Mexican regime is a strongly presidential system in which major political initiatives remain under the firm control of the federal executive.

The Mexican regime has generally been relatively restrained in its use of repression against opposition political groups and individual dissidents. Although major challenges to the existing socioeconomic and political order have been forcefully suppressed, the governing elite more frequently combines selective repression of regime opponents with negotiation, compromise, and policies designed to address protesting groups' demands. The comparatively low level of repression in Mexico is largely due to the effectiveness of regime control over mass actors such as labor unions and peasant organizations through a combination of state administrative controls on mass political participation and these more flexible strategies of governance.

Regime-initiated attempts at political restructuring in Mexico have generally responded to a combination of particular events or crises and the broad consequences of sociopolitical change. The 1977 political reform followed this pattern. The regime-sponsored liberalization measure addressed three closely related problems.

First, during the early 1970s, liberal elements in Mexico's governing revolutionary coalition became increasingly convinced that the regime suffered from a substantial erosion of its political legitimacy. The 1968 student strike and "Tlatelolco massacre" (in which police and army troops killed or wounded many protesting students) were watershed events in this regard. The significance of the 1968 crisis for subsequent political developments was largely due to the nature of political legitimacy in the Mexican system. Because the regime had originated in a revolutionary transformation rather than through an inclusive and widely accepted electoral process, public perceptions of regime legitimacy depended more on overall evaluations of government performance and the fulfillment of a comprehensive revolutionary program than on government adherence to particular procedural requirements.[2] Despite the governing elite's use of selective repression to silence political opponents and suppress popular movements that threatened the entrenched position of "official" mass organizations, until the late 1960s the established regime received widespread public support as the embodiment of the 1910–17 revolution's commitment to the progressive achievement of social equity and political democracy. Mexico's rapid economic growth between the 1940s and the early 1970s substantially reinforced the governing coalition's position.

The 1968 crisis significantly affected public perceptions of the established regime's revolutionary credentials and revealed broad sociopolitical pressures for change. Perhaps most important, the crisis demonstrated that the rapidly growing urban middle class could not be easily incorporated into the existing political system by traditional means. The protest movement called for democratization and the creation of new participatory opportunities: it did not immediately challenge the regime's labor and peasant bases, but it did pose a serious potential threat to the regime in its effort to link a radical middle-class leadership with opposition elements in the organized labor movement and among urban marginals. The violent attacks of the Díaz Ordaz administration (1964–70) on student protesters shocked the urban middle class—the ruling elite's most politically articulate constituency. The mass public protest that followed the Tlatelolco massacre condemned the government's action as a violation of accepted governing practices.

The 1968 crisis also initiated a sustained national debate on the shortcomings and contradictions of Mexican development. Although the events of 1968 did not challenge directly the underlying political-economic pact between the state and the private sector, they seriously undermined the "myth of the Mexican Revolution" and the assumption of the progressive achievement of socioeconomic and political justice officially associated with Mexico's post-1940 development model. Public attention subsequently focused on issues such as the shortage of productive employment opportunities for urban workers, limited access to public services, increasing relative.income inequality and stagnating agricultural production in rural areas, problems caused by the high rate of rural-urban migration, and the declining ability of the national education system to meet the needs of the expanding urban middle class.[3] Most of these problems were not new, and in some cases they took on important dimensions only after the 1968 crisis in public confidence. Nonetheless, growing concern with government policy performance on issues such as these contributed to public disillusionment with the established regime. One goal of the 1977 political reform was to reverse this tendency.

The emergence of several new opposition political parties outside the officially recognized party system constituted a second major motivation for the 1977 political reform. The Díaz Ordaz administration's violent suppression of the 1968 student movement drove many leftist political groups underground. In the next few years, leftist opposition to the established regime often took the form of urban and rural guerrilla actions, including bank robberies, kidnappings, and political assassinations. Violent attacks by paramilitary groups on student demonstrators in June 1971 further fueled guerrilla movements in several areas of the country, convincing many leftist groups that peaceful reform efforts were futile. The response of the Echeverría administration (1970–76) to this challenge combined systematic (and generally successful) efforts to repress urban and rural guerrilla movements with a more liberal government policy toward nonviolent political opposition, frequently providing political support and material assistance to nonviolent opposition elements as part of a "democratic opening" policy designed to reduce sociopolitical discontent. In this more open national political environment during the early 1970s, opposition movements among urban marginals, peasants, workers, and university students took on a new importance.

The opposition political organizations that appeared during this period represented forces on both Left and Right and in many cases their formation reflected the same sociopolitical pressures for regime change that had surfaced in 1968. The most important of these opposition organizations were the Mexican Democratic party (Partido Demócrata Mexicano, PDM, 1971), Socialist Workers' party (Partido Socialista de los Trabajadores, PST, 1973), Communist Left Group (Unidad de Izquierda Comunista, UIC, 1973), Movement for Socialist Action and Unity (Movimiento de Acción y Unidad Socialista, MAUS, 1973), Mexican Workers' party (Partido Mexicano de los Trabajadores, PMT, 1974), Mexican Popular party (Partido Popular Mexicano, PPM, 1975), Revolutionary Socialist party (Partido Socialista Revolucionario, PSR, 1976), and Revolutionary Workers' party (Partido Revolucionario de los Trabajadores, PRT, 1976).

With the exception of PDM (the most recent political manifestation of a conservative, Catholic agrarian movement dating from the 1930s), these were all leftist political organizations of various ideological tendencies. They joined the opposition Mexican Communist party (Partido Comunista Mexicano,

PCM, 1919) outside the official party system. The emergence of these opposition political organizations underlined the increasing difficulties that the PRI and established opposition parties had in incorporating important mass publics. The liberalization program initiated by the 1977 political reform sought to bolster the established regime's claim to political legitimacy by incorporating these elements of the political opposition into the officially recognized party system.

The third motivation for the 1977 reform was the governing political elite's increasing concern over the institutional health of PRI. A decline in electoral competition had eroded PRI's mobilization capacity and weakened its internal organization. During the 1960s and early 1970s the traditional registered opposition parties—especially the Socialist Popular party (founded in 1948 as the Partido Popular and reorganized in 1958 as the Partido Popular Socialista, PPS) and the Authentic Party of the Mexican Revolution (Partido Auténtico de la Revolución Mexicana, PARM, 1954)—became less and less viable as independent opposition political forces. PARM, formed by military veterans of the revolution in part as a reaction against the increasing centralization of Mexican politics, never operated as more than a factional electoral vehicle with limited regional support. It never nominated its own presidential candidate; instead, it regularly supported PRI's nominee. PPS was originally formed as a progressive alternative to the "official" PRI, but after 1958 it also regularly backed PRI's presidential candidate. Disillusionment with PRI's fraudulent electoral tactics and the impossibility of winning national office limited these parties' interest to competition in state and local elections. In part owing to these factors, the conservative National Action party (Partido Acción Nacional, PAN, 1939) took on new importance as a catchall opposition party. However, PAN did not field a presidential nominee during the 1976 presidential campaign because of a growing abstention movement within the party and severe internal division among party leaders. PRI then faced a presidential election without the participation of a legally recognized opposition candidate.

PRI had also encountered considerable difficulty in adapting to changing sociopolitical conditions. The gradual loss of its more easily mobilized rural support base due to continued rural-urban migration and the need to represent an increasingly urban, often middle-class electorate posed new challenges to the "official" party's organizational structure. Furthermore, liberal elements in PRI were concerned that the party's traditionally closed internal nominating procedures produced candidates without the broad-based political experience necessary to respond successfully to the demands of a changing electorate. They hoped that increased electoral competition would compel PRI to adopt internal reforms that would improve the party's ability to confront this problem.

Growing public disillusionment with the established regime, the decreasing viability of traditional opposition parties, and the erosion of PRI's mobilization capacity contributed to a steady decline in voter participation in the

electoral process. The historical political agenda set by the 1910–17 revolution's promise of "Effective suffrage; no reelection" gives the electoral process
special importance in the Mexican authoritarian regime as a legitimating
mechanism. Yet between 1961 and 1976 the percentage of registered voters
not voting in congressional and presidential elections rose steadily from 31.7
percent to at least 38 percent.[4] In addition, large numbers of citizens either
failed to register or invalidated their ballots. Although the regime places
important restrictions on independently organized mass mobilization, growing citizen apathy toward the electoral process was seen as a significant threat
to the viability of the PRI-dominated party system. The 1977 political reform
sought to revitalize the electoral process, reinvigorate PRI, and reverse the
trend toward rising voter abstention by increasing the effectiveness of opposition electoral competition.

The Mexican regime has over time relied on a combination of strategies to
respond to political problems and changing sociopolitical circumstances. In
addition to negotiation and compromise, elite rotation, the cooptation of
opposition leaders, and the selective use of repression against political opponents, the governing elite has engaged in massive fraud to deny opposition
parties an electoral victory on those occasions when they have posed a threat
to PRI's dominance. Various forms of electoral fraud (stuffing ballot boxes,
intimidation of voters, violence against opposition parties and their candidates, and so forth) are widespread at the state and local level. On several
occasions PAN has been denied what appeared to be a clear electoral victory
when the government invalidated the vote returns. PAN has succeeded in
winning some important local victories, but PRI's government ties and its
ability to shape the outcome of the electoral process have proved powerful
obstacles to electoral challenges by opposition political forces. For example,
PRI's candidates for the presidency, the federal Senate, and state governorships
have never been defeated.

The established regime has also demonstrated considerable flexibility over
time in reshaping the formal rules governing the electoral process in order to
accommodate diverse groups and adapt to change. Although serving somewhat different purposes at different times, several presidential administrations have reformed legislation regulating elections and political party registration so as to structure opposition parties' representation in elected
positions. Electoral legislation enacted in 1946, 1949, 1951, and 1954 set
requirements concerning party registration procedures and the minimum size
and distribution of party membership that reinforced the position of PRI by
making the formation of local and regional political parties more difficult. In a
partial reversal of this trend, electoral reforms enacted in 1963, 1972, and 1973
attempted to revitalize a party system in which registered opposition parties
(PAN, PPS, and PARM) played an increasingly marginal role by guaranteeing
these parties representation and a national political presence in the federal
Chamber of Deputies.

The 1963 reform (like the López Portillo liberalization measure) sought to defuse accumulated sociopolitical discontent following the government's repression of strikes by teachers and railroad workers in 1958–59, and to direct the internal political opposition sparked by the Cuban Revolution into established institutional channels. The reform provided minority political parties winning more than 2.5 percent of the total national vote with a minimum number of Chamber deputies (five each, plus one for each additional 0.5 percent of the vote, up to a maximum of twenty). And when PPS and PARM failed to win even this minimum percentage of the national vote in the 1964, 1967, and 1970 congressional elections, the national electoral college acted "in the spirit of the law" to grant them Chamber representation in any event. In 1972 the Echeverría administration enacted additional constitutional reforms to reduce the minimum required percentage to 1.5 percent. At the same time, the maximum number of "party deputies" was increased to twenty-five per party. A 1973 reform of the electoral law also reduced the minimum membership requirement for party registration.[5] However, none of these measures succeeded in transforming existing minority parties into a credible political opposition.

Given the diverse political problems confronting the Mexican regime in the late 1960s and early 1970s, one might ask why the Echeverría administration (1970–76) did not undertake a more extensive electoral and party reform. The governing elite's ability to delay broader political liberalization was due largely to the established regime's continued overall strength. Accumulated pressures for regime change remained diffuse; they did not constitute an immediate threat to regime stability. Although some response was clearly necessary to reduce existing tensions, the political elite retained the capacity to control and direct the liberalization process.

In addition, three other factors influenced the specific timing of a more extensive regime-sponsored liberalization program. First, from the political elite's perspective, insufficient time had passed since the 1968 crisis. A major reform that greatly expanded the political presence of the leftist opposition would have signaled regime weakness by drawing too direct a causal link between an attack on the established regime and its response to demands for change. Second, the status and organizational structure of the leftist opposition that emerged after 1968 were not conducive to a more extensive party reform. At the time of Echeverría's reforms, the government had not yet succeeded in suppressing leftist guerrilla groups. It was not until the second half of the Echeverría administration that the bulk of these new opposition forces had regrouped into reasonably stable party organizations. Although the Echeverría administration could coopt opposition leaders individually in order to respond to changing political circumstances, emerging leftist opposition forces had not yet evolved to the point at which they could be conveniently integrated into the existing party system according to established rules of the game.

Finally, a more extensive political reform might not have been possible at the time for reasons associated with Echeverría's own political career. As minister of the interior during the Díaz Ordaz administration, Echeverría had been the cabinet official directly responsible for the violent suppression of the 1968 student movement. Given the serious reservations that a number of leftist opposition parties expressed regarding participation in the López Portillo liberalization policy, it is possible that any major reform initiative by Echeverría would have been tainted by his own association with it. The reforms enacted in 1972 and 1973 sought to reinvigorate the political party system, but they were essentially limited modifications of the existing party deputy arrangement. The intended beneficiaries of these measures—PAN, PARM, and PPS—were unlikely to boycott Echeverría's reforms, as more radical opposition parties might have done.

Formulation of the 1977 Political Reform Law

Thus when the López Portillo administration (1976–82) took office in December 1976, several factors favored a broad reform of the political party system and the electoral process. López Portillo had actively discussed this possibility with his close advisers during the 1975–76 presidential campaign, and more detailed discussions concerning the general characteristics of a political reform measure continued after the July 1976 general election. Between December 1976 and March 1977, Minister of the Interior Jesús Reyes Heroles conducted high-level, confidential consultations with diverse groups regarding the content of the reform initiative. However, the first official announcement of the government's intention to implement a "political reform" came in a 1 April 1977 address by Reyes Heroles. López Portillo was personally convinced of the need for such a measure, and liberal elements in the established regime actively supported the initiative.[6] The fact that López Portillo had recently been inaugurated enhanced the administration's ability to present the measure as an important departure from previous electoral reforms.

Political reform constituted a basic part of the López Portillo administration's plan to confront Mexico's 1976–77 economic crisis. The end of the Echeverría administration saw massive capital flight as the private sector expressed its discontent with developments such as government-authorized emergency wage increases, heightened labor mobilization, inflation, and increased economic uncertainty. At the same time, rural violence and the incidence of land invasions rose sharply, and there was unprecedented public speculation regarding the possibility of a military coup d'état and the armed forces' renewed open involvement in national politics. In order to restore political balance in the revolutionary coalition, the López Portillo administration forcibly suppressed some opposition movements and implemented a series of economic policies designed to regain the private sector's confidence (including severe wage restraint and close government control over labor mobilization, the relaxation of price controls on basic commodities, tax and investment concessions, and a reduction in the number and importance of state-owned enterprises). By simultaneously opening the party system to new forces on the Left, liberal elements in the regime sought to counterbalance the resurgence of conservative groups and the overall conservatism of López Portillo's early socioeconomic policies. The prospect of renewed national economic growth on the basis of Mexico's recently announced massive petroleum resources may also have increased the administration's willingness to engage in political experimentation.

However, the revolutionary coalition was divided internally regarding the desirability of a political reform measure. Various conservative elements (including some representatives of the private sector) expressed reservations about the proposed liberalization project, but the most active opposition came from two principal sources.[7] First, the Confederation of Mexican Workers (CTM)—PRI's labor sector and the single most important representative of the organized labor movement—opposed a major reform in the electoral process and the existing party system because such a measure threatened its own privileged position. Political negotiations in PRI involved bargaining among the party's three sectors. In comparison to the heterogeneous agrarian sector and the even more amorphous "popular" (middle-class) sector, CTM's more easily mobilized membership, its greater organizational coherence under the strong leadership of Fidel Velázquez, and its comparatively closer ties between leaders and rank-and-file members provided it with important internal political leverage in PRI. To the extent that the electoral process became a major arena of political competition and the principal source of regime legitimacy, CTM's own political role would be diminished. Although CTM was apparently the first sector to voice its opposition to the political reform, conservative elements in PRI's other two sectors (the National Peasant Confederation, CNC, and the National Confederation of Popular Organizations, CNOP) soon lined up behind CTM on this issue.

The CTM leadership also feared the impact that the legalization of additional opposition political parties might have on its own membership.[8] With the exception of PDM, the minority parties most likely to win official registry under the political reform were leftist political organizations advocating a more aggressive, combative role for labor unions in economic negotiations and in the national political process. During the early 1970s opposition political groups had actively attempted to undermine CTM's control over its affiliates, especially in those more modern manufacturing activities where structural changes in labor force characteristics and limited competition from other "official" labor organizations for the allegiance of these relatively highly paid workers already threatened CTM's position. Quite predictably, then, CTM did not welcome the prospect of legal recognition for these same opposition political groups and their more active public organizational activities. Although the CTM leadership was divided over the likely consequences of the political reform,[9] the most intransigent opposition came from leaders of large industrial unions, who feared that the reform would reduce their access to political patronage (especially their share of PRI elective positions in federal, state, and local government) and expose their membership to increased competition, as opposition parties expanded their national political presence. Because these leaders controlled some of the most influential unions in the confederation, their reservations regarding the liberalization initiative accounted for CTM's opposition to the measure.

The second group in the governing coalition that sought to limit the scope of the political reform included state governors and local and regional political bosses. Their principal opposition to the initiative focused on the possible extension of the reform to state and local governments. In the past PAN, PPS, and PARM had been most effective in challenging PRI in local and state elections. Opposition party activities and mobilized citizens' groups at the local level often posed delicate political problems for state governors. Because guaranteed opposition party representation in state legislatures and local governments would have constituted a major expansion in these parties' political role, it was vigorously opposed by a large number of state governors, whose political power depended on PRI's continued domination of state and local politics. PRI sector organizations such as the CTM joined the state governors and traditional political bosses in opposing the extension of political reform below the federal level. These same groups also opposed liberal efforts to extend the political reform to the federal Senate because minority party representation there would have involved an important change in the balance of political power in the states affected.

The prospect of participating in a regime-sponsored liberalization project that maintained important state controls on the political process also posed a divisive issue for many opposition groups. Thus Reyes Heroles and the reform's liberal supporters faced an early challenge in the need to win previously unregistered opposition party participation in the reform process through formal participation in the 1979 elections for the federal Chamber of Deputies. Several of these political organizations (especially Marxist-Leninist groups and parties) had been founded on the basis of their ideological opposition to the governing revolutionary coalition, the established socioeconomic and political order, and PRI. Some favored participation in the 1979 congressional elections as the best available opportunity to advance their political cause. Despite its limitations, political reform would create a more open national political environment in which they could articulate alternative programs and expand their organizational bases. Advances such as these might open the way to broader political change at a later date.

However, other opposition organizations feared that participation in the reform would result in their cooptation by the established regime. They were fully aware that minority representation in the executive-dominated Chamber of Deputies offered limited opportunities to effect substantial change. Furthermore, they had misgivings concerning the corruptive effects that access to government resources and opportunities for individual political advancement might have on opposition leaders. This possibility was a particularly serious issue for parties with major internal factional divisions and for political organizations with a heterogeneous membership and no rigorous ideological orientation. Some opposition groups were also concerned that their participation in the official party system would strengthen the established regime's position and make fundamental change more difficult. In the end, however, PMT was the only major unregistered opposition party not to participate in the 1979 election, as a result of deep internal divisions regarding the relative merits of the political reform proposal.

Despite resistance from conservative elements in the established regime and objections by several opposition parties, the federal executive retained close control over the political reform process. The López Portillo administration had defined the principal characteristics of the reform measure through confidential consultations held before Reyes Heroles's April 1977 address,[10] but it was important to keep the reform process formally open-ended and subject to influence by the political opposition in order to maintain the spirit of the initiative. The Federal Electoral Commission held special public hearings to permit broad-ranging discussion of the issue by political organizations, academic institutions, and private citizens. These hearings began only four weeks after Reyes Heroles announced the administration's intention to implement a political reform. PAN, PMT, and MAUS had for some time advocated reforms in the existing law regulating electoral procedures and in the requirements for political party registration, and they were prepared to discuss these matters in some detail. But most opposition party presentations before the electoral commission were limited to an overall critique of Mexico's socioeconomic and political problems. There is no evidence that opposition party participation in the hearings had any significant effect on the final draft of the political reform law. Various opposition proposals for broader political reform—including full proportional representation rather than an expanded "party deputy" system, and opposition political representation in the federal Senate—were turned aside.

Conservative elements in the governing coalition were more successful in influencing the reform initiative's scope in exchange for their final support. Because of López Portillo's personal commitment to the political reform and the federal executive's tremendous political power, these groups could not flatly reject the proposal or publicly oppose it. But they did engage in active behind-the-scenes negotiations and internal bargaining in an effort to limit the impact of the measure. CTM's ability to bargain for concessions was greatly enhanced by Mexico's 1976–77 economic crisis. Wage restraint was a major element in López Portillo's economic stabilization program, and CTM's commitment to limit its demands was the key to controlling wage increases on a national scale. The CTM leadership argued that its support for the stabilization program merited special consideration for the confederation's concerns regarding possible consequences of political liberalization. In addition, CTM formulated a list of broad-ranging economic reform proposals against which it sought to negotiate concessions in the political reform.

As a result of these internal negotiations, the final reform proposal did not automatically extend minority party representation to the federal Senate. It also allowed each state to decide individually whether or not to provide guaranteed opposition party representation in state legislatures and local governments.[11] Moreover, in a clear effort to protect PRI's rural support base from the organizational activities of opposition groups, the reform measure limited opposition party representation to *municipios* (local politico-administrative units roughly equivalent to counties) with at least three hundred thousand inhabitants. These were important limitations on the scope of the liberalization project. López Portillo and Reyes Heroles's commitment to reform the electoral process and the political party system was realized, but the reform was not as comprehensive as its most liberal sup͡   ͡ ͡ had envisaged.

Thus the reform measure enacted on 31 December 1977 as the Federal Law on Political Organizations and Electoral Processes had the following principal characteristics:[12]

1. Liberalized procedures for political party recognition. Political organizations that presented a declaration of principles, program for action, and statutes could seek official registry as parties through one of two methods. A "conditional registry" could be validated if the party received at least 1.5 percent of the total national vote in the election during which registry was sought. This was a particularly significant change in existing electoral legislation because it substantially eased the registration process for opposition parties. "Definitive registry" could be achieved if the party officially enrolled the minimum required party membership (at least three thousand members in each of at least half of Mexico's thirty-one states and the Federal District, or at least three hundred affiliates in each of at least half of all single-member electoral districts, for a total of at least sixty-five thousand members) through a series of party assemblies. The reform law also recognized "national political associations"—groups with at least five thousand members throughout the country, a national directorship, delegates in at least ten states, and at least two years' political activity prior to requesting official registration—and it allowed electoral alliances to be formed for a particular election.

2. Reform of the federal Chamber of Deputies. The political reform law increased the size of the Chamber of Deputies to four hundred members and created a two-tier electoral structure: three hundred deputies elected by a simple majority of votes cast in single-member electoral districts, and one hundred deputies elected by proportional representation in party-list circumscriptions. These one hundred seats were reserved for minority political parties, but minority parties could also compete in single-member districts.[13]

3. Changes in electoral procedures. Registered opposition parties were first granted representation on the Federal Electoral Commission and state and district electoral committees under the 1973 electoral law. The 1977 reform extended representation to conditionally registered parties, although this did not include voting rights until the party in question won its definitive registry. Conditionally registered opposition parties did receive the right to name representatives to the supervisory committee at each polling place, with the authority to challenge questionable conduct throughout the electoral process. Political parties also became eligible to receive modest material support from the electoral commission to offset their campaign expenses, including financial assistance for campaign literature, meeting halls, and transportation.

4. *Expanded party access to mass communications.* Political parties were first permitted access to mass communications media during election campaigns under the terms of the 1973 electoral reform. The 1977 reform law granted parties permanent regular access to television and radio. The López Portillo liberalization measure also provided for support from the Federal Electoral Commission for party publications and retained the 1973 electoral law's provisions allowing parties free access to postal and telegraph privileges and exempting them from all taxes and duties.[14]

Consequences of Political Liberalization

The 1979 election for the federal Chamber of Deputies and the 1982 general election were the first major tests of the regime-sponsored liberalization program. The registration of new political parties created additional opportunities for the articulation of alternative programs and the expression of diverse ideological perspectives. Opposition parties increased their total level of electoral support in 1979 and 1982 in comparison with previous elections. The opposition's expanded presence in the federal Chamber of Deputies after 1979 renewed the Chamber's political importance and created a new forum for opposition party activity. The 1982 general election results also indicated that the presence of new parties increased citizen interest in the electoral process and helped reduce the rate of voter abstention. Nonetheless, opposition parties differ considerably in their size and importance. Their electoral support often varies greatly from one area to another, and the electoral strength of many opposition parties is concentrated in urban areas, where PRI's support base was already eroded. Although the participation of new opposition parties in the electoral process reduced the incidence of fraud, both the 1979 and 1982 elections demonstrated that this problem remains a serious obstacle to opposition political activity.

Registration of New Political Parties

Several new political parties won official recognition on the basis of their showing in the 1979 and 1982 elections. The Federal Electoral Commission granted conditional registry to the Mexican Communist party (PCM), the Socialist Workers' party (PST), and the Mexican Democratic party (PDM) for participation in the 1979 federal Chamber of Deputies election. All three parties won definitive registry by gaining more than the 1.5 percent minimum share of the total vote required by the political reform law. (See Table 6.1 for a summary of 1979 and 1982 election results.) The Social Democrat party (Partido Social Demócrata, PSD) appeared in 1981, primarily representing middle-

Table 6.1 1979 and 1982 Federal Electoral Returns by Party
(percentage of total valid votes cast)

| Political Party | 1979 Elections for Chamber of Deputies | | 1982 General Elections | | |
	Simple Majority Voting	Proportional Representation Voting	Presidential Voting	Chamber of Deputies Simple Majority Voting	Chamber of Deputies Proportional Representation Voting
Institutional Revolutionary party (PRI)	69.7%	66.6%	68.4%	69.3%	69.7%
National Action party (PAN)	10.8	10.6	15.7	17.5	17.0
Mexican Communist party (PCM)[a]	4.9	6.7	3.5	4.4	4.2
Socialist Popular party (PPS)	2.6	2.9	1.5	1.9	2.1
Socialist Workers' party (PST)	2.1	2.3	1.5	1.8	2.0
Authentic Party of the Mexican Revolution (PARM)	1.8	2.2	1.0	1.4	1.3
Mexican Democratic party (PDM)	2.1	2.2	1.8	2.3	2.4
Revolutionary Workers' party (PRT)[b]	—	—	1.8	1.3	1.5
Social Democrat party (PSD)[b]	—	—	0.2	0.2	0.2
Unregistered candidates	0.1	NA	0.1	0	NA
Annulled votes	5.9	6.6	4.5	0	NA

Sources: Federal Electoral Commission, *Reforma política*, 9 (1982): 128–29; for 1982 proportional representation voting (preliminary results), Federal Electoral Commission internal documents, August 1982.

[a] The PCM competed in the 1979 elections as part of the Leftist Coalition, including the Mexican Popular party (PPM), Revolutionary Socialist party (PSR), and Movement for Socialist Action and Unity (MAUS). In 1981 these four parties and the Political Action Movement (MAP) joined to form the Mexican Unified Socialist party (PSUM).
[b] The PRT and PSD were eligible for participation only in the 1982 general elections.
NA = not available

class professionals who had previously participated in other civic and political organizations. PSD recognized that it was not a mass-based party, and it encountered some difficulty in translating its programmatic statements into a clearly identifiable political position between the PRI and leftist political organizations. The PSD and the Trotskyist Revolutionary Workers' party (PRT) both received conditional registry to compete in the 1982 general elections, but only PRT won enough support to gain definitive registry.

The formation of the Mexican Unified Socialist party (Partido Socialista Unificado de México, PSUM) in November 1981 was the most significant development in this area following the passage of the political reform law. PSUM formally joined the Mexican Communist party with the members of its 1979 electoral coalition (the PPM, PSR, and MAUS) and the recently organized Political Action Movement (Movimiento de Acción Política, MAP, 1981). Although the PCM and other leftist political organizations had engaged in various forms of cooperation and had discussed several unification projects since the early 1970s, the creation of PSUM was the first major step toward uniting long-established leftist groups such as PCM with the opposition forces that emerged after the 1968 student movement. The PRT and the Mexican Workers' party (PMT) participated actively in discussions preceding the formation of PSUM. However, as a result of ideological differences and organizational and personal rivalries, neither joined in the creation of the new party. PSUM won its definitive registry in the 1982 general elections.

Although the 1977 political reform permitted the registration of several new parties, in January 1982 the López Portillo administration modified the original reform law so as to raise the barriers to electoral participation and prevent the formation of a large number of small political parties. The 1977 version of the reform law stipulated that an officially recognized political party lost its registry only after failing to win 1.5 percent of the national vote in three consecutive elections. But the 1982 modifications specified that any party failing to receive at least 1.5 percent of the total party-list vote in any given election would automatically lose its registry.[15] López Portillo's introduction to the 1982 legislation noted that it was unlikely that this change would affect political parties then registered, or those likely to be formed in the immediate future. Nonetheless, the Authentic Party of the Mexican Revolution (PARM) and PSD did lose their definitive and conditional registries, respectively, following a weak showing in the 1982 elections.

1979 and 1982 Electoral Results

The participation of new opposition parties in the 1979 and 1982 elections reduced somewhat PRI's total electoral support. PRI officially won 69.7 percent of the valid votes cast in simple majority voting for the federal Chamber of Deputies in 1979 and 69.3 percent in 1982; PRI received 68.4 percent of the 1982 presidential vote. (See Table 6.1.) The opposition's total share of simple majority votes for the federal Chamber of Deputies rose from 20.1 percent in 1973 and 13.9 percent in 1976, to 24.3 percent in 1979 and 30.7 percent in 1982; opposition parties together won 27.0 percent of the 1982 presidential vote.[16] PRI's percentage of the 1982 presidential vote was the smallest since its founding in 1929, smaller even than in 1940, 1946, and 1952, when the "official" party faced major opposition movements. Nonetheless, PRI remains by far the most important force in the Mexican party system. PRI's reduced share of the total vote in 1979 and 1982 reflected the combined impact of various opposition parties rather than a significant erosion of its electoral position. Most of the support for opposition parties came from areas in which PRI's strength was already in decline.

Political liberalization has not substantially affected PRI's internal candidate selection procedures. Between 1977 and 1979 political analysts frequently speculated that increased party competition might encourage PRI to reform its nominating procedures. There may have been some improvement in the quality of PRI candidates in 1979 and 1982, as the government sought to win convincing victories in the first campaigns against new opposition parties and to overcome the increasingly technocratic image of PRI candidates by nominating individuals with more diverse political experience. But the candidate selection process itself remains a series of closed negotiations between specific interests and political factions.

The 1979 and 1982 electoral returns also showed that the impact of the 1977 reform on opposition parties varied considerably. The National Action party (PAN) retained its position as the most important opposition party, winning 10.8 percent of the simple-majority vote in 1979 and 15.7 percent of the presidential vote in 1982. PAN was the only opposition party to win Chamber of Deputies seats in single-member districts—four in 1979 (two in the state of Nuevo León and one each in Coahuila and Sonora) and one in 1982 (in the state of Mexico). PAN's surprisingly large electoral showing in 1982 was largely due to its long-established role as a channel for urban middle-class discontent with the government/PRI apparatus. Although PAN's electoral platform called for structural change and a reduction in socioeconomic inequalities, most observers agreed that the campaign conducted by presidential candidate Pablo E. Madero was relatively colorless and uninspiring. Nonetheless, PAN won over 20 percent of the presidential vote in eight states in the Pacific North, North, and Center regions.[17]

PAN's anticorruption campaign found its widest audience in an urban middle class affected by rising inflation and sluggish economic growth. PAN may also have benefitted considerably in some areas from the exhortations of Roman Catholic officials to vote against leftist opposition parties because of Marxism's presumed incompatibility with Christianity. Given the extensive propaganda campaigns conducted by PSUM and PRT, PAN may well have benefitted from anticommunist sentiment among conservative factions of the middle class.

Other opposition parties fared considerably less well. Although the Mexican Communist party (PCM) won 6.7 percent of the proportional representation vote in 1979, it won no Chamber of Deputies seats by majority. The PCM was the only opposition party other than PAN to win more than 10 percent of the vote in a single state. The other parties' support ranged from 2.9 percent to 1.8 percent of the total national vote. In 1982, electoral support for these opposition parties ranged from PSUM's 4.4 percent of the Chamber of Deputies vote to 0.2 percent for the Social Democrat party (see Table 6.1). The Revolutionary Workers' party (PRT) won widespread attention in the 1982 elections principally because of its presidential candidate, Rosario Ibarra de Piedra—a woman and a long-standing critic of government repression against opposition political activists.

Finally, the 1979 and 1982 elections demonstrated that there is considerable regional variation in support for opposition parties. In both years, PAN's electoral strength was concentrated in the Pacific North, North, and Center regions. Similarly, the greatest support for PCM (1979) and the Mexican Unified Socialist party (1982) came from the Pacific North and Center regions. The vote for PDM and PRT was concentrated in the Center states. Although PPS, PST, PARM, and PSD showed less regional variation in these two elections, they also received far less overall electoral support. All the opposition parties mobilized quite heterogeneous backing in both elections, concentrated particularly in the principal urban areas.

Opposition Party Representation in the Chamber of Deputies

As a result of the political reform and the 1979 elections, opposition parties significantly increased their representation in the federal Chamber of Deputies. In the 1976–79 Chamber, the three opposition parties then registered (PAN, PPS, PARM) held 17.4 percent of the existing seats under the "party deputy" system. In 1979, with the inclusion of PCM, PST, and PDM, the opposition expanded its representation to 26.0 percent of the total four hundred seats. The proportional representation system used to distribute opposition positions (the Hagenbach-Bishöv system) biased the final distribution of Chamber seats in favor of the smaller opposition parties; PARM, PST, and PDM benefitted from this arrangement, while PAN and PCM were penalized.[18] Nonetheless, an ideologically defined political opposition appeared in the Chamber of Deputies for the first time since the early 1930s. The representation of diverse ideologies and political tendencies enhanced the national political prominence of the Chamber. Opposition parties won a total of 101 seats (25.3 percent) in the 1982–85 Chamber.[19]

Expanded representation in the Chamber of Deputies permitted opposition parties to play a more active role in congressional activities. The larger number of opposition deputies allowed them to participate on more committees and commissions. Opposition party deputies introduced new ideas and altered the character of Chamber debate. On some occasions the PRI majority modified legislative initiatives in order to avoid confrontations with the opposition. In the 1979–82 Chamber, the Mexican Communist party (leader of the Communist Parliamentary Group that also included MAUS, PSR, and UIC) pursued a strategy designed to generate maximum public awareness of PCM programs and the party's presence in the Chamber. Opposition activity such as this sometimes resulted in novel legislative alliances. For example, although leftist opposition parties have generally criticized the pro-government CTM's domination of the organized labor movement, PCM, PST, and PPS supported the confederation's 1980 demand for a general wage increase to counteract inflation.[20]

However, Chamber representation holds its own challenges for opposition parties. Participation in the federal Chamber of Deputies constitutes a major change for those parties that developed followings and based their legitimacy on long-standing opposition to the established regime. Despite the Chamber's new role in national political debate, the opposition's expanded presence there is in the short run unlikely to affect strong executive control over the legislature. Opposition party leaders have been hard-pressed to show their constituents substantive results from legislative action. Opposition parties with limited personnel may also find that election campaign activity and legislative participation absorb scarce resources that might otherwise be devoted to base-level organizational work and the expansion and diversification of party membership. Problems such as these have surfaced in several leftist parties, accentuating existing internal divisions and provoking debate on the appropriate focus of party activity.

The Problem of Voter Abstention

One goal of the 1977 political reform was to increase voter participation in the electoral process. However, voter abstention actually rose in the 1979 election for the federal Chamber of Deputies. The proportion of total votes cast as a share of total registered voters was officially only 49.3 percent, although the reported electoral results may have underestimated the true dimensions of the problem. The 1979 abstention rate (50.7 percent) was higher than that recorded in either the 1973 congressional election (39.7 percent) or the 1976 presidential election (31.3 percent), and the total number of abstentions exceeded the total number of votes cast for the first time. Observers attributed this outcome to the generally lower voter participation characteristic of congressional elections in Mexico and the lackluster, nonideological campaign conducted by a number of opposition parties.

This situation changed dramatically in the 1982 general election. The national voter registration lists included 94.9 percent of all eligible citizens; 74.8 percent of all registered voters participated. Both rates were the highest officially recorded since 1946, and all major political parties participating in the election accepted their general validity.[21] The unexpectedly large turnout was especially impressive because Mexico's growing economic problems (such as rising inflation) might have encouraged voters to boycott the electoral process as a form of protest.

Two factors produced this abrupt reversal of a long-term historical trend toward growing voter abstention. First, the 1981–82 presidential campaign included an intensive government effort to raise citizen interest in the electoral process and mobilize voters on election day. Under the slogan "The Great Civic Action," the government-supported PRI conducted a long and costly mass media advertising campaign and used opinion polling techniques on an unprecedented scale. For example, PRI produced television advertisements focusing on issues important in particular areas. Some of these involved question-and-answer formats featuring PRI's presidential candidate, Miguel de la Madrid Hurtado. PRI also used more traditional means to encourage voter participation, including the mobilization of the party's worker and peasant bases and the organization of large numbers of mass assemblies. Although PRI's ability to draw extensively on government resources makes it impossible to estimate the true cost of the campaign, its expenditures clearly dwarfed those of all other political parties.

Second, the presence of eight other political parties and six alternative presidential candidates (the PPS and the PARM once again supported the PRI candidate) stimulated voter interest in the elections. This was the highest number of presidential candidates in Mexican history. PAN, PDM, PRT, PST, and PSUM all conducted extensive campaigns to increase voter participation and expand their own electoral support. The Federal Electoral Commission divided some 500 million pesos (approximately $12.5 million) among all parties competing in the election in order to make this campaign effort possible.[22] Although some small opposition groups called for voter abstention as a gesture of antigovernment protest, PAN, PRT, PSD, PST, and PSUM all encouraged participation in the election. PAN, PPS, PST, and PSUM also ran complete candidate slates for the federal Chamber of Deputies and Senate races. Although there are no public opinion survey data available to evaluate voter participation in the 1982 general election, observers agreed that those citizens who had previously failed to take part in the electoral process distributed their votes among the different parties in rough proportion to their previously established strengths, with PRI and PAN benefitting most.[23] This suggests that much of the previously high abstention rate reflected a generalized disinterest in the electoral process rather than a form of protest against the established regime.

The Problem of Electoral Fraud

The 1977 political reform also sought to discourage electoral fraud by permitting all parties participating in an election to designate representatives on the supervisory committee attached to each polling place and by providing parties with access to documentation regarding election results. Although errors in national voter registration lists continue to be a serious problem, most observers of the 1979 and 1982 elections agreed that the electoral process in the principal urban areas was comparatively free of fraud. Despite the formal opportunities to oversee the voting process, however, the large number of polling sites throughout the country (some 43,000 in 1979 and 50,408 in 1982) meant that opposition parties faced substantial logistical problems in actually placing a representative on each committee. In 1982, PSUM had more success in this regard than most other opposition parties, but it could supervise only about 60 percent of all polling sites.[24]

Opposition party vigilance at the polls was thus important but not decisive in the conduct of the 1979 and 1982 elections. In many rural areas PRI conducted the elections much as it always had, mobilizing peasants *en masse* through local political bosses and engaging in various forms of electoral fraud. In addition, close collaboration between local government officials and PRI made it extremely difficult for opposition parties to document fraud, voter intimidation, and other electoral abuses. The opposition of local government officials to political liberalization and continued electoral fraud in many areas remain significant problems.

Prospects for Future Regime Change

The liberalization process initiated by Mexico's 1977 political reform has remained under close government control. Although the established authoritarian regime faced significant challenges in the late 1960s and early 1970s, the López Portillo administration undertook the reform from a position of strength. The political opposition's relative weakness and the diffuseness of pressures for regime change contributed to the federal executive's ability to determine the timing, structure, and speed of the reform process. Political reform removed an important potential source of instability by incorporating recently emerged leftist opposition forces into the existing party system under government-defined rules. The inclusion of new political forces and ideological tendencies in the existing party system expanded the regime's representative capacity and demonstrated its flexibility in response to sociopolitical change.

The 1977 political reform nonetheless marked an important departure in Mexican politics. The López Portillo liberalization measure acknowledged for the first time the existence of a legitimate opposition to the left of the PRI-led "revolutionary coalition." The registration of additional opposition parties expanded the mobilization channels available to opposition political forces, particularly on the Left. Increased access to mass communications (especially television and radio) and more active participation in the electoral process significantly improved the ability of opposition parties to articulate alternative public policies and widen their membership base. Expanded representation in the federal Chamber of Deputies gave these parties new prominence in a national political forum and offered them a chance to influence the legislative process. Whether opposition parties will be able to exploit these opportunities so as to promote broader sociopolitical and economic change remains to be seen. However, the liberalization that began with the 1977 reform has altered Mexico's national political map in ways that are not easily reversible.

Despite the importance of the 1977 reform, there are significant obstacles to further liberalization in the established regime. Mexico's continuing economic crisis constitutes the most immediate challenge to future progress in this area. The sharp 1981 downturn in international petroleum prices produced a sudden decline in Mexico's oil export revenues, cut short the 1978–81 economic boom, and contributed directly to the August 1982 debt crisis. These economic reverses produced tensions in the governing coalition and heightened public discontent with government economic policy performance. At the same time, the country's financial difficulties drastically reduced the resources available for government social and economic programs designed to resolve long-standing development problems and build popular support for the established regime. Although recent developments suggest that there is no linear causal relationship between economic downturn and political closure in the Mexican case, the challenge that economic crisis poses for the established regime makes further political liberalization more difficult.

The abruptness and severity of the 1981–82 economic crisis eroded the López Portillo administration's commitment to continuing political liberalization. Indeed, the administration attempted to use the 1982 general election to reinforce the government's position at the expense of opposition parties in order to maintain firm political control as the economic crisis deepened. The administration perceived an impressive PRI victory and increased voter participation as necessary political components in the construction of a stabilization program to confront Mexico's growing national and international economic problems. The 1982 election offered an opportunity to prove the continued strength of the Mexican political system in order to retain the confidence of the U.S. government, the international financial community, and foreign investors. The PRI presidential candidate, Miguel de la Madrid Hurtado, had been criticized as a politically inexperienced technocrat whose career in the economic policy-making bureaucracy (he had never served as an elected public official) provided him with few ties to the traditional party apparatus. Many observers considered his candidacy and early campaign effort to be uninspiring and politically weak. A convincing PRI victory in the 1982 election was thus an important step in building a political base for the new de la Madrid administration. The Mexican government's effort to demonstrate continued national political stability and the viability of its single-dominant party took on special meaning in the context of escalating violence in Central America.

These considerations explain the attempt of the López Portillo administration to hold the opposition's 1982 electoral success to a minimum. There is convincing evidence that the National Action party (PAN) was the victim of significant electoral fraud in Nuevo León and some other areas.[25] PAN won four single-member districts in 1979, but in 1982, despite a substantial increase in its share of the total national vote, the party failed to win any single-member seats in areas of traditional electoral support. Subsequent events underlined the relationship between the administration's conduct of the election and its plans to address a deteriorating economic situation. Four days after the Federal Electoral Commission provided preliminary official validation of PRI's convincing victory, the administration had announced a substantial reduction in government subsidies for basic commodities and the dramatic 5 August 1982 devaluation of the peso.

In contrast, in the first half of 1983 the de la Madrid administration felt compelled to recognize a series of local-level (*municipio*) opposition victories, marking the first time that the government officially recognized opposition party victories in major cities in the Pacific North, North, and Center regions. They included five state capitals (Chihuahua, Durango, Guanajuato, San Luis Potosí, and Hermosillo) and a major border city (Ciudad Juárez). All but one of these elections were won by PAN and the other (in Guanajuato) was captured by PDM in coalition with PAN. Furthermore, in the elections of a somewhat less important city of the Pacific North (Ensenanda, Baja California), the government recognized PST as the official victor. This support for opposition parties reflected widespread popular dissatisfaction with the government's harsh austerity measures rather than an endorsement of opposition parties' platforms or ideologies.

The de la Madrid administration's decision to respect local opposition victories in 1983 reflected its perception that a limited political opening was essential at a time of severe social and political tension. Like López Portillo's implementation of the 1977 political reform, de la Madrid's handling of the 1983 elections was part of an effort to balance stringent economic austerity measures with policies designed to diffuse widespread public discontent. However, volatile sociopolitical conditions in 1982–83 and the prospect that Mexico's economic crisis would persist for the indefinite future made more extensive political liberalization too risky. Instead, the de la Madrid administration attempted to restore public confidence in the established regime through a series of other measures. These included a widely publicized "moral renovation" campaign whose goal was to reduce corruption in the government bureaucracy and the police forces. A cabinet-level Comptroller General's Office was created to investigate suspected government corruption, and the anticorruption campaign resulted in the prosecution of several senior officials in the López Portillo administration (including the former director of the state-owned petroleum company and the former chief of the Mexico City police).[26]

Although the Mexican regime's political response to economic crisis has varied over time depending on specific circumstances, the challenge posed by economic crisis has generally constrained the liberalization process. The government's 1983 decision to recognize opposition victories in major cities was an important precedent, but it did not imply a broader commitment to political liberalization. So long as the governing elite retains firm control over liberalization, specific decisions such as this are reversible. Opposition victories in 1983 occurred in areas of traditional opposition strength, and continued federal government control over local budgetary resources limited opposition parties' ability to use their position as incumbents to expand their local support base. Moreover, official recognition of conservative parties' electoral triumphs was balanced by a successful government effort to end by force PSUM's control over the municipal presidency in Juchitán, Oaxaca. In 1984 the de la Madrid administration granted conditional registry to the leftist Mexican Workers' party (PMT) and the conservative Authentic Party of the Mexican Revolution (PARM, which had lost its registry after a poor performance in the 1982 election) for participation in the 1985 congressional and state elections in order to demonstrate its commitment to continued political opening. However, electoral results in 1984 state and local elections in Baja California, Michoacán, Oaxaca, Puebla, and Sinaloa may have been manipulated to guarantee PRI victories.[27]

Even if the tensions resulting from Mexico's economic crisis eventually ease, conservative elements in the governing revolutionary coalition are likely to oppose further regime liberalization. From their perspective, the 1977 reform measure's relative success in resolving several specific political problems reduced the need for additional political opening. The leverage that entrenched interests are able to exert in internal regime negotiations gives these groups a significant role in shaping regime-sponsored liberalization projects. The election of an opposition candidate as state governor or the loss of a major industrial union to opposition political control would probably increase conservative resistance to regime change. Developments such as these might challenge the existing system by introducing major new policy and leadership alternatives. The effectiveness of conservative opposition to future political liberalization would be substantially increased if heightened sociopolitical tensions resulting from prolonged national economic crisis and widening regional military conflict in Central America led to more active political participation by the Mexican armed forces.

Liberal elements in the governing political elite will therefore be challenged to maintain regime flexibility in response to ongoing sociopolitical change. Flexible adaptation to change (including the possibility of more extensive institutional reforms) may be a particularly important means of addressing popular discontent in a period when the material resources available for coalition maintenance are severely limited. This approach will be especially significant if the commitment of leftist opposition groups to political participation through established institutional channels is to be preserved. Over the longer term, liberal reformers must also address the underlying tension between traditional political actors' vested interest in maintaining the existing system and demands for alternative political arrangements, including increased emphasis on broadly inclusive competitive elections as a basis for regime legitimacy.

Opposition forces will also encounter major challenges in their efforts to promote broader political opening. The 1977 political reform incorporated the most important unregistered opposition organizations into the existing party system without greatly increasing their real political influence. The direction of future political change will depend in large measure on their ability to press for further regime liberalization. The need to develop a broader political base is particularly urgent for leftist opposition parties, which have fared less well than conservative parties in recent elections. The governing political elite's continued commitment to maintaining an overall Left-Right balance in the liberalization process makes leftist parties' electoral viability especially important as a condition for additional political opening.

Opposition parties' first task is to develop coordinated strategies advancing alternative programmatic proposals and to increase their electoral support. In many cases strategy coordination may require opposition parties to establish innovative ties with local groups and organizations that increase their combined mobilization capacity and electoral strength. The 1979 and 1982 election campaigns provided important lessons in this regard. Opposition parties continue to experiment with tactical alliances that often cut across Left-Right political divisions, but factionalism, organizational rivalries, and personal jealousies often hamper these efforts.

More important, opposition political forces on both the Left and the Right must also substantially expand their mass organizational bases if they are to develop an effective national political presence. In well-institutionalized, broadly based authoritarian regimes such as Mexico, where the degree of political liberalization is still limited, opposition forces must challenge the established regime's sociopolitical support bases on a variety of fronts in order to push liberalization forward. Efforts by opposition parties to develop identifiable constituencies are especially important in Mexico because the inclusive nature of the established regime has made existing opposition forces heterogeneous and diffuse.

Opposition parties in general have made only limited progress in this area so far, but leftist parties have had particular difficulty in organizing a coherent membership base outside their traditional sources of support (university employees, the intelligentsia, teachers, white-collar employees, some industrial workers). Conservative parties have been much more successful at translating the sociopolitical discontent resulting from government austerity measures into electoral support. Indeed, leftist forces were to some extent disoriented by the economic crisis of the early 1980s and the conservative parties' relative electoral success. Leftist parties frequently disagreed with each other on appropriate responses to government austerity measures and the Left's relationship with the "official" organized labor movement. Leftist opposition groups were also divided over the government's 1982 nationalization of private banks and its implications for potential leftist alliances with progressive elements in the established regime. The emergence of coalition protest movements linking urban marginals, peasants, and some labor groups (which resulted in major popular protests in October 1983 and June 1984) for the most part occurred independently of leftist party efforts. Although the Mexican Unified Socialist party (PSUM) has had some success in establishing local political alliances in states such as Chiapas, Guerrero, Oaxaca, and Puebla, this work has been slow and subject to frequent reverses.

The lack of opposition-party access to significant resources and power, the small probability that this situation will change substantially in the near future, and resistance by existing "official" labor and peasant organizations all make mass organizational work difficult. However, only the creation and consolidation of independent social bases and durable ties with popular sector organizations will allow opposition parties to develop the identifiable constituencies that can serve as a basis from which to work for the substantive fulfillment of formally guaranteed individual and collective rights. Progress in this area is also a prerequisite for opposition efforts to promote more far-reaching regime change.

7 •

Military Interventions and "Transfer of Power to Civilians" in Peru

Julio Cotler

The history of Peru has been plagued with military coups and subsequent transfers of power back to civilians. This chapter examines the last two "interventions" and their respective "transfers," which present a number of contrasts with the country's preceding experience.[1] The military interventions of 1962 and 1968 took place with little resistance. They were precipitated by a military leadership that wished to head off various social movements, emanating from a crisis of the society and of the oligarchic state; otherwise, the military anticipated that a state of severe social disorder might arise. On both occasions (but more drastically in 1968) the military governments applied a policy which sought to subordinate the popular classes to the state apparatus, by adopting nationalist and antioligarchic policies. The 1963 handover to civilians, like that which began in 1977 and culminated in 1980, took place in a context of intense social and political struggle and also, in the second case, of acute economic crisis, which obliged the armed forces to seek a constitutional escape route which would permit them to channel conflicts in an institutional direction, while assuring military autonomy.

These two experiences prompt a number of questions. Why was the representative regime so easily eliminated by the military, and then fairly smoothly reinstated, with the collaboration of civilian forces? In what ways are the new institutions different from the preceding ones? What social forces secured the restoration of constitutional government, in what type of internal and external conjunctures, and by what means? Finally, what is the likelihood that the new regime installed in July 1980 will survive and succeed in consolidating democratic institutions?

The first part of this chapter will examine these two recent experiences, indicating, in a general manner, their comparable and contrasting features. The second part will more closely analyze the military intervention of 1968 and the actions of the self-proclaimed Revolutionary Government of the Armed Forces (GRFA), together with the reactions they produced and the reasons the military eventually returned to barracks.

Military Interventions and Withdrawals, 1962–80

On 3 October 1968, army general Juan Velasco Alvarado, with the support of a small group of officers whom he had placed in key positions, carried out a coup d'état that had been in preparation for months. That night, the troops of the principal military garrisons in Lima marched to the Presidential Palace, seized and deported to Buenos Aires the discredited and unresisting president Fernando Belaúnde (who was subsequently reelected in 1980), and occupied the principal points of the city. On the following day, as the last of Belaúnde's many cabinets was disbanded, General Velasco was busy urging the chiefs of the country's military regions, as well as the naval and air force commanders, to recognize the new situation created without their consent. These officers soon joined Velasco in the government, which therefore became an expression of the armed forces as a collectivity.

In the face of this renewed military intervention, the political parties showed themselves, as in 1962, unable to create a movement of opposition. In contrast with the enthusiastic support given to the government at its initiation five years earlier, the population showed a singular apathy and disinterest in events which were taking place only at the apex of the power structure. This apathy also reflected public disenchantment with Belaúnde's government after 1963.

The government deposed in 1968 had emerged in 1963 with the endorsement of the armed forces, after a one-year interregnum during which the armed forces had constituted an "institutional" government, the first in Latin America. In 1963, as in 1980, Fernando Belaúnde and his party, Acción Popular, came to power as a result of a "transfer of power to civilians," decided on and prepared by the leaders of the armed forces.

These two military interventions, and the two withdrawals, both exhibit certain parallels that suggest some constants in Peruvian society and politics, notwithstanding the intervening transformations. In 1962 and again in 1968, the military coups occurred on the eve of presidential elections. In both cases the military authorities sought to head off a confrontation between diverse social forces and the state which might have been expected if events were allowed to unfold freely. Political disintegration and even the possibility of a revolutionary denouement were anticipated unless the military acted. The governments of the 1960s confronted growing popular and middle-class protests against a decrepit oligarchic leadership, dating from the 1930s. Although the popular movement was characterized by weak organization and political inexperience, the massive and unprecedented incorporation of the peasantry was transforming the political landscape. Lower-class demands were becoming a central issue on the political agenda, and organized groups were appearing which, under the influence of the Cuban Revolution, put forward revolutionary socialist policies.

The first military government, of 1962, sought to contain popular mobilizations, which included a generalized peasant insurgency, the development of a vigorous working-class movement linked with the new and broader middle strata, and a series of partisan organizations demanding antioligarchic and nationalist reform measures. In contrast to previous military interventions, the 1962 government did not try to block all reforms, but, rather, tried to ensure that such change did not come about by direct action from below, as had occurred a few years earlier in Cuba. Thus the military government rounded up hundreds of peasant leaders and brutally repressed their movements. The same happened to working-class, student, and party activists, especially those belonging to the revolutionary Left. The military also annulled the elections which, weeks earlier, had given a narrow victory to the APRA party of Haya de la Torre. In order to channel reforms that were both widely desired and also accepted as necessary according to its military ideology, the government created bureaucratic agencies headed by officials who later played a crucial role in the coup of 1968. (In particular, they were to implement agrarian reform in the most troubled regions.) Moreover, the National Institute of Planning was founded to organize the budget and plan the economic and social development of the country. Some of the key officials involved would also participate in the 1968 coup. Finally, the government announced the imminent nationalization of the International Petroleum Company (IPC), initiating talks on this with the enterprise and with the U.S. government.

However, the military soon found themselves obliged by domestic and international pressures to withdraw from government, after convening new general elections. The popular movement contrived, albeit in a disorganized manner, to push its claims in all spheres, surpassing the limits imposed by the military. Even more decisive in persuading the military to withdraw was the role played by the middle strata and their parties, as well as by various sectors of the bourgeoisie, which threw their weight behind the confrontations with the government. The military's wish to impose their own plan without consultation signified a closing of the political channels previously open to the different classes and interests, resulting in governmental isolation and the emergence of a broad and heterogeneous front opposed to military rule. This phenomenon would be repeated in the 1970s.

The military regime of 1962 also encountered powerful resistance from Washington. In accordance with the Alliance for Progress, Kennedy's administration visibly supported APRA, encouraging a project for social reforms within the framework of institutional legality and with reliably anti-Communist credentials (that is, rejecting the example of the Cuban Revolution). Washington was also tenaciously opposed to plans for nationalizing the IPC. Bilateral aid and military assistance were suspended, and loans from international organizations were vetoed until the government relented in its campaign against this enterprise. In order to resolve these problems, one member of the military junta attempted to seize power, thus disturbing the precarious institutional character of the government. The military command dismissed him, and the remaining junta decided to withdraw from power. But this military withdrawal was linked to a decree specifying ground rules for an election under which the subsequent civilian government would find it difficult to obtain a parliamentary majority. In this way the military ensured that their successors would be unable to subordinate them to the sphere of civil power and that, on the contrary, the autonomy achieved by the armed forces would be preserved.

From 1963 on, the officer in command of each service would be designated by seniority, and the president of the republic would have to appoint his defense ministers from a slate of names put forward by these commanding officers. Moreover, each service would present the economy minister with the total budget it required, without providing any breakdown of expenditure, which would be kept as a state secret unknown even at cabinet level.

On these conditions the armed forces lent their support to the election in 1963 of Belaúnde. He stood for the social reforms recommended by the Alliance for Progress, on which the military were also agreed. But above all, they supported him because, in contrast to APRA, Belaúnde was not backed by a militant, organized body of partisans, and had no history of confrontations with the army. In this way the military assured themselves that social reforms would be carried out within a strictly legal framework, and, above all, that they would be executed administratively—in other words, from above and without any mobilization of the potential beneficiaries. However, the initial optimism of the military following the accession of Belaúnde rapidly evaporated when it became evident that he was incapable of resolving the growing social crisis. Within the army this realization strengthened the influence of the intelligence services. Between 1963 and 1968 the reformist parties of the middle strata demonstrated very clearly their inability to adapt the political system to the growing demands for political and social participation. At the same time the dominant class experienced sharp fragmentation, conflicts of interest, and disagreements over the political and economic development of the country. Disrupted by the impact of foreign investment and the rise of new industrial and urban groups, the dominant class was incapable of uniting around a strategy of social and political hegemony that would subordinate the middle and popular strata.

In this context of crisis, both civil society and the state manifested their fragile constitution, unable to organize and mobilize the resources to create a relatively coherent and consistent new order. In such conditions a democratic conception of social relations could only take on (then as now) an abstract and vacuous form.

It was under these conditions that the armed forces, especially the army, achieved an important advance in "professionalization." A military "intelligentsia" developed, with a new ideology designed to legitimate an enhanced role for the armed forces as a response to the new internal and international conditions facing Peru.[2] Owing to the particular ethnic configuration of the country and to the backwardness of its capitalism, associated with an ostensible "foreign" domination of capital, this intelligentsia literally appropriated the revolutionary positions and solutions proposed in the 1930s by Haya de la

Torre and the Aprista party. To these they added some propositions borrowed from both the old and the new positions of the church, thus creating an ideological hodgepodge designed, on the one hand, to justify the new doctrine and, on the other, to forestall any accusation of "Communism."[3]

This military ideology focused on the issue of national integration, understood as the assimilation of the ensemble of the society's interests in a common objective that the state would incarnate. This assimilation was intended to rally the population around some unifying principles, thus diluting the society's class and ethnic particularities and facilitating a strengthening and expansion of the functions of the state.[4] With this increased social support, the state would acquire the resources and leverage to exercise a margin of autonomy from imperialist enterprises and foreign governments. This would enable Peru to free itself from the two nightmares that have historically weighed upon its existence: first, the risk of social disintegration, due to the existence of a large indigenous population lacking much sense of "nationality" and the growing antagonism between the social classes; and secondly, the permanent threat from bordering states, especially Chile, which might be disposed to repeat the annexationist adventure of 1879 the moment Peru presented signs of internal division.

This reasoning presumed the achievement of profound social transformations which would definitively eliminate the "antinational" bases ensconced in Peruvian society, politics, culture, and economic structure. In short, this analysis concluded that a revolution was urgently required and that a revolutionary will had to be forged. But how and with whom could such a revolution be made, when the bourgeoisie was foreign or under foreign influence, the indigenous peasantry lacked much sense of nationality, the organized groups of the middle and popular sectors demanded the satisfaction of their sectoral interests, and the political organizations dispersed rather than concentrated the feeble energies available? The military intelligentsia viewed the same armed forces with their vertical organization, centralized command, capacity for deployment, experience in organization, apoliticism, and patriotism as the appropriate prime mover of this nationalist revolution. A revolutionary transformation of the society could, it was thought, be effective only if liberal-democratic practices were eliminated, for these arrangements simply granted political space to "antinational" groupings and "alienated" popular interests. For this reason, the military envisaged a revolution that would not be based on the popular masses, whose leaders might wish to compete with the military, impeding the construction of a state above sectional interests. The military project was therefore characterized by an antiliberal and particularly an antipopular slant, in that it rejected the rights of different social interests, and especially those of the immense majority, to be represented within the proposed revolutionary state.

Both in 1963 and again in 1977, military decisions to hand back the government to civilian authority occurred in a context of generalized political mobilization in which wide sectors of society, for a variety of different reasons and motives, confronted the government and a military apparatus that, especially in the latter period, found itself exceptionally isolated and discredited. In addition to failures of political and economic management, the 1970s junta faced serious pressures and international threats of a politicoeconomic nature. From 1974 onwards, there were also military threats that placed the country in an exceptional situation of crisis.

Paradoxically, then, the establishment of military governments in 1962 and 1968 in order to prevent the mobilization of popular forces instead gave rise to greater political mobilization and also led the country into international isolation. Consequently social opposition and international pressures split the military leadership both in 1963 and in 1977–80, with the result that those officers prevailed who favored withdrawal from government, so as not to compromise politically the organization and the future of the armed forces. Even so, in each case withdrawal was made conditional on a series of provisions laid down by the military high command to ensure the future of the military institution and the privileges of its members. Thus, the date of elections and their legal form were determined by the military high command. Furthermore, the elected rulers were again required to guarantee the armed forces' autonomy and to prevent any political upheaval which would affect the "public order." Finally, the armed forces maintained veto powers over any measure which might compromise "national security." It is evident that these conditions were stipulated with much greater clarity and firmness in 1977–80 than in 1963, owing precisely to the experience and institutional knowhow acquired in the course of the preceding twelve years of military government.

The Military Intervention of 1968

The small group of officials which in 1968 constituted the Revolutionary Government of the Armed Forces (GRFA), on attempting the revolution which had been in the making since the failed attempt of 1962, sought to monopolize political activity. However, they neither repressed nor shut down the political parties and union organizations, wishing to avoid unnecessary confrontations and to leave open channels of communication. Although the GRFA did deport and persecute a small group of leaders and functionaries from the preceding government, their basic aim was to immobilize the party system while the government put through the "structural changes" which the political parties had proposed for so long. In this way, the loyalties of the population might be focused on the government and its institutional base, the armed forces. A series of institutional changes widened popular participation, at a time when official rhetoric legitimized long-established antioligarchic and nationalist demands, and challenged the demo-liberal foundations of the ancien régime.[5] All this, contrary to the expectations of the military planners, served to stir up and inflame the popular movement, and the government proved unable to control the results of such mobilization.

Traditionally, the Peruvian Communist party had established a strong position in the urban labor movement. In exchange for lending "critical" support to the military government, the party was tolerated to the extent that it mediated popular pressures and isolated APRA. (APRA, in turn, went along with this situation in that, in the words of its leader, Haya de la Torre, it adopted a posture of "wait and see.") But neither the Communist party's bureaucratic control over the General Confederation of Peruvian Workers (CGTP), nor the support which the government received from the USSR, from China, and from Cuba, and in concrete form from Fidel Castro, could serve to immobilize popular agitation. Nor were the revolutionary organizations immobilized, in spite of their international Maoist or Castroist affiliations. They united with the peasant and workers' movements, seeking full implementation of the new social legislation and elimination of its bureaucratic limitations. Between 1971 and 1975, different branches of the government announced the creation of a series of "popular" organizations which would be directly controlled by military officers. But this apparently corporatist tendency was ineffective because of political and bureaucratic rivalries between these organizations. They ended up in competition with each other, and this left room for the rank and file to expand their margins of maneuver and to respond to the resistance and opposition coming from already established popular organizations. Thus, the military government found itself unable to coopt the popular movement, notwithstanding the apparent radicalism of official measures, or the government's fiery speeches, or the international support given to General Velasco's government.

At the other social extreme, the bourgeoisie and international capital had the same reaction as the popular strata. Owing to the drastic nature of the reformist measures and to the government's refusal to recognize the legitimacy of the dominant class's organizations, the latter felt itself seriously threatened. Ownership reforms, official encouragement for the labor and peasant movements, a socializing rhetoric, and talk of a tendency to "Yugoslavianize" the military revolution—all these were taken as signs of an arbitrary and dictatorial regime with a Communist hue. Thus the dominant classes soon sought a military withdrawal to barracks and the return to a constitutional regime. Notwithstanding the economic concessions granted to the bourgeoisie, it joined with the "traditional" parties (APRA and Acción Popular) in demanding a prompt return to liberal constitutionalism.

To reinforce their political strategy, the military adopted a typically populist economic policy, but this did not succeed in satisfying the different interests in play. Instead it rapidly produced a violent economic crisis, unprecedented in the country's history.[6] This crisis in turn reinforced the regime's problems of political participation. Whereas the ownership reforms threatened to eliminate both those landholders engaged in precapitalist exploitation of the indigenous peasantry and oligarchic sectors of the bourgeoisie, the overall economic policy tended to favor the expansion of the state and to promote industrial development, granting indiscriminate incentives for the substitution of imports, favoring consumption by high-income sectors, and boosting the profitability of capital. Thus, "structural change" favored the development of dependent capitalism. The relatively well paid generally benefitted from the government's policies of social reform, increased remunerations, and a doubling in the number of public employees. Public enterprises found themselves free to determine their structure of production and employment and the distribution of personal and regional income, as well as of consumption. This tended to favor the middle strata and worked to the detriment of the more impoverished sectors of the population, the peasants and the urban underemployed.[7] Nevertheless, for a long period overall domestic demand grew substantially faster than internal production, giving rise to inflationary tendencies. The exchange rate became progressively more overvalued, leading to a spectacular and uncontrolled growth of imports. On the other hand, exports stagnated, the substantial rise in commodity prices being offset by a decline in volume of Peruvian exports. The widening trade deficit was financed via heavy borrowing from the international banks, the proceeds of which were often earmarked for large investments, frequently with very long gestation periods, or in some cases inspired by objectives of a strategic-military rather than financial nature. Following the military coup in Chile in 1973, the Peruvian military government became committed to sustained and costly arms purchases, using international credit and very seriously compromising the public finances.[8] The expectation of major oil finds and the boom levels attained by many mineral prices nourished the illusion that all this was sustainable.[9]

In order to favor the organized urban sectors, many basic imported foods and fuels were subsidized, while rigid price controls were imposed on internationally traded agricultural goods. The results were a violent increase in the fiscal deficit on the one hand, and, on the other, a rapid fall in already very low peasant earnings, accelerating the secular process of impoverishment among the rural majority.

In summary, by 1974 the revolutionary military government had produced a major economic crisis. In these circumstances the government, and General Velasco in particular, began to adopt desperate measures. Faced with evident disequilibria in the economy, a select group of technocrats proposed, "with all due respect, General," a set of readjustments: reduced subsidies, the regulation of imports, devaluation, higher prices for foods produced in the country, and a reduction in arms purchases. President Velasco not only vehemently rejected this advice, but also ordered a reduction in the price of gasoline and resolved to continue with the existing economic policy, confident that in a race against time, the necessary resources to resolve existing difficulties would be forthcoming. This decision may have reflected a wish to counter the government's social isolation and to generate domestic support ahead of a seemingly inevitable confrontation with Chilean troops.

However, the popular sectors, with a strengthened capacity for organization, continued to press the authorities with their own autonomous demands, which for the first time began to express regional problems. These pressures met with selective repression, while the government also formulated new initiatives to attract popular support, such as a law on "social ownership." The bourgeoisie, relying heavily on the media as its last political refuge, mounted a fierce campaign against the government, seeking to block such reforms and to undermine the government's apparent success with the popular movement. The rightist media interpreted the government's policies as aimed at establishing a totalitarian regime. This campaign incited General Velasco to expropriate the mass media in June 1974, despite opposition from important sectors of the government and the armed forces, especially the navy. When it became evident that Velasco and the group surrounding him were intent on making decisions without concern for the collective interests of the military, deep divisions occurred. It was recalled that from the outset General Velasco had bypassed institutional dispositions and promoted his personal followers to key positions in the government and the armed forces.

In February 1975, the Guardia Civil joined a wave of strikes demanding both wage increases and its inclusion as an organization in the composition of the government. Only after repression by the army were these strikes ended. During the absence of these "guardians of order" from the streets of Lima, there was rioting and looting in the city, which was stopped only by the use of tanks and which left more than one hundred dead. No one was defending the Peruvian Revolution except the armored division.

These crises came on top of a succession struggle, originating when Velasco became gravely ill in 1973. The military junta was composed of the commanding generals of the three services, who in turn were to designate the president. Under these arrangements, General Velasco should have retired from the government in 1970, but he succeeded in holding onto the presidency because of his role as leader of the 1968 coup and because of the sophistries he resorted to in order to eliminate his rivals and opponents. Consequently, the duration of his mandate was never specified, nor was the form of succession laid down. Thus, when Velasco became seriously ill, the government found itself without a head for several days, and an open struggle for the succession began. Against this background and the increasingly personalist leadership of the government, the expropriation of the media and the police strike initiated an institutional crisis. The expropriation of the media silenced the dominant classes. The newspapers were handed over to various organizations grouped around the government, who established a limited competition among themselves. The government hoped by this means to incorporate the popular movement. But the results were the opposite of those intended, since a broadening of the information available concerning worker and peasant demands reinforced the dynamism of the popular movement. Eventually, the government decided that the time had come to silence, crush, and otherwise domesticate the popular organizations. In effect, the government concluded that the ownership reforms, the subsidies, the socializing discourse, the creation of corporatist organizations, and the expropriation of the mass media had failed to coopt popular dissent. Thus one sector of the government opted for an open confrontation with the organized masses, forming the Revolutionary Labor Movement (MLR), in conjunction with Aprista factions on the margin of trade union life, in order to destroy the popular movement. Whereas in 1974 the government had silenced the bourgeoisie, in 1975 it hoped to do the same with the popular classes, thereby assuring itself of full control over society. But in the course of this confrontation it became clear that it was not as easy for the government to crush the popular movement as it had been to silence the bourgeoisie. The popular movement put up a strong opposition and allied itself with sectors of the bureaucracy which favored a radicalization of the process initiated by the military, aided by some of the groups now controlling the press. This confrontation came to a head in August 1975 with the deportation of nearly thirty journalists, leaders of the trade union movement, and militants of the revolutionary Left. Nevertheless, the MLR and its followers within the government were defeated.

Things were going badly for the junta not only on the internal front but also on the external front. At the same time that this state-society confrontation was taking place, General Velasco decided (again without consultation) to expropriate a mining enterprise, hoping to offset the antipopular image created by the activities of the MLR. In 1974 the Ministry of Foreign Relations had signed a contract with the U.S. State Department determining compensation for the North American enterprises that had been nationalized by Peru, but Velasco's impulsive action reopened tension between the two governments. Simultaneously, the military regimes of Chile and Bolivia opened negotiations about Bolivia's access to the sea, a step which disturbed the relations between Peru and its neighbors, even bringing tensions to the brink of war.

In summary, in August 1975 a number of serious problems converged, problems whose solution would require an important readjustment of internal and external policies. At the end of August, after various military ceremonies relating to the War of the Pacific, the commanders of the military regions deposed General Velasco and appointed the army commander and minister of war, General Francisco Morales Bermúdez, as the new head of state. In his first communiqué Morales Bermúdez announced a "second phase" of the Peruvian Revolution, so called because the military high command would resume the direction of the government and would seek to adjust the reforms in the light of the experience gained over the previous seven years.

The Second Phase: Crisis and Withdrawal

General Velasco and the small group around him had subordinated the cabinet, the public administration, and the officer corps, labeling opponents as "counterrevolutionaries" and "infiltrators." In the second phase, by contrast, the military junta sought to legitimize itself in the eyes of the high command by keeping senior officers informed and consulting them on the problems facing *their* government. That is, the personalization of power was cast aside, and indeed, those officers who had originally directed the military revolution and their ideological advisers were marginalized, on the grounds that they had strayed from their role as delegates of the armed forces. At the same time problems of defense and security were reemphasized, especially since the possibility of military action by Chile was perceived to be increasing.

The deposing of Velasco generated expectations in all social spheres. The bourgeoisie and the traditional political parties considered that an era of arbitrary rule had ended and a return to constitutionality was in prospect. The popular organizations and the revolutionary Left breathed a sigh of relief, given that the MLR was being dismantled and the officers who had organized and directed it were being demoted, while the deportees began to return, and opposition news media were reestablished. The new government's heterogeneous composition and imprecise orientation (it still included some "progressive" generals) encouraged the various social sectors to harbor conflicting expectations of it. Thus, whereas Velasco had constructed an image as "undisputed and indisputable Head of the Revolution," the image of Morales Bermúdez was that of a weak figure, vacillating between the divergent tendencies contained within the new government.

The first step was a series of economic readjustments weakly resembling a policy of stabilization, along with concessions involving various social reforms demanded by the popular forces. Official rhetoric continued to insist on the socialist, humanist, and Christian orientation of the Peruvian Revolution—neither capitalist nor Communist. But nothing placated the inflamed spirits of the popular classes, who intensified their protests. Although the Communist party and the CGTP still asserted the need to support "progressive" sectors of the government, other working-class organizations escaped their control and expressed the popular discontent. The government therefore reinforced its policy of "selective repression," to use a term coined by the minister of the interior. Certain popular organizations and leaders faced persecution but without a wholesale closure of the channels of communication and negotiation, since such a move might have led to an open, total confrontation between popular classes and the state. (After all, it was precisely this that the military had tried to avert with the interventions of 1962 and 1968, which were intended to put an end to the type of confrontation that had threatened Peru since the APRA risings of the 1930s.)

On the other hand, the second phase also signified an opening by the government toward the capitalists, the APRA, and Acción Popular. Belaúnde and other figures from his government were permitted to return to the country. In this way the government sought to establish a political alliance that would counterbalance the weight of the popular movement and obtain general endorsement and support for economic recovery. These returning forces joined the government in a chorus of denunciations of the errors and "excesses" of the first phase, especially the strikes and the "politicization" of trade unions, which were presented as determining factors in the country's economic and political crisis. Such denunciations opened the way for a campaign to purge the government of those responsible for the first phase, to restore the "freedom of the press," and to return the country to constitutionality. These steps were presented as prerequisites for economic recovery and tranquil political development.

Faced with this campaign, the government continued to vacillate. In January 1976, it deported those officers who had constituted General Velasco's main support when they denounced the "counterrevolutionary" character of the second phase. But the following month, contrary to all expectations, General Fernández Maldonado, one of the principal revolutionary figures of the first phase, was promoted to commander general of the army, minister of war, and prime minister, causing widespread speculation that the military government was about to return to its starting point. But then the government dismissed the officials who had been running the state-owned communications media, which had remained inclined to support popular interests. In March 1976, President Morales Bermúdez sought to explain this zigzag course in an address to the nation which took up the official rhetoric of the first phase, insisting on the need to free the people from exploitation and to end "external dependency." He advocated a united socialist, humanist, and Christian society which would forge a "social democracy with full participation" and which would consolidate national sovereignty. But he added a new ingredient to this message: a gradualist "new methodology" was needed to assure the route and to prepare each step. He also warned of the imminent danger of a totalitarian dictatorship aimed at erasing all the social advances made by the Peruvian revolution since 1968. In short, the president appealed to the popular classes and organizations for a political truce, threatening that the alternative might be a military "Pinochetazo." This appeal went unheard.

On 30 April 1976, following the same tack of seeking accord with different political forces, the president spoke openly to APRA sympathizers, asking them to forget the old hatreds and proposing a political détente, since the current aims of the party had much in common with those of the military government. Thus Haya de la Torre's prolonged wait seemed to bear fruit, in that the GRFA was admitting its own impotence and calling on his APRA party for assistance. The answer was not long in coming. Haya announced that the president's "unfinished symphony" could end only with general elections and a return to constitutional government. Shortly thereafter, ex-President Belaúnde, on his return from exile in the United States, endorsed the demands of Haya de la Torre.

Thus, each new step taken by the president to establish interlocutors and to negotiate a truce with the various political forces ended up by widening the political spectrum without validating the government's proposals.

While the APRA, Acción Popular, and the bourgeoisie focused their demands on a "redemocratization" of the country, the popular movement and its trade unions and parties pressed for a radicalization of the social reforms, postponing the problem of democracy in the political sphere. This sector considered that social and economic democratization would automatically result in a new political order, freed from the system of class domination.

However, the military rejected as premature the possibility of transferring power back to the civilians. First they would need to put the country's economy on a sound basis, and to consolidate and adapt the structural reforms in such a way that the armed forces could withdraw "with the satisfaction of a mission accomplished." Secondly, they wished to pursue rearmament in order to face down the Chilean threat. The supposed ignorance and negligence of civilians concerning matters of war served as a powerful argument to postpone discussions on a possible redemocratization.

But the failure to secure support for the political truce proposed by the military meant that government strategy had to be changed, the vacillations cease, and the state retreat from its isolation and autonomy in relation to the underlying social classes.

This change in strategy toward a political opening was also connected with the economic crisis which had begun in 1974 and had obliged the government in 1976 to enter into negotiations with the IMF in order to obtain international credit. As was to be expected, the Fund recommended its usual prescription, including restraint on public spending and a reduction in arms purchases. Since the government was very reluctant to reduce military spending, it postponed negotiations with the IMF and attempted to set up its own stabilization policy. Among the measures taken were the outlawing of strikes in the profitable mining and fishing sectors (April 1976) and, in June, a decree introducing the first "package" of price increases and subsidy cuts. Paradoxically, General Fernández Maldonado was given the task of explaining these measures. Directing himself to the popular strata, he underlined the necessity for a "pause" in the Peruvian Revolution to avert tendencies which might otherwise result in a military dictatorship or in a civil war.

The popular response was not long in coming, in spite of the divisions in the labor movement and on the Left. There was a unified call for a national stoppage. The government responded by declaring a state of emergency and imposing a curfew, measures which were continued for eleven months. At the same time repression was intensified and generalized, and directed not only against labor leaders, but also against peasant, neighborhood, student, journalism, and political leaders, thereby disarticulating the popular movement. Trade union advisers and representatives and political leaders from the revolutionary Left were sent into exile and their periodicals closed down. But to balance the account, the government also closed some rightist newspapers which were attacking the government, with the result that the repressive political conditions of early 1975 were re-created. The first attempt at political opening seemed to have ended abruptly. However, the following month (July 1976) General Bobbio headed a rising in the military complex in Lima, demanding the resignation of General Fernández Maldonado and of the last remaining "revolutionary" generals still in the government. In short, Bobbio was demanding a drastic change in the government's direction and orientation. The high command responded—Solomon-like—by dismissing both contending figures and at the same time sending the remaining Velasquista officers into retirement. Thus, a new and more homogeneous military leadership seemed in prospect.

In spite of the repression, the forces of the revolutionary Left and of the popular classes continued to gain strength, as indicated by the proliferation of meetings, discussions, publications, and protests expressing resistance to the government. At the same time the bourgeoisie and its political parties continued demanding the elimination of the "excesses" of the first phase and a return to constitutionality, accusing the military of provoking a situation of class warfare which could end in uncontrollable violence.

Faced with these vigorous signs of social effervescence, General Morales continued to tour the country trying to promote a "front for the defense of the revolution," but this tired revolutionary argument convinced nobody. At the same time, he also sought to win over the bourgeoisie and to promote an anxiously awaited "economic reactivation." To this end, the legislation on the workers' communities and job security was modified; the fishing industry was returned to private hands; and the communications media were restored to their original owners under a "gentleman's agreement" that their activities would be tolerated provided they did not promote opposition to the military government. In fact, the government followed a contradictory strategy, combining populist speeches with frankly antipopular economic measures.

However, all these steps proved insufficient. At the beginning of 1977 General Morales, in the presence of the high command of the three armed services, made public the Plan Tupac Amaru, by which the armed forces promised to hold early elections for a Constituent Assembly which would be dedicated exclusively to the drafting of a new constitution and which, moreover, would legitimize the structural reforms introduced by the military government. This step facilitated the initiation of cautious and reticent talks between the government, APRA, and the Popular Christian party (PPC), this last being a party which explicitly reflected the interests of the extreme Right and of the bourgeoisie. This move by the government succeeded in dividing the political opposition and creating room for maneuver within which the regime could negotiate and arrive at compromises with the main political forces. Since ex-President Belaúnde continued to argue for an immediate return to civilian rule, without accepting conditions imposed by the very military who had overthrown him in 1968, the only valid interlocutor available to the military was APRA, which, it should be said in passing, became the regime's favorite for the succession. There were two cardinal reasons for this. First, APRA was an organized party, unlike Acción Popular. Secondly, APRA concurred with the military's wish to maintain the structural reforms associated with the Peruvian Revolution. Meanwhile, the citizenry showed itself sceptical about the possibility of holding genuine elections, and the popular movement and the revolutionary Left concentrated on denouncing the new

APRA-military pact. But with the establishment of this accord between the two life-long enemies, APRA and the military, the two most compact organizations in the country's modern history, it seemed that the government had found the institutional way out it had been seeking.

It was not so easy for the government to sort out its relations with the international banks. When the first round of negotiations with the IMF were broken off, Peru sought to implement the first stabilization measures independently, and the private commercial bank creditors set up a committee to evaluate this policy. This committee concluded that the June 1976 package of measures was incoherent and insufficient to resolve the country's economic problems. Moreover, it stated that in order for Peru to receive international credit it had to bring the payments to the private banks up to date. Finally, owing to the lack of confidence in the government in international circles, Peru had to accept the supervision of its fiscal dealings by a body to be nominated by the original committee. Incredibly enough, all these demands were accepted by the government, even the last. The government's promise to comply secured it an immediate loan of $400 million. But a short time later, the bankers learned from the *New York Times* that Peru had acquired Russian airplanes. Lima's deception over these purchases caused the private banks to break off their dealings and to demand an IMF role in the future to reinstate any negotiation.[10] Consequently, in November 1976 conversations were renewed between the government and the IMF. The IMF proposed a policy of "shock treatment," which was immediately rejected by the functionaries of the Central Bank and by the military command. The Central Bank proposed a gradualist policy in order to reduce the "social and political costs" which the state and society would otherwise incur. But the decisive reason for a second rejection of the Fund's proposals was the military decision to concentrate on facing down the threat from Chile. Hence relations between Peru, the IMF, and the international banks were not reestablished until May 1978.

Although the economy was collapsing to the point that Peru might have to default on its international payments, President Morales Bermúdez persisted in the search for political alternatives, while struggles between different tendencies in the government and confrontations between civil society and the government threatened to break up the precarious institutional order. The president seemed to sway to and fro seeking to balance multiple contradictions. The announcement in February 1977 of forthcoming elections fitted into this framework.

Then in May 1977 the minister of the economy resigned in protest over the authorities' unwillingness to adhere to a rigid austerity plan. He was replaced by a prominent entrepreneur who promised to generate an economic recovery following the economic stabilization policies. Within a month, the new minister had discovered the impossibility of establishing authority over the military ministers, not only in relation to arms purchases but also with regard to ministerial budgets in general, and he followed his predecessor by resigning.

In the meantime, an important event profoundly altered the panorama of Peruvian society and politics. In spite of the multiple divisions between the different groups of the revolutionary Left and within the leadership of the labor movement, the popular movement succeeded in uniting around the national strike of July 1977. This strike received tacit support from APRA, Acción Popular, and the bourgeoisie, all of whom sought to force the military government's withdrawal. In turn, each group took advantage of the strike to blackmail the military, whom they accused of allowing the Left and the trade unions to hold the country to ransom at a time of grave economic crisis. They argued that the only valid and effective alternative was a return to democratic life, of which they were the representatives.

The government's first reaction was to decree that employers could dismiss those workers who had incited, led, or participated in the national strike. Employers eagerly took advantage of the occasion to dismiss many trade union activists. This meant laying off around five thousand workers, an event which had a marked impact on workers in general, particularly since unemployment was worsening. For this reason, one of the leading demands of the popular movement would henceforth be a "labor amnesty" and job security. Once the regime had granted one of the most important of the employers' demands—breaking up the trade union apparatus, which had served as the crux of the popular movement—it proceeded in August 1977 to call elections for a Constituent Assembly, which would be held in June 1978.

The Constituent Assembly and Economic Stabilization

With the calling of elections for the Constituent Assembly, the government found a means to divide the political opposition and shift public attention, from popular struggles concerning social issues toward interparty competition. The government hoped that this would free it to implement an economic stabilization policy. Lastly, the military aimed to use the elections as a means of testing the distribution of political opinion and evaluating the scope for a slow and cautious transfer of power to civilians, under a new institutional system containing guarantees of the armed forces' rights.[11]

Acción Popular, led by ex-President Belaúnde, opposed the calling of these elections, which Belaúnde described as both unnecessary and illegitimate. His party declared that it would abstain from the electoral competition and would reject the conditions imposed by the military. This left the field clear for APRA and the PPC to explore the advantages of cooperation with the military. At the other end of the spectrum, Patria Roja, a Maoist group, also refused to take part and launched a campaign against the other leftist groups, calling them "electoralists" and "bourgeois reformists," and urging revolutionaries to join its campaign for electoral abstention. At first, therefore, it seemed that the military initiative might fail. Nevertheless, it soon became evident that the popular desire for a return to open political life would prove too strong for the success of the position of these "maximalist" leaders. The franchise was extended to eighteen-year-olds, meaning that a majority of electors would be voting for the first time, since the previous election had been in 1963, fifteen years earlier. The radio, television, and the newspapers, all controlled directly or indirectly by the government, were instructed to give broad coverage to the contending parties, which increased general interest in the issues.

As the military had apparently foreseen, the popular movement was fragmented by the increase in party competition. The National Electoral Commission would grant official recognition to any party demonstrating the support of forty thousand citizens, a measure aimed at eliminating the multiple groupings of the revolutionary Left and leaving the field clear for the traditional parties. However, this measure obliged the different groups within the revolutionary Left to seek a system of interparty alliances that would enable them to enter the electoral game and propagate their views.

The calling of elections signified a relative democratization of the country's political life, favoring a revival of civil society and the incorporation of vast social sectors into political life, together with the development of new sectoral and regional institutions. Suddenly there was a proliferation of magazines carrying debates between national figures; throughout the country there was a multiplicity of meetings, discussions, courses, and seminars. Speakers not only fearlessly attacked the "military dictatorship," but also proposed different remedies for the country's complex economic and social problems.

The PPC and its leader, Luis Bedoya Reyes, proposed a "managerial" alternative which would establish order via strong measures to put the country "on the right path." The Pinochetista flavor of the measures proposed by Bedoya on the advice of "Chicago boys," ensured he would acquire an ultraright image. At the other extreme, the left-wing groups, competing with each other, accused the military dictatorship of colluding with APRA, and described both as representing the "feudal-bourgeoisie," "the grand bourgeoisie," and imperialist interests. Some proposed a return to the nationalist reformism of the "first phase" of the military government; others advocated the construction of a Socialist society (with the consequent sovietization of the army and the means of production). Some leaders of the Left saw the development of a "revolutionary situation" and anticipated a state of insurrection.

Between these two extremes, Haya de la Torre presented himself as a conciliator, disposed to find formulas for coexistence both among the civilians and between them and the military. He aimed to draft a constitution that would emphasize the state's role as mediator between the social classes. To this end Haya reasserted his old postulates of the 1930s, centered on the creation of a "National Economic Congress" representing all the forces of production in order to plan the country's development. Haya and the APRA party presented themselves as the democratic successors to the military government. According to the Aprista leadership, the immediate political debate should be restricted to constitutional issues, relegating more substantive policy issues to a later date. Haya had accepted the military's conditions for a restoration of civilian authority, and in this he could count on the support of Bedoya. Thus, in practice these two parties were allied with the government in isolating the labor movement, the revolutionary Left, and the popular movement more generally.

Nevertheless, this alliance suffered from serious limitations. It had reached no agreement on an economic stabilization policy, and there was still no agreement with the international banks. The government had succeeded in fragmenting the opposition and had even established a political alliance in opposition to the popular movement, but it still had to confront the economic problems. Now that the main political parties were lending it their tacit support, the government was no longer alone in accusing the popular movement of seeking to destroy the transition to democracy.

Finally, in May 1978, one month before the elections and with the Peruvian exchequer literally on the verge of bankruptcy, a provisional agreement with the IMF was finally reached, on the basis of an oral statement prepared by the minister of economics, Javier Silva Ruete, and the president of the Central Bank,[12] Moreira Paz Soldán. They obliged the military junta to adopt the first of a series of stabilization measures. The popular movement was quick to respond: the labor movement and leftist organizations called for a new national stoppage. But this time the government could rely on the support of the political parties, especially APRA, to frustrate this move. This left the military free to carry out a new wave of antiunion repression; it also deported political leaders and left-wing journalists, including some candidates for the Constituent Assembly elections. APRA and the PPC supported these measures, arguing that "public agitation" was a threat to redemocratization and might provide the pretext for a coup, this time of a Southern Cone type. They were, in fact, accepting the government's offer of a transfer of power in exchange for economic stabilization. These parties went further and justified the new economic measures as a necessary restorative after the excesses and stupidities of Velasquismo and "its allies, the communists." By charging all left-wing groups with complicity in the errors of the first phase, they hoped to strengthen their electoral appeal.

The military government also counted on a powerful external ally. A career ambassador, de la Puente, was appointed foreign minister with the aim of "normalizing" Peru's international relations with Argentina, Chile, and especially the United States. Peru abandoned its virulent attacks on the rich countries in the North-South dialogues and avoided militancy in the nonaligned movement. This changed international posture and the summoning of a Constituent Assembly caused the U.S. State Department to take a positive interest in Peru. Faced with the dictatorships of the Southern Cone, and instability in Central America and the Caribbean, the United States thought the direction in which Peru was moving might offer a way of avoiding political polarization and its uncontrollable consequences. Therefore, each step toward a restoration of civilian rule received a positive response from the U.S. government: increased support from AID, U.S. government loans, and so on. Above all,

U.S. embassy officials had explicit orders to resist advances from military officers and leading elements of the grand bourgeoisie proposing a military coup on Southern Cone lines. Moreover, the embassy made it clear that any such move would meet with direct repudiation by the United States. Thus, military conspirators found themselves internationally isolated.

The electoral results contained various surprises: The Aprista party obtained the largest vote (35.4 percent), a good result but one which suggested its inability to surpass its historical share. Diverse groupings on the Left did unexpectedly well in that, added together, they obtained about a third of the vote, whereas their previous showings had been insignificant. The PPC came second with 24 percent, thanks to its skill in appealing to the middle-class electorate that would normally have voted for Acción Popular, had that party not abstained from the election. Finally, parties of the old oligarchy disappeared from the country's political map. Thus a clear political spectrum was established, represented on the Right by the PPC, in the Center by APRA, and on the Left by groups ranging from "first phase" nationalists to Trotskyists. Furthermore, the system of proportional representation used in these elections permitted representation of a range of minorities.

The Constituent Assembly elected Haya de la Torre to its presidency, an act with great national impact. This was a major step in the transfer of power. Well-known figures from APRA and the PPC resumed their seats in Congress, together with some new personalities, mainly political, trade union, peasant, and urban neighborhood leaders affiliated with the leftist parties. As soon as the Constituent Assembly opened, the left wing, led by the Trotskyists, put forward a "red motion." This attributed sovereign powers to the Constituent Assembly and disavowed the military government. As was to be expected, APRA and the PPC rejected this motion and confined themselves strictly to the drafting of a new constitution that would replace that of 1933. While Haya concentrated on this task, the leftists kept trying to bring up social issues and repudiated the specific activities for which they were elected. The government and the majority parties responded by accusing the Left and the popular movement of causing strikes by miners, teachers, and public employees in order to overturn the legal process and provoke a military coup. However, Haya de la Torre also expressed a continuing interest in achieving agreement with what he called the "responsible Left," in order to isolate the most militant groups and to increase APRA's leverage over the PPC. But owing to APRA's long history of conflict with the Left, its reformism, and its conciliatory behavior with the military, these overtures were never successful, and APRA was left to deal alone with the PPC. The Constituent Assembly proceeded with its work, but soon acquired a tarnished public image, while the leftist representatives took advantage of their parliamentary immunity to promote their organizational goals to mobilize the opposition. Thus it happened that the assembly, contrary to official expectations, proved a poor instrument for encapsulating and institutionalizing the political conflicts occurring in society at large.

APRA's dependence on the PPC for forming a majority in the assembly signified that the structural reforms of 1968 would not be incorporated into the constitution and that the state's role in the country's economic life would be minimized. Haya's long-cherished purpose to integrate all the productive forces in one congress was discarded. At the last moment, however, the vote was extended to illiterates, and unanimous backing was obtained for a chapter devoted to human rights. Another of the important constitutional provisions strengthened the executive and gave it a presidential character, in order to avoid the instability and paralysis that had contributed to the overthrow of the earlier Belaúnde government. APRA was not disposed to yield over the formula for electing a president. On this aspect the fight was intense, and different methods were considered in which the interests of each group were obvious. The final arrangement was favorable to APRA: in the 1980 election, 36 percent of the vote would be sufficient to elect the president, and in later elections a minimum of 40 percent would be necessary. The PPC accepted the compromise because of its belief, fairly widespread in the country, that it would be difficult for any one candidate to obtain this proportion of the vote, in which case the presidential election would be decided within the Congress, where the PPC would play a decisive role.

In order to speed the transfer of power and take advantage of the influence it had gained, APRA asked the government to call elections the moment the Constituent Assembly had completed its task. The government rejected this proposal, arguing that the National Electoral Commission would require several months to update the electoral register and to incorporate illiterates. The elections were therefore fixed for May 1980, with the new government taking office in July. Only then would the new constitution come into effect. Meanwhile, the government would continue operating under the 1968 Revolutionary Statute. The military also refused to approve four of the Transitory Clauses, including the clause concerning human rights. Furthermore, it requested modification of certain dispositions limiting military powers in civilian spheres, but this request was unanimously rejected. Haya signed the constitution from his sickbed; the Assembly adopted it unanimously and closed in an atmosphere of tension and expectancy. Feelings of frustration were marked, both within APRA and the PPC, on the one hand, and within the military, on the other, once again raising fears of a possible coup.

With Haya soon on his deathbed, struggles for succession began within the leadership of APRA. This probably influenced the military in their decision to postpone the elections. For pro-APRA officers such as General Morales Bermúdez, the general secretary of the party, Armando Villanueva, would need time to assert his leadership and establish his position as the party's presidential candidate. Villanueva, supposed heir to Haya's tradition, would support consolidation of the structural reforms and would aim to establish a "social-democratic" regime. This regime, thanks to APRA's strong organization, would seek popular support and be capable of restricting the role of the Left and controlling the popular movement. For officers opposed to APRA (to be found in all services, but particularly in the navy and the air force), Bedoya and, above all, Belaúnde needed time for the infighting within APRA to develop, and time in which to organize their own campaigns. Finally, the military as a whole wanted another year before returning to barracks—among other things, in order to commemorate the centenary of the beginning of the War of the Pacific (1879) and also in the hope that an economic recovery might weaken the political momentum that had been achieved by the Left.

The economic stabilization policy seemed to be successful: after a year the trade balance had substantially improved, influenced by the increase in international mineral prices and the rise in the price of nontraditional exports. However, inflation and domestic recession continued to wreak havoc with popular living standards, occasioning continuous mobilizations and protests. But the economic-policy makers had to face criticism from the armed forces who wanted to increase spending on armaments, now that dollars were again accumulating in the coffers of the Central Bank. Silva Ruete and Moreyra were able to contain these demands, however, thanks to the backing and prestige which they received from the international financial community[13] and from the Peruvian bourgeoisie.

The other point of tension over economic policy concerned the industry minister's proposals to reactivate internal production and counter inflation and unemployment by means of renewed state spending now that the "emergency" was over. This issue was once again resolved in favor of Silva, Ruete and Moreyra. Their repeated threats of resignation unless their economic policy proposals were accepted resulted in the removal of an industry minister from the cabinet.

Silva Ruete and Moreyra went even further, linking the economic recovery with the restoration of democracy and the development of "market forces." They argued that it would not be possible to control the personal and corporate arbitrariness that had created the economic crisis in the first place unless constitutional government was restored. This posture reinforced the line taken by the U.S. government and helped to ensure that there was no backsliding after the closure of the Constitutional Assembly, notwithstanding the restlessness of various *golpista* currents within the military.

The Transfer of Office

The "transfer of government, not of power" proposed by the president in December 1977 was decisively affected by the illness and death of the octogenarian Aprista leader, Haya de la Torre, a few days after the Constituent Assembly completed its activities. His burial was a national event which brought together, for the first time in the country's contemporary history, a whole range of public figures who united in recognizing Haya's contribution to Peru's political development. The armed forces—in an irony of history—rendered him the highest posthumous honors. Nevertheless, the man who had created and dominated the most important mass party of the last fifty years, and who came to symbolize popular struggle against the oligarchy and the division of the country between Apristas and anti-Apristas, left his party with a difficult legacy. Prior to his death, internal divisions had already become obvious: as one party leader had said, APRA's problem was how to pass from absolute monarchy to a republic. All this made it very difficult for the party to present a clear and consistent image which would arouse national support, at a moment when Peru was undergoing an intense social and political recomposition.

Shortly after Haya's death, the party chose Villanueva as his successor, with the support of the party apparatus and the youth sector. The defeated rival was Andrés Townsend, whose group consisted of older men, experts in the parliamentary arts and in negotiating with the military and the bourgeoisie. This group would have sought to conciliate the Right and to seek the support of the urban middle strata. Deep contradictions within the party, previously silenced by Haya, emerged publicly after his death to reveal a totally different image from the APRA Haya had projected as a party of discipline, fraternity, and ideological coherence. Moreover, the violence used by the rival factions seemed to foreshadow the means that the party might use in government.

In order to reestablish a semblance of party unity and to salvage APRA's impaired image, Villanueva insisted that Townsend run as first vice-presidential candidate. He also arranged for Luis Negreiros, a respected labor leader, to stand as candidate for the second vice-presidency. Thus, Villanueva attempted to employ Haya's old tactic of using intermediaries who would broaden the party's radius of influence both among the popular sectors and with the bourgeoisie. But in the new conditions of social and political polarization, this tactic involved competition both with leftist groups who rejected APRA's search for a "responsible left," and with Belaúnde's Acción Popular. APRA immediately embarked on an expensive election campaign, supported by German social democracy. Villanueva tried to present himself as a conciliator, prepared to resolve national problems by acting as a mediator between the interests of the popular classes and of the bourgeoisie, and between the state and international capital, and by improving the reforms decreed by the military government. Thus APRA's positions did not move far from official discourse, nor from what the military expected of Villanueva's candidacy. As a result, the government sought to favor APRA through a series of electoral devices concerning the distribution of congressional seats among the different electoral subdivisions.

The PPC competed with APRA in wasteful electoral spending, seeking to attract some of Belaúnde's natural support: the middle strata and the bourgeoisie. To this end, Bedoya presented himself as a man at the head of a qualified team of technicians, capable of running the state in a "managerial" manner, hard and inflexible, without relapsing into the indecision and weakness shown by Belaúnde in the 1960s.

Belaúnde, by contrast, engaged in a countrywide campaign, promoting the slogan "work and let work," building on his reputation as an architect, a constructor of works endowed with imagination and knowledge of the national territory. Likewise, he emphasized his independence from the military and his party's refusal to enter the Constituent Assembly, while underlining his respect and deference for the professionalism and modernization of the armed forces. He placed particular stress on his "pluralism," always referring to his colleagues and opponents courteously in his speeches.

Meanwhile, the left-wing parties devoted their energies to organizing demonstrations against the military dictatorship, denouncing APRA's collusion with the military and the economically and politically repressive nature of the state, and describing the other parties as servants of bourgeois and imperialist interests. Attempts to create a united left-wing electoral front, first initiated on the eve of the 1978 elections, were resumed in late 1979. At a succession of interminable meetings of numerous small groups, two fundamental points were discussed. The first, and most important, concerned the weight each group would have within the proposed Revolutionary Association of the Left (ARI). The second concerned setting out a common program. To complicate negotiations further, the Trotskyist Hugo Blanco (who had achieved third place in the 1978 vote) demanded that a united front should be formed "without generals or the bourgeoisie"—in other words, that the inheritors of Velasquismo should be excluded. These lengthy negotiations continued to the very last moment, when the registration of candidates was over, without ever reaching agreement. The Left was divided, with its inability to agree on candidates and a minimum program apparent, much to the disappointment of the rank and file, whose interests had not been taken into account by those negotiating at the leadership level. This division of the Left prevented coordination of the labor and popular movements, which were further weakened by uncoordinated strikes and mobilizations that confirmed the inability to construct a political platform.

The electoral results produced a surprise: Belaúnde won overwhelmingly with 45 percent of the vote, surpassing all expectations. APRA dropped from its 1978 figure of 35 percent to 27 percent, suffering a substantial loss of its traditional social base; the PPC fell from 24 percent to 10 percent; and the left-wing groups fell from the 36 percent they had obtained in 1978 to only 17 percent. Some tentative explanations may be offered. As mentioned already, the PPC had won support in 1978 in the absence of Acción Popular. Moreover, in a heated political campaign the presentation of Bedoya as an "ultrarightist" raised fears that he would polarize politics. APRA, for reasons outlined above, lost a proportion of its sympathizers, who preferred the "pluralism" of Belaúnde. As for the Left and the popular forces, the tremendous switch of its vote toward Acción Popular was due not only to organizational weaknesses, but also to the fact that Belaúnde seemed to many in the popular movement preferable to an APRA government that would strongly promote its own trade union and party machinery.

The Prospects for Democracy in Peru

Following the installation of Belaúnde's government, on 28 July 1980, economic policy continued to stress austerity. The industrial recession persisted, while emphasis was given to dynamizing primary exports and expanding the financial system, in the manner of the Southern Cone dictatorships.[14] This economic policy implies continuing unemployment and a squeeze on lower-class and self-employed incomes, and bankruptcy for many medium-sized enterprises. Those affected could form a "nationalist" opposition against a government and big business interests that are seemingly committed to further internationalization of the economy. However, the Belaúnde government has also sought to create mechanisms of political intermediation which would permit negotiation and compromise with strategic sectors of society, at least partially relieving the most acutely felt grievances.

On the other side, the popular movement has had serious difficulty achieving political integration and coordinated action. The various attempts to make the General Confederation of Peruvian Workers (CGTP) into a unified labor leadership have foundered, primarily because of the Communist party's interest in retaining full control over it. The efforts to make the united Left into a *political*, and not just an *electoral*, front have been impeded by the competing interests of the various party leaderships. Added to this, the divisions within APRA have further impeded efforts to broaden and consolidate an opposition front against the government.

The redemocratization process began with the establishment of the "second phase" in 1975. At first, the military government sought to end its self-imposed isolation from civil society and to build bridges with the surviving civilian organizations. To this end, it proposed a "truce," while still repeating the old official discourse and at the same time dismantling some of the reforms undertaken in the "first phase." Initially, big business viewed these developments with satisfaction but hesitated to lend any direct support.

Since the military government was determined to pursue rearmament, and since it also hoped that the economy might soon be stabilized, the next step was to recognize APRA and Acción Popular as valid interlocutors who might cooperate with the government and assist it in obstructing the autonomous development of the popular movement and the strengthening of the Left. In return the traditional political parties—which had for seven years been banished and anathematized by the military—demanded assurances that there would be an eventual return to barracks. Meanwhile, the growing forces of the Left rejected a purely political redemocratization and worked instead for the overthrow of the military apparatus and the "deepening" of the social reforms. Pressures from President Carter's administration, together with the demands of the political parties and the bourgeoisie, obliged the military to take a third step, that of holding elections for the Constituent Assembly. But it was the national strike of July 1977 that really compelled the military government to hold to its schedule for withdrawal. The repression of the strike and the holding of elections gave rise to an implicit bargain between APRA, Acción Popular, the bourgeoisie, and the government. There would be a transfer of office to civilians, and in return, these parties would withdraw from the opposition, leaving the popular movement in isolation and giving the government scope to introduce its economic stabilization policy.

After the military had restored the government to civilian hands, the problem of democracy in Peru became once again to determine what kind of political participation would be possible for the popular and middle sectors, in an economic context favoring the reconcentration of power in the hands of a few big financial groups and the reincorporation of Peru into the international markets via renewed emphasis on primary exports. Under these conditions, the capacity for intermediation of the parties now in government (Acción Popular—PPC) seems limited, and their resources for resolving this type of contradiction appear very slender.

Once in office, the Belaúnde government did not resort to straightforward "shock treatment" for the economy, nor has the popular opposition proved able to confront the state effectively and challenge the political boundaries set by the 1979 Constitution. The nation's political prospects and the consolidation of democracy will depend upon the state's capacity for intermediation among sharply conflicting interests and demands in economic conditions that are hard to reconcile with political participation by broad sectors of society.

The obstacles to an effective consolidation of Peruvian democracy became more pronounced as the Belaúnde administration approached the end of its five-year term. With the economy in a disastrous state (aggravated by the continent-wide debt crisis that began in 1982) and a very severe problem of guerrilla insurgency (the Sendero Luminoso movement, based mainly in the Indian highlands of southern Peru), Belaúnde's remaining ambition became to hand over his sash of office to an elected successor.

8 ·

Uruguay's Transition from Collegial Military-Technocratic Rule

Charles G. Gillespie

Introduction: The Development and Crisis of Uruguayan Democracy

For the first time in Uruguay's history, in 1973 the military as an institution implemented a coup, which resulted in the displacement of the country's politicians by high-ranking officers. Despite the retention of a civilian president as figurehead, power lay with the Junta de Oficiales Generales and the top brass, who were installed as directors of Uruguay's myriad state agencies, public corporations, and ministries. There had been militarist dictators during the last century, but they identified with the Colorado party, which dominated the government uninterruptedly from 1865 to 1958. The military played no part—beyond acquiescing at its inception—in the "mild" authoritarian regime of 1933–42. Those who study Uruguay and Chile traditionally dispute which country was the "most democratic" in Latin America before their similar fates in 1973. However, the absence of militarism made Uruguay the more politically envied nation by Latin Americans during this century. The Left was weak, and class struggles failed to manifest themselves in heroic, or even very overt, political conflict. Yet the endurance of the moderate and often conservative "traditional" parties (Colorado and Blanco) almost since independence in 1828 cannot be ascribed to the survival of an "oligarchy" by means of clientelist electoral cooptation of the masses, and the country's artful but dubious electoral laws.[1] In contrast to Argentina, Uruguay's "oligarchy" was exhausted by the repeated civil wars between the two parties during the nineteenth century, leading to the formation of what Real de Azúa has called the patriciate. The state remained in the hands of a relatively autonomous political class, while the booming export economy based on beef and wool was controlled by less *criollo* nouveaux riches. The population, unlike that of Chile, was homogeneously European, and political participation reached high levels earlier.[2]

No understanding of Uruguayan democracy is possible without reference to Batllism, the Krausian ideas of Don José Batlle y Ordoñez, who took over the Colorado party and used his two presidencies (1903–7 and 1911–15) to promote social and political reforms favoring women, children, and labor. Although the Batllist political project was to transform the country's political economy, and defy the neoliberal ideologues half a century later, it was resisted both by conservative factions of the Colorado party and by the traditionally antistatist and prorural Blancos. While Batlle pressured for the enactment of the 1918 Constitution (which for the first time introduced direct presidential elections by secret ballot), his opponents were able to exploit his plans for a collegial executive by incorporating the idea of "coparticipation" by the minority party (always the Blancos) in government. Thus, paradoxically, while Batlle was to achieve far greater success in implementing reforms than Yrigoyen, leader of Argentina's Radical party, the survival of political spaces for the opposition made Uruguay's democracy the more pluralist and enduring. Batlle's failure to create a disciplined, centralized party organization, and his reliance on rival factions in order to ensure victory over the Blancos would, however, become the Achilles heel of Uruguayan democracy.

After Batlle's death in 1929, the Colorado party became increasingly factionalized, as dynastic disputes erupted between his sons and nephew. In the great prosperity of the post-World War II decade, Luis Batlle, the nephew, was able to revive the populist content of Batllism, extending the country's welfare state provisions and, above all, favoring labor by implementing a classic model of import-substituting industrialization (ISI) along CEPAL lines. He, too, was restrained by the reintroduction of a collegial executive in 1952–67, but even more by the exhaustion of ISI within the confines of Uruguay's market and the trade crises which began after the end of the Korean War boom. For the first time in almost a hundred years the Blancos won the 1958 election, committed to more liberal economic policies. The dictates of electoral strategy, however, were to result in the continued growth of the public sector, increasing inflation, and fiscal crisis, resulting in the bank crash of 1965. The republic's checks "bounced" overseas.

Ever since the 1931 "Pork-Barrel Pact" established the principle of appointment to public-sector jobs on a spoils system for both government *and* opposition, the Blancos had matched the Colorados in the extension of patronage networks into the rapidly growing urban electorate by means of political clubs loyal to individual bosses (*caudillos*).[3] Rural-urban migration, the relatively large public sector, and the closeness of elections made the practice of clientelism not only possible, but increasingly indispensable. One result was the absence of class voting, and the crucial factor that links were not forged between the trade unions and the main parties.[4] Another was the accelerating disarticulation of the traditional parties and the increasing bureaucratization and paralysis of the state. Perhaps inevitably, the deepening crisis was blamed on the cumbersome collegial executive, which was replaced by a much tougher presidentialist constitution in 1967, to some extent modeled on that which de Gaulle had given France in 1958.

The creation of a strong presidency merely exacerbated the contradictions of the system and did nothing to promote more disciplined or cohesive parties. The electoral law allowing vote-pooling among competing lists loyal to rival leaders within the same party was retained, making rational voting extremely difficult and sometimes impossible. In the 1971 elections, liberal and democratic Colorados helped to elect a man who had almost no previous connection with the party, but who was chosen by President Pacheco as his proxy, given the constitutional ban on reelection of incumbents. Because the six Colorado candidates together polled 13,000 votes more than their three Blanco rivals, the traditional electoral law known as "double simultaneous vote" led to the proclamation of the Colorado with the most votes—Bordaberry—as president, despite the fact that the leading Blanco, Wilson Ferreira, had far more votes. After assuming the presidency, Bordaberry used his power to escalate political repression, decree emergency powers against strikers, and finally to stay on as figurehead for the military regime.

Elsewhere I have argued that the growth of terrorism, strikes, inflation, and ideological extremism and the authoritarian and ultimately military reaction to these are best seen as *symptoms* of the crisis of Uruguayan democracy from 1968 to 1973. The underlying causes were rooted in a simultaneous crisis in the political economy of the "relatively autonomous" state, and its interaction with the failures of the party system. The degree of "threat" to the existing capitalist order was far lower in Uruguay than in Chile.[5] The Left was able to regroup for the 1971 elections, following the example of the trade unions, which had formed a unitary federation, the Convención Nacional de Trabajadores (CNT). Yet Uruguay's Broad Front was a far more moderate coalition than Chile's Unidad Popular, stretching from the Communists and Socialists, to elements which had left the Blanco and Colorado parties and even the Christian Democratic party (PDC). The 18.3 percent which the Broad Front polled was a historic leap forward, but it represented less than half of the votes which Allende had achieved in Chile the previous year. Nevertheless, the operation of the electoral system, and increasing violations of civil liberties, provided ideal conditions for the extreme Left to propagate their view that bourgeois democracy was a sham and that an urban guerrilla strategy could bring about a revolution. Addressing university students in Montevideo early in the 1960s, Che Guevara had explicitly criticized both halves of this argument, but the generation of young Uruguayans who idolized him forgot his warning. Conversely, the spectacular successes of Latin America's most sophisticated guerrillas, the Tupamaros, provided maximum grounds for the absorption of national security doctrines by the increasingly U.S.-trained military, and a widely exaggerated climate of panic among the middle and upper classes.

As a result of a stalemate between Wilson Ferreira and President Bordaberry, a political space for the military opened up and grew rapidly in line with public dissatisfaction with politicians. It is interesting to note the increasing numbers of businessmen who joined governments, and of retired generals who ran for president. General Liber Seregni, the Left's candidate in 1971, surrounded himself with the cream of the army's top-ranking teachers from the officer school (IMES). Senators and deputies were subject to virulent attacks from the military for alleged corruption and links with the terrorists, although the terrorists were effectively eliminated by infiltration and confession under torture during 1972. The military became convinced that they could promote development and eliminate "subversion" more successfully than the president. His isolation was demonstrated by the fact that no other parties came to his aid when the army refused his choice of defense minister in February 1973. Chastened by the experience, Bordaberry decided that if he could not beat them, he would join them. When the National Assembly refused to suspend the immunity of a senator from prosecution for alleged terrorist links, it was closed "for grave violations of the Constitution."

Exactly eleven years later (27 June 1984), Uruguay was paralyzed by the second illegal general strike in less than six months. This one was rather special, however, in that it had the wholehearted support of the Colorado and Blanco parties. The authoritarian regime was dead: all that remained to be decided was what would replace it. The political actors in the transition were apparently very similar to those of the breakdown: a somewhat radicalized Blanco party, and the Colorado and leftist parties both converging on the Center from opposite directions; a reconstituted labor movement that openly claimed continuity with the banned CNT; the hardline army, softline navy, and middle-of-the-road air force. Terrorism had not reemerged. The party system had not been recast by the creation of an officialist party along Brazilian lines, nor had the conservatives and rightists disbanded and thrown in their lot with the regime, as had happened in Chile. The rest of this chapter will explore the failure of the Uruguayan military's attempt at "political engineering," and the manner of the politicians' survival. I shall emphasize the dilemmas and inconsistencies in the strategies pursued by those on both sides.

Particularities of a Collegial Authoritarian Regime

Although proportionately far fewer Uruguayans were murdered or "disappeared" in the war against the guerrillas than in Argentina, or during the destruction of unions and leftist parties following the coup, as in Chile, human rights groups estimate that the proportion of the population that passed through or remained incarcerated in jails was the highest in the region. The CNT labor federation was banned for calling a two-week general strike against the closure of Parliament. Bordaberry insisted, however, that the traditional parties remained the "essence of democracy and the formation of our nationality." One year later his response to an open letter signed by hundreds of congressmen was to insist they give up hope of once more "using their perverted political apparatuses." By this time, the parties of the Broad Front had been systematically dismantled, their presses confiscated, and their leaders arrested, while the traditional parties remained merely suspended. A document of the armed forces approved in May 1974 abolished the double simultaneous vote and stated that each party must henceforth have only one presidential candidate, the goal being to "fortify, moralize, homogenize and effectively democratize future political parties."

The early years of the military-dominated regime were characterized by repeated crises (especially over economic policy disagreements) and chronic uncertainty that came to a head in 1976—the year that Bordaberry's elected term of office expired. The president circulated a memorandum proposing the permanent abolition of political parties and his continuation in office. The military, on the other hand, were reluctant to break with the line that they were merely intervening to restore the country's traditional two-party democracy and displeased by Bordaberry's suggestion that they abandon public administration and return to the barracks, which they no longer considered the proper locus of the "war against the roots of subversion." When Bordaberry accused them in a second memorandum of leading the country toward "totalitarianism," he was deposed.[6]

This fascinating and rare moment of audibility in the internal discourse of the regime marked a turning point. The military remained loyal to the traditional parties as part of their *orientalidad* (patriotism), believing that a corporatist adventure would be neither successful nor legitimate. In their press communiqué they bluntly denigrated the idea, affirming that sovereignty resided in the nation as expressed in the popular vote, adding that it was wrong to "blame the system for personal errors and deviations." It would be false, however, to conclude that they fully espoused (or even understood) the free-market neoliberalism of Alejandro Végh Villegas, the man who had been made minister of the economy in order to calm the fears of the international financial community. Partly, it was the case that Uruguayan political culture (and Batllism) had historically forged a very resilient bond between liberalism in politics and statism in economics, and this characteristic mixture entered the military's thinking. The public sector of the economy was not reduced, but made more efficient. Unions were not coopted into the state, as in Argentina or Brazil, and when elections did not weaken the alleged hold of the Communists, they were suspended. In other words, the military were not impressed by abstract models such as corporatism or neoliberalism.

It has been speculated that Végh's decision to resign when Bordaberry was replaced by the gray figure of Aparicio Méndez in 1976 was due precisely to frustration with military checks on his more radical free-market policies (such as removing tariffs on cars, and thus on the fledgling automobile industry).[7] In his own memo, however, he expressed concern that the growing void between state and civil society might favor the renewal of subversion, adding that "consolidation of a durable regime necessitates a civic consensus far broader than that which a group of technocrats can form." This was a particularly significant comment, coming from a Harvard-trained engineer and technocrat par excellence. His preferred solution was the Brazilian one of bypassing, rather than abolishing, constitutional provisions. Even though the resultant legitimacy was more apparent than real, it gave the regime greater resilience than reliance on (economic) efficiency alone.

On the day he took office, 1 September 1976, Méndez signed the Fourth Institutional Act, which banned fifteen thousand former politicians from engaging in any political activity for fifteen years. Here the kind of subtlety that Végh had called for was clearly lacking. In Brazil, about five hundred citizens (only some of them politicians) were selectively deprived of their political rights, less than one-thousandth as many as in Uruguay, relative to population. The conditions were toughest for the Uruguayan Left: anyone who had stood for office was deprived of his or her vote and banned from engaging in politics. On the other hand, only those Colorados and Blancos who had actually held office were thus banned; they were not disenfranchised. Other institutional acts had postponed elections *sine die*, and the legislative function had been transferred to a new body called the Consejo de la Nación, consisting of the Consejo del Estado (twenty-five nominated civilians, principally "unknowns") plus the Junta de Oficiales Generales (twenty-one top-ranking generals) in joint session. Further acts abolished the immunity of civil servants from being fired, subordinated the judiciary to the executive, and intervened in the machinery for the future holding of elections.[8]

In many ways, the situation inside the parties was no less confused. Important sectors of the Colorado party (principally the Pachequistas) operated within the framework of the new institutions. Most of the Blancos, however, resisted such overtures, with the exception of some aged ultra-conservatives. Debates on tactics divided both the traditional parties and the Left, with exile and repression complicating the problems. In the Blanco party, exiled leader Wilson Ferreira made the controversial decision to forge an alliance with the Left, the Convergencia Democrática en Uruguay, which included strong Communist representation. No Colorados went into exile, however, and they refused to support Convergencia, although leaders such as Jorge Batlle made their opposition to the regime explicit.

Confusion on the Left was severe, given the failure of both the guerrilla struggle and the electoral road. The Broad Front was able to operate its clandestine executive sporadically, though never with all delegates present. Liber Seregni continued to smuggle out political pronouncements from jail, presumably because the government found it convenient to tolerate this. Perhaps belatedly, the Left placed democracy in the forefront of their creed, though the Communists and Christian Democrats had always been critical of terrorism and ultraleftism. Under leader Juan Pablo Terra, the PDC went so far as to state that the Broad Front no longer existed. Until Seregni was released in March 1984, atomization and confusion meant that the Left was not well positioned to profit from the crisis of the regime after 1980, and the reemerging politicization of youth.

Deprived of access to state resources, the traditional parties were unable to operate the patronage networks that provided many of their sectors with votes. Politicians were still discredited for their failure to solve long-term economic problems, and in some cases by their ambivalent attitude to the coup. Unfortunately, explanations for the parties' survival in "suspended animation" inevitably tend to be either circular or negative: they survived because they were central to political culture (due to their longevity) and also because of the absence of any military program to displace them. Furthermore, the proscription of even minor leaders and the ban on political activity paradoxically froze their leadership.

Despite the militarization of administration, which tended to jeopardize attempts to cut spending, the regime did not attempt to found its own clientelist support base either within an existing party or through establishing a new one. This is surprising, given the very large size of Uruguay's public sector and the number of posts to be filled. The problem was not so much lack of resources, but the fact that citizens had come to see state benefits as an entitlement. The crucially powerful mayor of Montevideo, elected in 1971, stayed on as a technocrat to boost capital investment while maintaining jobs and resisting the witch-hunt against alleged leftists. The military were probably influenced by their own rhetoric of "house-cleaning" and their aversion to "dirty" party politics. They were also hampered by the lack of a preponderance of ties to any one party and the absence of a clear leader.

Official concern that the "politicization" of the armed forces might subvert the internal hierarchies and discipline on which they relied (either by trickling down from the top, or by spreading up through the ranks as a result of any residual porosity with respect to civil society, as had happened in Portugal) led to occasional purges and the decision to disenfranchise police and servicemen, later reversed. Generals who amassed too much power, such as Chiappe Posse in the early years, were ousted. Uruguay lacked a large rural population previously marginal to political participation and therefore "available" to be incorporated from above in alliance with traditional elites into a proregime party. Furthermore, national security ideology never achieved the same degree of legitimacy, as can be seen by the contrasting role of middle-class professionals in the strikes that swept Chile and Uruguay during 1972 and 1973, and the fact that support for the coup from Uruguay's parties was mainly tacit. As elsewhere, the military were torn between nationalist and neoliberal visions of the country's reconstruction, with the latter winning but remaining strongly at variance with the Batllist political values that many retained and the political economy of the state they had inherited.[9]

Between 1974 and 1980, Uruguay's GNP grew at the historically high rate of 5 percent per annum; despite the oil shock, trade surpluses were achieved. The social cost, however, was enormous, as measured in emigration, falling real earnings, income concentration, and physical repression of all trade union activists. Macadar has shown that the rapid growth was not so much the product of neoliberal economic policies—for instance, there was almost no privatization of public industries—as it was the result of a boom in construction (brought about by changing government policies and an increase in public investment compared to consumption), the promotion of "nontraditional" exports by subsidies (until the U.S.A. threatened countervailing duties), and a boom in tourism from Argentina.[10] Financial liberalization brought, not an influx of foreign investment into productive areas of the economy, but an expansion of the financial sector. From 1978, Uruguay decided to make the reduction of inflation the number one target and allowed the peso to devalue only very gently according to a preannounced schedule (*tablita*), as international monetarists had advised. Since this led to an import boom and a wave of industrial bankruptcies, the earlier hopes of drastically reducing protectionist tariffs had to be given up. The wave of bankruptcies, in turn, caused banks to collapse. The Central Bank then adopted a policy of buying up bad loan portfolios in order to act as midwife in the acquisition of these banks by foreign banking groups. This ultimately led to twenty out of Uruguay's twenty-two banks being in foreign hands.

In practice, the military refused to sponsor consistently particular economic interests, as a result of pressure from the free-market advisers and technocrats, although they could occasionally be persuaded to intercede to protect an industry on the grounds of national security. One business sector after another was alienated: manufacturers for the domestic market by tariff cuts, exporters by overvalued exchange rates from 1978, petty commerce by the massive contraction of real earnings, construction by the military's refusal to mitigate the slump that began in 1981 with countercyclical public investment, and practically everyone—but especially ranchers—by the high interest-rate policy and the unwillingness to help firms that had taken on heavy debts in order to invest.

Many problems were external: the massive rise in oil prices, trade barriers to non-traditional exports, such as shoes, and the collapse of the Argentine peso in 1981 and 1982, which ruined the important tourist trade, sending it into reverse. Until 1980 the regime could derive legitimacy from the revival of growth for the first time in two decades. After the second oil shock it lost that legitimacy, and the high costs of the regime's policies in terms of living standards became apparent, though free-market policies were, if anything, intensified. Uruguay's foreign debt almost quadrupled between 1972 and 1983.[11]

Bordaberry's memorandum to the military had warned them that by assuming the tasks of administration, they would also have to assume public responsibility for success or failure ("as if they were a party"). Not only was this "improper," but it would also lead to "frequent clashes and friction with civilians," introduce divisions, and threaten the military's esprit de corps. Actually, one of the few areas of agreement between Végh's and Bordaberry's memos had been that military power was potentially threatening to the armed forces as an institution. They disagreed on the solution, Végh charging that Bordaberry's corporatist plan would in fact increase the danger of an "internal rupture" of the military. Ironically, the alternative of avoiding a permanent formalization of military power without building a proregime party produced precisely the two problems that both had correctly identified: a political vacuum and a vacillating, divided military. Chile and Brazil solved the problem of military dissension and lack of coordination by establishing strong, independent secret services—mechanisms which did not emerge in either Argentina or Uruguay. In both cases, interservice rivalries were crucial, but in Uruguay, this was really just another result of collegiality. The price of collegiality, however, was a tendency toward the "feudalization" of public administration, and problems of coordination.

The first cautious attempt to break out of the circularity of power-without-accountability fell far short of liberalization, let alone redemocratization. In fact the real "transition" did not even appear on the horizon until after this attempt at controlled reinstitutionalization had failed. Partly as a result of pressure from the Carter administration, the power struggle in the army resulted in a complex victory for the proponents of what was called the *Cronograma* (timetable). Generals such as Esteban Cristi, who were thought to oppose resort to any type of electoral legitimation, lost power, and the military's Political Affairs Commission (COMASPO) announced that elections would indeed be held in 1981. First, however, a constitution would be drafted and submitted to a referendum in 1980. The traditional parties were eventually permitted to organize a very limited last-minute campaign before the November 1980 plebiscite. The Colorados managed to publish two issues of an opposition magazine, *Opinar*, in time for the vote, while the parties were permitted to hold two meetings that took the form of historical lectures. For the first time, Uruguayans heard of Dr. Enrique Tarigo, a new Colorado leader who became the figurehead of the "no" campaign. The military saturated radio and television with commercials for a "yes" vote, and controlled the vast bulk of the press, including the main dailies: the Colorado *El Día* and the Blanco *El País*. Such was their hubris that at the last minute they included the provision that there be only a single candidate agreed upon by the two parties and acceptable to the National Security Council, COSENA. It has been hypothesized that given the continued proscription of almost all politicians, certain generals hoped to commandeer the Blanco party as their platform. In any case the constitution retained the National Security Council as part of the executive and gave the president new power to declare a "state of emergency" without parliamentary approval. It was a case of overkill.

Uruguay after the Plebiscite: From Suspended Animation to Animated Suspension

The announcement that the *Cronograma* had been defeated by 57.2 percent to 42.8 percent, in a turnout of 87 percent, stunned the military as much as the opposition. Given that government propaganda had attempted to sell a "yes" vote as a vote for the orderly return to democracy, it was surprising that only 2 percent of voters had cast blank or spoiled ballots, and even more surprising that the parties had been able to organize adequately in the very limited time available to counter the regime's propaganda. Yet it was inevitable that the military would not win the support of politicians whom they had banned until 1991. The only major leader to call for a "yes" vote was the Colorado Pacheco, so that the military's strategy had depended on the electorate ignoring, or being unaware of, the position of the banned politicians. In practice, surrogates sprang up, allowing little doubt as to whom they represented. According to one theory, the government was so convinced that victory would be theirs—as it was in Pinochet's Chile—that they waited too long to falsify the results. Perhaps, too, they had been misled by opinion polls owing to the reticence of interviewees. It is at least plausible that one factor in the defeat was the severe compression of real wages that had occurred after the abolition of Consejos de Salarios under Pacheco, followed by the banning of the CNT union confederation after the military intervention and the erosion of minimum wage levels due to the fixing of increases below inflation. Unemployment, however, had declined, and there was a consumer boom. Yet it was not true that only the heartland of the Left had voted "no" (as investigation of the ecological pattern of voting shows), and of course, the total "no" vote was over three times higher than the Left vote in 1971. It was also found that young and first-time voters had voted overwhelmingly "no."[12]

The continued weakness of the political parties meant that they were unable to capitalize on their unexpected victory: the major development of the ensuing months was the growth of the opposition press, including the advent in July 1981 of *La Democracia*, clearly aligned with Wilson Ferreira, who was banned and in exile, as well as subject to a military arrest warrant. At about this time the neoliberal magazine *Búsqueda* became a weekly with a news and politics orientation, more critical of the delay in returning to democracy. The traditional sectors of Batllism brought out *Correo de los Viernes*. All magazines were subject to arbitrary and unpredictable sanctions, especially closure for a number of issues if they mentioned the names of banned politicians. Significantly, however, the introduction of *prior* censorship, in January 1984, eventually had to be abandoned under the weight of protests by politicians, editors, foreign governments, and domestic and international associations of journalists.

Within the military the power struggle intensified between those who argued that redemocratization must continue with more input from the "valid interlocutors" of the traditional parties and those who thought democracy should be taken off the agenda. The latter group claimed that the victory of the "no" in the plebiscite was a victory for international Communism. Out of this bitter conflict, retired General Gregorio Alvarez finally achieved the goal of becoming the regime's first noncivilian president—but only by ruthlessly exposing the corrupt dealings of his opponents. This betrayal of esprit de corps probably earned him further enemies.

The editors of these volumes have stressed the importance of the first phase of the transition, or its birth, which is referred to as the "military moment" out of which a leader emerges with the full confidence of the high command. Alvarez did not have the total support of the Junta de Oficiales Generales, given the manner of his succession and the apparent opposition to his candidacy among the navy. Supposedly, this could have paved the way for a concentration of executive authority to isolate the hard-liners and permit a belated liberalization, especially an end to illegal acts of repression. As subsequently became clear, the vaulting ambitions of President Alvarez actually stood in the way of confidence-building and finally a more or less smooth handover of power. In fact—anticipating our story somewhat—the armed forces slowly came to realize that he did not serve the long-run interests of their institution. The traditional parties did not demand a full-scale amnesty for terrorists and the legalization of all leftist parties as a condition for compromise over the military's project. What would, however, have helped a great deal was a clear commitment to restoring habeas corpus, freedom of expression and association. In the absence of this, the traditional parties could not be sure that the transition had really begun. Above all, President Alvarez's intentions remained ambiguous, while the military remained inflexibly wedded to their demand for a limited democracy (*democradura*), even though this maximalist model had been rejected in the plebiscite.

The election of Ronald Reagan had reduced U.S. pressure for accelerating the transition, although the Armed Forces Commission on Political Affairs, headed by General Rapela, was to begin talks with the traditional parties. One month after Alvarez's inauguration in September 1981, it was announced that new machinery for primary elections would be set up so that the traditional parties might choose new leaders. The same month *La Democracia* was temporarily closed down for publishing a letter from a banned Christian Democrat. When the Christian Democrats' magazine protested, it too was closed. Thus had begun the clear pattern of stick and carrot which we may interpret either as a deliberate (if counterproductive) regime strategy or as a sign of increasing divergence between Alvarez and the Junta de Oficiales Generales.

As a result of talks held in the headquarters of the joint chiefs of staff, ESMACO, the traditional parties succeeded in winning the restoration of the electoral system known as "double simultaneous vote," and thus multiple presidential candidacies. The draft of the new Statute of Parties was submitted to the Council of State in January 1982. It forbade parties "with foreign links" and those "advocating violence," and stipulated that in order to register for elections, parties had to be internally democratic. The Council of State relaxed a number of provisions of the statute, presumably because they regarded their future as obscure politicians who had collaborated with the regime as bleak. In order to blunt the opposition, direct election of the permitted parties' leaders was dropped in favor of nomination by the five-hundred strong conventions each was to elect in open primaries at the end of November. Candidates for the convention could appear on an electoral list in one department only; the lists could not use the old numbers by which voters knew the *sublemas* of each party; and the pooling of votes among lists was banned. Thus it was intended to disrupt the ability of leaders to form cohesive blocs, to reduce the clarity and public impact of the whole process, and (as a result) to increase the power of the smallest local clientelistic bosses and patrons. How far the regime as a whole subscribed to such a tactic is unclear. The traditional parties decided they had no choice but to accept manipulation of the terms. The government began to downplay studiedly the significance of the vote—which, unlike the plebiscite, was not compulsory—and to step up harassment of the opposition press. At the eleventh hour, five candidates, four Blancos and one Colorado, were arrested on charges of attacking the honor of the military.

The turnout of 60.5 percent for the November 1982 primaries was not as low as it might have been, given the silence of the media, the confusion surrounding the names on the new lists, the abolition of absentee voting, and the high level of recent emigration. Nor can there be any doubt that this time economic conditions played an important role in the regime's defeat: just forty-eight hours before the poll, the government was forced to announce the free floating of the Uruguayan peso, undoing at a stroke the centerpiece of their anti-inflation policy since 1978.

The Left was banned and in some disarray, with the Communists committed to their alliance with Wilson Ferreira in the Convergencia Democrática (headquartered in Mexico City and Washington) and imprisoned General Liber Seregni convincing the *Mesa Ejecutiva* of the Frente Amplio in Montevideo to call for a blank ballot. The Christian Democrats eagerly, and the Socialists (under Jose Pedro Cardozo) reluctantly, agreed. In practice, a call for the endorsement of those within either party who were the most ardent opponents of the regime would largely have meant voting for the Wilsonistas inside the Blanco party, as the leaders of Convergencia had calculated. Some former leftists probably did opt for the latter strategy, and the Communists' support for the blank ballot was half-hearted at best. The other parties, however, were determined to protest their exclusion from the primaries and to avoid the charge that they were attempting to take over the traditional parties. Nevertheless, in Montevideo the Wilsonista "ACF" list won in every district, while nationally the blank vote was 7.0 percent, well down from the 18 percent of the Broad Front in 1971.[13] Furthermore, in all but four departments of Uruguay's interior, the Blancos outpolled the Colorados, nationally attaining 49.2 percent to the Colorados' 42.1 percent.

The clear message of the primaries was an even greater rejection of the regime than two years previously. Despite some ambiguities in the alliances of the many local *caudillos* (bosses), the proregime followers of ex-president Pacheco Areco (Pachequistas) achieved a surprisingly low 27.8 percent of the Colorado vote. Proregime Herreristas did even worse in the Blanco party— 18.9 percent according to their magazine *El Debate*, only 13.7 percent according to a Wilsonista magazine, *La Razón*.

In the antiregime Colorado camp were leaders such as Julio María Sanguinetti (originally a stand-in for Jorge Batlle, banned leader of the fifteenth list); Dr. Enrique Tarigo (who founded a new sector, Libertad y Cambio, on the strength of his fame in spearheading the "no" vote in the plebiscite and the success of his magazine, *Opinar*); and various other leaders who disputed the Batllista legacy. The three main strands of the antiregime Blancos were Por la Patria (their leader the exiled Senator Wilson Ferreira), Movimiento de Rocha (led by banned Senator Carlos Julio Pereyra), and the Consejo Nacional Herrerista (led by Luis Alberto Lacalle).

Although bearing in mind the limitations of ecological regression analysis, Luis González has shown that support for the "no" vote in the plebiscite did not come exclusively from the modern sectors of the country and did not bear any very close relation to the previous support for politicians in the 1971 elections. The unspoken conclusion that a major electoral realignment had taken place appeared to be confirmed in the results of the primaries. Least surprising was the close correlation between blank-voting in the 1982 poll and the result of the Broad Front in the 1971 elections. Far more interesting is the absence of any statistically significant correlation between the votes for Wilsonista Blancos in the primaries and the pattern of his votes in the last presidential election. His vote, or that of his allies and proxies, jumped 11.5 percentage points in Montevideo and 16.6 percent in the neighboring department of Canelones. Equally, the correlation between Pacheco's votes in the primaries and support for his reelection in 1971 is insignificant. There is, however, a relatively strong association between his primary support and the "yes" vote in the 1980 plebiscite, implying that the authoritarian Colorado vote had shifted earlier on. Where Wilsonistas made strides, Pachequistas slumped (down 21.2 percentage points in Montevideo, 19.1 in Canelones), though we cannot assume that voters directly transferred from one to the other. The pattern of Jorge Batlle's support also shifted markedly, presumably because of the slump in Pachequismo and the rise in Tarigo's Libertad y Cambio. The Batllistas, who had run joint lists in many interior departments, put up a joint slate for the National Executive Council when the convention met, thereby reducing the Pachequistas' representation to a minimum and effectively excluding them from talks with the military. To an even greater extent, the antiregime Wilsonistas were able to dominate the Blanco leadership. Significantly, however, two conventioneers who were closely associated with Wilson and his radical son failed to get into the executive, which was elected by secret ballot.

The military's strategy originally had been to call into being a new generation of political leaders, while older adversaries remained banned, though politicians who had favored the aborted 1980 Constitution had their rights restored. Yet those new faces that had emerged from the elections—such as Dr. Enrique Tarigo in the Colorado party and Professor Juan Pivel Devoto in the Blanco party—were strongly committed to restoring a fully democratic system, free from military tutelage.

Wilson Ferreira was against attending the talks with the COMASPO, to be held in the Parque Hotel. While his supporters were still subject to harassment in the form of arrests and the closure of their weekly magazine, *La Democracia*, he argued, they could not negotiate from a position of strength. In exile he continued to promote Convergencia, which did not exert much influence in Uruguay, and was widely criticized, even by Blancos, who became worried at the apparent leftism of its major figure, Wilson's son Juan Raúl. Enlightened elements in the military had unsuccessfully been arguing even before the primaries that at least *some* leftist parties had to be legalized; otherwise, their activists would infiltrate the traditional parties, and their voters distort the results of the process of candidate selection.

The major flaws in the military's strategy during 1983 were their overestimation of their negotiating strength and their inability to recognize the advantages of divide-and-rule tactics. As a result of Wilson's opposition to even talking to the military and his criticism of Convergencia, a crucial gulf opened up between him and the bulk of the Blanco leadership. The Por la Patria delegates pulled out of the talks after turning up merely to denounce them, but the closely allied Movimiento de Rocha faction (led in less verticalist style by Carlos Julio Pereyra) stayed on until one of its leaders was arrested. In June the Blanco Directorio voted 12 to 3 against pulling out of the talks; later, on 4 July, it voted 14 to 1 in favor, and was quickly joined by the Colorado party, anxious not to be discredited. Wilson's strategy was vindicated.

According to most politicians, the military had not budged from their 1980 proposals, which the electorate had rejected, and were not really committed to handing over power. The military argued that their proposals—retaining the National Security Council, allowing Parliament to declare a "State of Subversion," the holding of suspects for ten days, and incorporation of military judges into the judiciary—would be placed in the hands of a democratically elected president. They also complained that inflammatory speeches were made outside the talks in order to provoke them into reacting, in effect admitting that they had played into the hands of those who wanted the talks to fail. The military also had difficulties with the political negotiating style, used as they were to giving orders. The fact that the talks were public rather than private (despite the Blancos' requests) made the negotiators extremely cautious of appearing to compromise.

The politicians' trust had not been increased by a speech the president made well before the talks began, calling for the rallying of conservative politicians from all sides into a new officialist party. The response to such a tardy venture had been a deafening silence among those who might have been tempted to sympathize. Nevertheless, in the wake of the collapse of the dialogue, there was a definite hardening of sectors of the regime, those most closely associated with President Alvarez. A decree of 2 August temporarily "suspended" all public political activity until further notice, while a new institutional act permitted the arbitrary banning of further politicians. The Armed Forces Political Affairs Commission leader, General Rapela, stated that the transition would not begin until March 1985 and that, since the parties had walked out of the talks on revising the constitution, the regime would reserve the right to decree the changes that it saw fit. Hundreds of students were arrested for demonstrating, some remaining in jail over a year later. According to the London *Times*, however, the moderates in the military had succeeded in staving off a worse showdown between the government and the opposition, preserving the commitment to elections in November 1984.

Surprising vacillations had begun. The students' union, ASCEEP, was allowed to hold a week-long celebration of the twenty-fifth anniversary of the law which had granted the university autonomy. Some had wondered whether the decision to allow the renascent trade union federation, PIT (Plenario Inter-sindical de los Trabajadores), to hold a May Day rally had been designed to bring back the specter of the Left and scare the middle class. It was clear that such a strategy was futile when, on 27 November, an organization formed by all parties, legal and illegal, plus social movements, held a stunningly large rally at the foot of Montevideo's obelisk. The organizers made a point of inviting all parties' leaders and calling for all to take part in the elections. A belated strategy of wooing back the traditional parties by lifting the ban on all remaining leaders except Wilson had clearly failed. The president attacked the return of "Communists" to public life, but his successive attempts to promote a crackdown were frustrated, for example during the sudden general strike of 18 January 1984. The strike was forced prematurely by pressure from militants at the grassroots, and the Colorados refused to endorse it, arguing the time was not right. In the event, however, the reaction of the regime was mild: PIT was formally made illegal, but its leaders were not arrested.

Tragic incidents continued to show sinister signs of a struggle inside the armed forces. In April, a doctor from a small town in the interior was arrested for the last of several times. He was returned to his family allegedly after a "heart attack" but showing signs of torture. Many hypothesized that the whole incident was an elaborate provocation designed to discredit General Medina, commander of the military region where the case occurred, but about to ascend to the key post of army commander in chief. If so, the plot backfired, as Medina made personal assurances that the officers involved would be court-martialed. In his inaugural speech he committed the army to an honorable exit.

A hundred thousand demonstrators were (optimistically) held to have attended the first May Day rally since the coup, and four hundred thousand to have heard the proclamation at the obelisk on 27 November 1983. The wave of opposition publications grew, and openly leftist ones appeared for the first time. Apart from the unions of workers and students, other social movements began to flower; these included FUCVAM, bringing together cooperative housing tenants, and SERPAJ, a group opposed to human rights violations. Despite the continued "suspension" of public political activity under the decree of 2 August 1983, the feverish debates at the Blanco and Colorado conventions showed that the traditional parties had emerged from suspended animation into a state of animated suspension.

Limited Democracy or Negotiated Reform?

The Blanco party convention overwhelmingly endorsed the presidential formula of Wilson Ferreira, with Carlos Julio Pereyra as running mate. Wilson, however, remained in exile, banned, and wanted for arrest on charges of "attacking the Armed Forces' morale," "exposing the Republic to foreign reprisals" (for campaigning for the end of U.S. military aid), and alleged links with subversives. The Colorados chose Julio María Sanguinetti and Enrique Tarigo as their candidates, the moderation of their strategy becoming increasingly apparent. Tarigo controversially reneged on the obelisk declaration by suggesting elections without the Left were better than no elections at all. The Colorados were the more concerned about a possible "Chileanization" of the situation, as pot-banging protests developed and sporadic violence began. Cadets and high-school students clashed, businesses advertising in leftist newspapers were bombed, carnival ended in a riot, and the police beat up demonstrators at a street fair.

Two crucial events occurred in March, starting with the release of Liber Seregni, who was reaffirmed as leader of the Broad Front. Though deprived of political rights, he called for national reconciliation and pacification. It was clear that his strategy would be compromise to achieve the rehabilitation of the Left. In the same week the Colorados accused the Blancos of having secret talks with the president, in which the idea of indirect presidential elections was discussed. Combined with a postponement of the vote (denied by the Blancos) this might have been a face-saving way for the military to accept Wilson as president. With the Left rehabilitated, as the Blancos favored, their senators and deputies might tactically vote for Wilson, thereby preventing a repetition of 1971, when the Colorados achieved a narrow win.[14] The revelations were damaging to the Blancos, despite their denials, and led to a deterioration in their relations with the Colorados. These events were also further evidence of the military's split and the isolation of the president.

In April, Wilson moved to Buenos Aires, where he made the brilliant gesture of offering *not* to run for president if there was an immediate, unconditional return to the 1967 Constitution. The military countered with a new draft for certain modifications and called for the traditional parties to discuss them. This document called for the election of a Constituent Assembly in the November general election but provided that the assembly would not meet until 1986 and that meanwhile all institutional acts would remain in force and there would be no amnesty. The Blancos denounced the draft as worse than the Parque Hotel terms, while the Colorados cautiously welcomed the recognition that the constitution should only be democratically redrafted. After an agonizing hiatus, Wilson announced that he would return to Montevideo in a chartered ship, surrounded by the press and politicians—not, as had been claimed, to destabilize the government but to "defeat tyranny." When the ship docked, he was taken by helicopter to imprisonment in a barracks over two hundred kilometers from the capital, effectively putting an end to hopes that the Blancos might negotiate with the military.

On the eve of the 27 June "civic strike," the multiparty alliance voted to empower Colorado leader Sanguinetti to meet the commanders in chief. The Blancos promptly withdrew. The decision to negotiate without them was made possible by the strategy mapped out by Seregni: mobilization, concerted action, and negotiation. Mobilization meant reestablishing the impressive street-presence of the Left in Montevideo. Concerted action meant reaching a consensus with other parties and social movements on the correct way forward. The tactics of the Colorados favored concerted action and negotiation, because, they argued, the military's monopoly of armed violence made talk of insurrection dangerous madness. The Blancos also claimed to favor concerted action (bringing out a new magazine called *Concertacion* and another called *Unity*), but since they had left the alliance, their entire strategy rested on mobilization against the Naval Club talks as those talks moved inexorably toward agreement. (See Table 8.1 for an outline of the parties' positions.)

In an internal newsletter of the Broad Front, Seregni wrote: "It was our line to say 'no' to the dialogue, but 'yes' to discussion of the 'climate' necessary to negotiate. . . . This means not only winning political space for the Broad Front, but also winning space for freedom. . . . We take the liberty of recommending to our militant comrades that they read the record of the Parque Hotel, and also the press of just a few months ago, when there were those who came forward to accept proscriptions which the regime saw fit to maintain, and others were offering a pact with the Armed Forces to make the elections indirect." The Blancos replied with a vicious attack on Seregni in the magazine *Unidad Nacional*, dredging up his involvement in the breaking of strikes as a general in the late 1960s. Thus began the "pre-dialogue" or "pre-negotiations" with the joint chiefs of staff, the Colorados, the Broad Front, and the small Unión Cívica.

At each step, the parties favoring dialogue extracted concessions, to avoid Blanco attempts to outmaneuver them. Institutional Act No. 16 allowed the lifting of the proscription of the leader of the Socialist party, Dr. José Pedro Cardoso, who represented the Broad Front at the ESMACO talks along with Juan Young, leader of the Christian Democratic party. Ten days later, Institutional Act No. 17 (AI 17) repealed the former institutional acts which permitted the firing of civil servants (AI 7) and the proscription of new politicians (AI 14). At the end of July, AI 18 rehabilitated the Broad Front and most of the parties that had formed it, except the Communists, restoring political rights

Table 8.1 **The Strategies of the Three Major Parties after Wilson Ferreira's Return and Imprisonment**

	Mobilization	Concerted Action	Negotiation
Colorados	Impossible, as a cadre party	Implement to avoid isolation	Offer military honorable exit
Blancos	Radicalize opposition	Impossible, due to isolation	Reject until Wilson freed
Broad Front	Increase presence and bargaining strength	Appear on an equal footing with traditional parties	Get back into the political game

to 6,500 former politicians and militants. A verbal commitment was made to release 411 prisoners who had served more than half their sentence. The same act also restored the vote to the military, adding seventy thousand (presumably conservative) voters to the electorate.

Although no formal document was signed at the conclusion of the Naval Club Agreement, the participating parties implicitly (and explicitly) subscribed to the Nineteenth Institutional Act, published a year and a day after the decree which had, at least in theory, suspended all public political activity. The provisions of the pact were as follows: (1) for army promotions, the president will choose the commander in chief from a list of three chosen by the generals (two in the other services); (2) the National Security Council survives in an advisory capacity, meeting at the request of the president, with a majority of government ministers; (3) Parliament may vote a "State of Insurrection" suspending individual guarantees; (4) a new legal mechanism, *recurso de amparo*, allows individuals and organizations to appeal government decisions to the courts; (5) military trials continue only for those arrested under the "State of Insurrection"; (6) the National Assembly elected in 1984 will act as a Constituent Assembly; (7) the text, if amended, will be submitted to plebiscite in November 1985. The plenum of the Broad Front voted in favor of these terms 31 to 14 with 6 abstentions.

The Blancos immediately denounced the pact as being repressive and amounting to the prolongation of military rule. Public opinion, however, showed a strong majority in favor of the terms of the deal, despite the fact that army commander in chief General Hugo Medina made it clear that there would be no more lifting of proscriptions. In other words, Wilson and the Communists would not be allowed to run, leaving about five thousand citizens without rights either to vote or run for office, and about three hundred political prisoners at the time of the elections. On the other hand, almost overnight politics flooded the media, and demonstrators were allowed to fill the streets. Nevertheless, the Blancos continued to threaten to cast blank ballots or abstain, arguing that the results were being manipulated. Strictly speaking it could be argued that the military had achieved their goal of a limited democracy, but they had drastically watered down their terms. Even the Communists and extreme Left were allowed to run lists within the Broad Front. When the Communist leader, Rodney Arismendi, returned from exile in Moscow, he was greeted by a mass rally, a motorcade from the airport into Montevideo, and a platform from which to speak. The irony of this reception, compared to Wilson's only a few months earlier, could hardly be lost on anyone.

The original model proposed by Guillermo O'Donnell for successful transitions from authoritarian rule required the existence of moderate oppositions willing to compromise with "soft-liners" within the regime. The trick had to be to isolate and outmaneuver both extremists and opportunists who would too easily be bought off by those in power. A further condition was that supporters would remain loyal to the agreement reached and the compromises that their leaders had been forced to accept. Similarly, the soft-liners in the military had to be sure not to lose power vis-à-vis the hard-liners. In essence, Uruguay did conform to this model but with the quite extraordinary twist that no one had predicted a year before, when all parties declared their commitment to free elections at the foot of the obelisk. In their determination to prevent Wilson from becoming president, the military were willing to rehabilitate the Left and to keep him in jail.

Flisfisch has analyzed the strategies open to parties in regime (non)transitions.[15] Each party's strategy depends on that of its rivals and is the product of their interaction. He thus classifies opposition systems *en masse* according to their predominant strategies—first, their flexibility (willingness to compromise); second, the breadth (inclusiveness) of their alliances. Thus, at the beginning of 1984, Chile's parties were inflexibly opposed to any negotiated reform (rather than rupture) with the authoritarian regime, and split into several narrow alliances. While Brazil's parties showed the symmetrically opposite combination of flexibility and inclusiveness, Uruguay's parties had forged a strong inclusionary alliance (i.e. the multiparty alliance and the intersectoral organization) but were inflexibly opposed to compromising over the holding of totally free elections. In fact, Flisfisch was writing on the eve of a crucial divergence between the three main Uruguayan parties. While the Blancos felt obliged to shift to an exclusionary and inflexible strategy, the Colorados and Broad Front moved toward flexibility in their dealings with the regime. Had the Colorados attempted to move on their own (i.e., flexibility in complete isolation), they would have been dangerously exposed to a campaign of criticism from the other parties.

The Blancos charged the other parties with "opportunism"; the other parties retorted that the Blancos were "free riding" by leaving the "dirty work" to them. In fact, though altruism was not in evidence, there was an advantage for all in the Blancos' intransigence, in that it greatly strengthened the negotiating position of the other parties. Furthermore, the incorporation of the Left into the transition had the added bonus for the future of Uruguayan democracy that it committed the leftists to a peaceful and democratic (i.e., electoral) road to socialism. The contrast with the Chilean Left was stark.

Alfred Stepan has argued that transitions require parties to unite behind procedural democratic pacts, and leave contentious social and economic issues for later, to avoid divisive policy debates. The Uruguayan case was extremely ironic, in that the distance between the parties on a democratic procedural pact was enormous, but relatively bridgeable in terms of actual policies. This may have been the result of gradual ideological convergence between the Broad Front, the Blancos, and even the Colorados with respect to the quite polarized options that they offered voters in 1971. The Blancos, in fact, rejoined the Concertación Programática Nacional, which basically took over from the defunct intersectoral organization and the multiparty alliance.

In discussing the political future of Brazil, Cardoso came to the gloomy prediction that transitions might not lead to full democracy, but merely to liberalization of the regime. This was essentially the controversial accusation of the Blancos and the basis for their opposition to the Naval Club Pact.

Coda: The Elections Go According to Plan

Almost all of the military's attempts at political engineering had failed. Most of the old politicians had survived, and most of the new ones were strongly antiregime, but the military remained chained to their commitment to hand back power. As their opponents threatened to sweep the board, the military revived the electoral system permitting multiple candidacies in each party, to protect their feeble supporters. The threat of founding a new party remained empty. After the hardening of positions at the end of 1983, President Alvarez began to attempt to boost the officialist sectors of the traditional parties instead, by appointing civilian governors in interior departments and a new mayor of Montevideo. A decree of April 1984 increased the chances of Alvarez's civilian nominees of being able to run for office from zero to feasible despite the low level of their support in the convention. There thus emerged two new Blanco presidential tickets: the conservative but antiregime Ortiz/ Ferber and the demagogic rightist and promilitary Payssé/Maeso (headed by the favor-distributing Montevideo mayor). This was a risky and somewhat perverse strategy, since it was inconceivable that these candidates would win if the Wilsonistas took part in the elections. This the Wilsonistas were eventually forced to do, since according to the new law, they would otherwise lose control of the party name and, reality suggested, many of the local bosses in the interior as well. However, with the Wilsonistas running a substitute formula, their rivals' votes would go to them under the "double simultaneous vote," quite possibly ensuring their victory over the Colorados. Hence the need to boost the aging Colorado second ticket, led by the former president, Pacheco. The seventy thousand soldiers, their families, and those of an authoritarian disposition in general thus had a favored option. Pacheco's votes would also be transferred, this time to Sanguinetti. In order to repeat the miracle of a Colorado win over the Blancos, however, the military had to swallow the bitter and ironic pill of legalizing the Left, which they had spent over a decade attempting to eradicate. The only serious risk was that the Left might win the Montevideo mayoralty, but this specter could also be harnessed to scare Blancos into voting for the Colorados.

As the election results trickled in late on 25 November and early the following day, it became clear that the strategy had triumphed. The Colorados came in well ahead of the Blancos, making it hard for the critics of the pact to say that they would have won under fully free elections. The Colorado percentage of the national vote was almost exactly the same in 1984 and 1971—41 percent—but this disguised a loss of votes to the Left in Montevideo and a gain from the Blancos in the rural interior. The Blancos slid from 40 percent to 35 percent nationally, while the Broad Front grew from 18 percent to 21 percent, mostly in Montevideo, though they did not win city hall.

The only surprises were the encouraging growth of newer lists within the traditional parties and the strong support for moderates generally. The two Colorados most associated with the authoritarian reaction and neoliberal economics of the crisis of democracy—Pacheco and Batlle—fared poorly. The Communists' vote stagnated, the extreme Left slumped, and the undogmatic "99th list" surged forward to dominate the Broad Front.[16]

Conclusion: Problems of Political Renovation and "Party Government"

What are the facts of the Uruguayan transition and the lessons for those studying (or even promoting) processes of redemocratization?[17] It is necessary to emphasize that Uruguay's transition really is a case of *re*democratization— that is, a return to democracy. Other transitions from authoritarian rule have come in countries where periods of democratic government had previously been very short, partial, or crisis-ridden. The most striking feature of the Uruguayan case was the fact that the minimally acceptable terms upon which the military, Colorados, and the Broad Front were able to agree were little different from a wholesale restoration of the *status quo ante*. Insofar as Uruguay's former democracy was in crisis, its wholesale restoration has been seen as cause for concern.[18] The simple hypothesis suggests itself that the degree of restoration of the democratic ancien régime is proportional to the length of the previous democracy's life, and inversely related to the length of the authoritarian interlude. Nevertheless, two other factors must be taken into account— and in Uruguay they mattered a great deal. On the one hand, the regime lacked a "foundational plan": those who favored a systematic rupture with the old two-party system were isolated and defeated. On the other hand, the processes of party renovation through participation "from below" were truncated by the preservation of the main precoup political leaders, who (with the exception of Wilson) reemerged willing to reach a deal, if mainly as an expedient.

"Renovation" is a convenient summary term which it is now necessary to split into several different components: emergence of new leaders; changes in parties' and factions' electorates; changes in party organization; changes in party platforms; and changes in the decision-making processes inside parties reflecting an altered internal power structure.

The military insisted that Uruguay's traditional parties needed new faces, new organization, new ideas, and (rhetorically) demanded they become more internally democratic. In practice there arose no "new faces" that were simultaneously popular with the voters and disposed to humor the military. Wilson's sway over the National party was symbolized by the wholesale replacement of his right-hand men and thus those who appeared in prime positions in his list for deputies and the joint Senate list with Movimiento de Rocha. The new Colorados in two cases began as "proxies" who—unlike those in the Blanco party, such as the respected professor of history Pivel Devoto—developed into leaders in their own right. An important sector of new deputies from the "list 85" came along as supporters of one of these—Enrique Tarigo. Tarigo was a bitter opponent of the failed 1980 Constitution, but in some ways his role as a soft-liner vis-à-vis the military (e.g., by favoring elections with proscriptions if necessary) and his key role in the Naval Club talks suggest that the military's original aim of eliminating the old politicians and making a deal with their replacements might have worked had the terms offered originally been more tempting. Tarigo's "85" does not offer renovation along any of the dimensions that we previously mentioned apart from leadership and organization: its program and electorate are clearly within the (historical) mainstream of Batllism. Nor is Sanguinetti such a new face; he was education minister before the coup. Although he has somewhat outgrown Jorge Batlle's "list 15," he remains identified with the list whose leading candidates were without exception survivors from precoup politics.

The major source of renovation, as we saw, came from electoral shifts between factions *within* parties. Apart from that, Uruguay's party system in 1984 was apparently very similar to that of 1971. Yet there are reasons for cautioning against concluding that the country is returning to the old stalemates and crises. For one thing, there may be a more subtle learning process at work that has taught major political actors certain lessons about how to avoid the kind of chaos which might bring a return to military rule. This is very clear in the Broad Front under Seregni's moderate strategy. The Left, however, is engaged in a deadly fight between Communists and non-Communists, which often destabilizes moderate leadership positions in the long run, whoever wins. The same rivalry is currently recurring in the union federation. A Communist victory is not necessarily the most dangerous outcome for the newly elected government, since the legendary discipline of party members can be useful should the party line be to stabilize the new democracy by agreeing to try to reduce strikes and negotiate centralized anti-inflationary wage agreements. This line of reasoning is at least publicly reflected by the new government, which wants secret ballot elections in all unions. These would probably reduce Communist influence, given the relative stagnation of their votes in the elections. But it does not follow that this would dampen militancy or wildcat strikes, or make the explosive wages issue easier to handle.

One of the more clearly unfavorable factors in Uruguay's democratic restoration is the return to the old asymmetry between a strong Left-led labor movement and a simultaneous tendency toward the traditional parties' dominating presidential races.[19] So far, outside the Left, only the Blancos have made serious attempts to work within the union movement. Those who credit the Colorados with a sophisticated degree of *Realpolitik*, however, argue that the new government's naive rhetoric about "nonpolitical" unions and democracy may be an aggressive ploy to strengthen its hand in talks with the opposition. Perhaps at the last moment a "corporatist"-style wage deal of the kind that proved crucial in Spain will emerge. The specter of Argentina is a soberingly close one.

The job of dealing with Uruguay's crisis-ridden political economy has been handed firmly back to the politicians. The $5 billion debt is clearly their major problem, but solutions, if any there be, lie largely outside Uruguay's borders. Greater cooperation among debtors proved an elusive aim. This must be the most frightening reality facing those who won the elections. It was a frequent Colorado charge that it was not in the country's interest to waste time on the details of the transition once the main principles had been assured. This is certainly true: the real story of the reconstruction of stable democracy in Uruguay (or its failure) would begin when Sanguinetti was inaugurated president on 1 March 1985. The Blanco charge, however, was that there was no need for a pact, at least not with politicians still banned, since the military were too far committed to elections. Neither side was really "right"; they were merely behaving logically given the constraints imposed by the military.

Were there any secret agreements at the Naval Club, as the Blancos claimed? Publicly the Colorados are committed to releasing political prisoners under amnesty or parole, and the military seem to be tolerating the idea. They have also promised no "Nuremberg trials" against those who tortured or swindled. They will allow private citizens to bring civil actions, however. This will produce potentially dangerous confrontations. Nevertheless the signs are more favorable than in Argentina, where the scale of assassination was so much higher. Furthermore, the Uruguayan military's parting gesture was to promise military trials for corruption, whereas the Argentine military had issued a vain self-amnesty. This leaves a question mark over torturers and the actions that opposition senators take in launching parliamentary inquiries. These proved particularly destabilizing to the last elected governments.

The military seem to think that the major danger to the new democracy, however, is the threat of "ungovernability": parliamentary turmoil, strikes, and a resurgence of terrorism. A reappearance of terrorism seems to be unlikely in the short run; with regard to strikes, an attempt is being made, however doomed, to reduce labor unrest. I end, therefore, by stressing the need to avoid executive-legislative deadlock, a built-in danger of presidential constitutions that has been exacerbated by the arrival of the three-party system. The real political problem would seem to be the absence or weakness of *party government* in Uruguay. Reform of the electoral system can reduce the parties' factionalism and incoherence, as Luis González has argued.[20] Party government, however, is impossible until the executive is responsible to the legislature, as in the parliamentary system.[21] For Latin Americans such political solutions seem too exotic; their loyalty to the U.S. model may, however, bear a high price.

9 ·

Petroleum and Political Pacts: The Transition to Democracy in Venezuela

Terry Lynn Karl

The tentative reemergence of democracy throughout Latin America has encouraged scholars and policy-makers to take a new look at the "older" democratic experiences on the European continent in their search for viable political models. Just as Chile and Uruguay were once considered the "Switzerlands" of Latin America, so Venezuela has now become the political darling of the development set. As Peter Merkl writes, "It appears that the only trail to a democratic future for developing societies may be the one followed by Venezuela. . . . Venezuela is a textbook case of step-by-step progress."[1] Praxis, however, has produced a certain wariness toward "textbook cases." The sudden demise of past democratic regimes warns that the search for models is fraught with perils. In addition, the development experiences of another country are not easily replicated: the choices and strategies of political actors can seldom be superimposed upon different conditions to produce similar outcomes. Venezuela, despite its current status as a country with an established party system, cannot be expected to provide a formula for those who seek paths to democratization.

Yet the Venezuelan experience of regime transformation in 1958 can yield important lessons for democratization. Specifically, a close examination of the interaction between petroleum and political pacts can illuminate the dynamic relationship between structure and statecraft in moments of political transition. This relationship is the focus of a central debate in political analysis: To what extent is a successful democratic outcome the product of structurally determined factors arising from the world capitalist economy, the international system of states, or the process of dependent development which are beyond the control of political actors in late-developing countries? What role do skillful statecraft, leadership, collective choice and organization, voluntaristic action, or mere *fortuna* play in the institutionalization of a political party system?[2] In order to clarify this debate a structural approach must be systematically related to purposive political action to demonstrate how socioeconomic and political structures at both the national and international level are worked out in a transition to democracy.

196

In the Venezuelan case, petroleum is the single most important factor explaining the creation of the structural conditions for the breakdown of military authoritarianism and the subsequent persistence of a democratic system. The particular economic organization and societal change fostered by petroleum definitively stamped Venezuelan politics and political institutions as well as the organization and class capacities of landlords, peasants, business, and labor. In this manner, it will be argued, an oil-mediated integration into the international market created the necessary structural conditions for a party system. The hypothesis underlying this argument is that different export commodities produce distinct social configurations which, when located in an historical context, shape the propensity for various regime types to emerge. In primary commodity exporters dominated by a single product, this staple affects social class formation, the rise and decline of different groups, the structural potential for organization and consciousness, the development of the state, the relative importance of various political actors, and, finally, the types of sociopolitical alliances that can or cannot be forged. Over time, staple-led development can discourage the emergence of certain regime types at a particular moment while increasing the likelihood of the appearance of other types. Contrary to some previous analyses of Venezuela, this approach places oil in the center of an explanation of regime change.[3]

Yet if petroleum fostered the broad transformations that created the necessary conditions for a democratic outcome in Venezuela, these structurally induced changes are not a sufficient explanation of the successful construction and consolidation of a competitive party regime. Here political pacts play an essential role. The emergence and subsequent character of Venezuela's party regime have been defined by carefully designed agreements among elites that embody a negotiated compromise and establish the future rules for governance. These pacts, whose importance to Venezuela was first highlighted by Daniel Levine, share the distinguishing features of elite cooperation and compromise which characterize "consociational" democracies.[4] As Levine ably demonstrates in his discussion of the Pact of Punto Fijo, they permit elites to develop new norms and operational codes for the regulation of partisan and interest disputes. In the context of petroleum-induced structural change, the presence of pact-making locates statecraft and the successful management of conflict at the heart of an understanding of Venezuela's democratic arrangements.

If Venezuela is to be defined and understood as a "pacted democracy" (*democracia pactada*), however, this conceptualization must be differentiated from consociational or other elite frameworks of democratization. In the consociational literature, attention is focused upon engineering or pact-making at the strictly political level: negotiations between political and economic actors are treated as separate or subsidiary issues rather than as an integral part of the rules for elite accommodation. Since political actors are viewed as the leaders of identity groups, they are not analyzed in the context of concrete socioeconomic interests. The result is a systematic underestimation of the economic component of these political arrangements. In this analysis, however, political actors are viewed as the functional representatives of concrete socioeconomic interests—a relationship that may be indirect and even unintentional. The assumption is that pact-making promulgates regime norms and state structures that channel the possibilities for economic change in an enduring manner. In Venezuela, as we shall see, the set of negotiated compromises embodied by pacts establishes political "rules of the game" which also institutionalize the economic boundaries between the public and private sectors, guarantees for private capital, and the parameters of future socioeconomic reform.

Once this economic component is granted its proper place, it becomes apparent that political pacts have a dual role. On the one hand, they provide a degree of stability and predictability which is reassuring to threatened traditional elites. The rules they establish limit the degree of uncertainty facing all political and economic actors in a moment of transition and therefore are an essential element of successful democratization. On the other hand, this stabilizing influence can have serious consequences for the nature and parameters of the democracy which is established. In relying upon elite negotiations to reconcile the interests of preexisting traditional elites with new challengers, a democracy by pact can institutionalize a conservative bias into the polity, creating a new status quo which can block further progress toward political, social, and economic democracy. Indeed, as the Venezuelan case will demonstrate, pacts can exemplify the conscious creation of a deliberate socioeconomic and political contract that demobilizes new social forces while circumscribing the extent to which all actors can participate or wield power in the future. This is a logical outcome since pact-making among elites, often conducted in secrecy, represents the construction of democracy by antidemocratic means.

The following discussion places the petroleum-induced structural transformation of Venezuela and the formation of elite pacts at the center of an explanation for the successful transition to democracy in 1958. It begins with a broad overview of the structural determinants which increase the likelihood of a democratic outcome in the Venezuelan case. A description of the so-called *trienio* experience and the subsequent transition year of 1957–58 then attempts to clarify the actors involved in regime change, their motivations, their resources, and the actual context of their immediate actions. The analysis next turns to an examination of the elite pacts themselves, highlighting the specific compromises and concessions underlying the modern democratic states as well as the structural and nonstructural conditions allowing political pact-making to occur. Finally, the discussion concludes with observations concerning both the cost and the durability of current democratic arrangements.

The Structural Determinants of Regime Change

Pérez Jiménez's flight from Caracas on 23 January 1958 marked the end of the military rule which had characterized Venezuela since independence. Yet sultanistic authoritarianism was historically dead as a political form long before the general escaped from La Carlota airport, taking with him a significant share of his country's fiscal revenues. The long-term impact of oil, a commodity which initially served to buttress existing regime arrangements, undermined the social basis for authoritarian rule, laying the groundwork for political change.

A historical perspective demonstrates the irony of this statement. The birth of the modern Venezuelan state during the twenty-seven-year rule of the caudillo Juan Vicente Gómez (1908–35) coincided with the discovery and exploitation of oil by foreign companies. As a result of this historic accident in timing, both U.S. multinationals and the U.S. government would become essential props to the formation of modern authoritarian arrangements. Colliding with a weak and fragmented civil society, their impact was overwhelming: petrodollars became the major bulwark of an alliance which included a hierarchy of military caudillos, the coffee and cacao producers of the Andes, and the Caracas commercial and financial elite. The foreign relationship was direct: Gómez himself seized power through a U.S.-backed coup in 1908 and subsequently used the oil companies to maintain the stability of his rule for almost three decades. In return for accommodating the companies through cheap oil concessions and favorable legislation, Gómez received rapidly growing revenues which allowed him to equip the first national army, expand a loyal state bureaucracy, lift the tax burden from elites, and develop a sophisticated repressive apparatus.[5]

Oil initially protected this oligarchic alliance from the disruptive strains of industrialization. Since an oil-mediated integration into the world market provided the revenues for a continuous expansion of the country's import capacity, petrodollars delayed indigenous industrialization in this financially rich country. One manifestation of this structural dynamic was the consistent appreciation of the bolivar in relation to the dollar, a currency movement which created the incentives for imports rather than for domestic production. Although the Depression encouraged manufacturing in Argentina, Chile, Brazil, and Mexico, and brought powerful pressures to expand political participation in these countries, Venezuela was insulated by its unusually strong capacity to import. Accelerated import substitution and the populist strategies that accompanied it in the rest of Latin America did not begin in Venezuela until the end of World War II, almost two decades behind Venezuela's neighbors. This difference in world timing would prove essential for the construction of Venezuela's democracy.

Yet oil eventually set in motion the long-term structural changes in the economy which undermined the organization of the society and polity. The petroleum economy hastened the decline of Venezuela's stagnating agriculture. Oil-induced, overvalued exchange rates destroyed the international competitiveness of coffee and other traditional exports, while the country's high import capacity for foodstuffs hurt the domestic market for agricultural products. With the collapse of coffee and cocoa exports during the Depression, Venezuelan agriculture virtually died: that sector's share of the gross domestic product (GDP) sank from one-third in the mid-1920s to less than one-tenth by 1950, the smallest contribution in all of Latin America. Since petrodollars provided easier ways to keep the economy alive, there were few major efforts to revive the agricultural sector.

The oil-induced agricultural decline had a profound impact upon both the social structure and political behavior of Venezuela's elites—a particularly small and tightly knit class by South American standards. If the condition of the landed upper class is a key variable in the type of political outcomes that arise in the transition from agrarian societies, as Barrington Moore has argued, this class in Venezuela experienced a rapid transformation with the foreign introduction of an oil enclave. As the attractiveness of rural investment declined, the impulse to commercialize agriculture and thus maintain elite control over rural areas also diminished. In "the dance of the concessions," Venezuelan landowners sold their property to the oil companies, converting themselves into the commercial and financial urban bourgeoisie that had once been their nemesis. Rather than continue to mortgage their coffee and cacao to Caracas middlemen, they snapped up the lucrative offers of the multinationals and turned to trading activities. At the same time, this growing mercantile class switched from handling traditional agricultural exports to goods imported from the United States. Thus a close and stable set of relationships evolved between foreign capital, local capital, and the state—frequently held together by the threads of corruption.

But the political price of the decline of the landlord class was high. Without a rural base, the Venezuelan agrarian elite lost the opportunity to have an autonomous political impact. Although it would support the formation of a conservative Christian Democratic party in 1946 and consistently provide this party with its major base in the Andean coffee-growing region, a weak agrarian elite in the postpetroleum era could never supply the social underpinnings for a conservative rural political party comparable to a Partido Nacional in Chile. Even an alliance with the church, another weak force, could not overcome the political results of this structural change. Thus Venezuela lacked a party organization that could shift the political spectrum to the Right in a future electoral arena.

The social and political impact of agriculture's demise was extensive at the mass level as well. The proportion of the work force engaged in rural activities declined rapidly—from 71.6 percent in 1920 to 33.5 percent in 1961. As the stagnation of agriculture forced peasants off the land and into urban areas (see Table 9.1), they became prime targets for political action. The rapid disintegration of strong traditional rural ties, propelled by the lure of jobs in the cities and the oil camps, created the opportunity to organize the peasantry. These peas-

Table 9.1 Population Distribution in Venezuela, 1941–71

Year	Rural	Urban
1941	69%	31%
1950	52	48
1961	37	63
1971	27	73

Source: Daniel Levine, "Venezuela since 1958," in *The Breakdown of Democratic Regimes: Latin America*, ed. Juan Linz and Alfred Stepan (Baltimore: Johns Hopkins University Press, 1978), p. 87.

ants, however, were not propelled toward revolutionary activity, since factors conducive to radical action were lacking in Venezuela. Strong peasant communities did not exist; the rapid commercialization of agriculture had been blocked by food imports paid for through oil revenues; and most important, the zero-sum conflict necessary to produce peasant revolutions in other countries was absent. Oil eased the virulence of landlord-peasant disputes, providing a permanent "exit" from the land for both elites and masses. If political change was unlikely to be authoritarian owing to the weakness of the rural elite, a revolutionary turn was arguably doubtful as well.[6]

In this context, the growth and transformation of urban Venezuela provided fertile ground for a reformist democratic regime. Once again, oil played a decisive role, creating the first significant internal market as well as the urban social forces which have historically provided the backbone of party systems in Latin America. As agriculture declined, the import and service sectors expanded rapidly, fueled by petroleum revenues. Total wages and salaries paid to the oil sector alone increased eightfold in the decade of the 1920s, while imports soared; between 1913 and 1926 alone, they leapt in value from U.S.$2,372,000 to U.S.$14,297,000. The most important social phenomenon resulting from the introduction and consolidation of the oil enclave economy was the emergence of a middle class composed primarily of propertied and salaried small artisans and white-collar workers in the service sector. Their numbers were complemented by a rapidly expanding state bureaucracy that swelled from 13,500 to 56,000 in a mere fifteen years. This middle class continued to increase following the death of Gómez, rising from 36.8 percent to 54 percent of the nonagricultural work force between 1936 and 1950.[7]

Of necessity, the aspirations and demands of these *capas medias* dominated the political arena. The oil economy fostered the emergence of an inverted pyramid of social classes: the generation and rapid circulation of petrodollars, a function of rent rather than real productive activities, meant that a largely nonproductive urban middle class actually preceded and outnumbered a slowly growing working class. In addition to the advantages of its size and political experience, this middle sector could control mass politics because of the weakness of the working class. Although the petroleum industry had created a modern industrial force, the capital intensity of the industry kept the number of oil workers to less than 26,000. While militantly organized, primarily by the Communist party of Venezuela, their small numbers and isolation in camps far from urban centers hindered workers' ability to make a powerful political impact. They could not unite with their industrial counterparts in the cities until the 1950s, since a politically significant working class in manufacturing simply did not exist before that time. A small and geographically fragmented proletariat was not conducive to the formation of large Socialist or Communist parties like those of Argentina or Chile. Since petroleum workers had to align with forces in the urban areas in order to win their labor demands, they became prime organizing candidates for reformist parties based in Caracas.

The beginning of significant industrialization, an event which did not take place in Venezuela until the 1950s, was the final structural condition for a reformist regime change. Once again, an oil-mediated integration into the international system was the motor for economic transformation. As a result of soaring demand for petroleum in the postwar period, the Iranian crisis of 1954, and the closing of the Suez Canal, Venezuela experienced a phenomenal economic boom which literally forced the country into industrialization. In the period between 1950 and 1957, Venezuela accumulated more foreign exchange than any other nation in the world except West Germany. As treasury reserves tripled and oil exports increased $2^{1}/_2$ times, the impact upon the domestic economy was immediate. Fueled by a high level of public expenditures that created a parallel expansion of aggregate demand, manufacturing grew 313 percent; the average investment rate was a staggering 28.3 percent.

This industrialization (see Table 9.2) carried the prospects for democracy a step further. While the decline of agriculture and the creation of new urban social classes undermined the old regime, manufacturing provided the necessary material base for a qualitatively new alliance. The timing of this industrialization was particularly important. Since it did not begin until the 1950s, a period of international expansion, rather than the 1930s, a period of international contraction, direct foreign investment played an unusually large role

Table 9.2 **Growth of Manufacturing Output in Venezuela, 1948–57**
(index: 1948 = 100)

1948	100	1953	251
1949	118	1954	286
1950	154	1955	333
1951	186	1956	364
1952	205	1957	413

Source: John Salazar-Carrillo, *Oil in the Economic Development of Venezuela* (New York: Praeger, 1976), p. 119.

from the beginning—contrary to the experiences of other Latin American countries. In this decade, direct foreign investment increased from $938 million to $3.71 billion, the largest concentration in any Latin American nation. Investment in manufacturing grew most rapidly. The political implications of this close intertwining of foreign and local capital were profound: by 1958, there were specific national and international interests that could be convinced of the need to defend an industrialization program. Although their numbers were small, they were united, highly concentrated, and economically powerful.

The Lessons of the Trienio Years

In 1946, Acción Democrática (AD), a new political party, was given an unexpected chance to govern, a mere two years after the party's founding. Invited to share power with the military (which utilized the new party to avoid an internal succession struggle after the ouster of General Medina), AD ruled for three crisis-filled years before its overthrow by the armed forces. This three-year period, the *trienio*, proved to be an important training ground for political leadership as well as a valuable educational experience for other Venezuelan elites. The military rule of Generals López Contreras and Medina Angarita, the successors of Gómez, had been characterized by pendular swings between liberalization and repression, reflecting the slowly growing collision of new urban social forces with a dying but unyielding oligarchy. The trienio experience, following in the wake of World War II, tipped the balance toward a new regime by changing the perceptions and ideologies of elites, particularly with regard to industrialization and a political party system.

The vision, leadership, and organization provided by Acción Democrática and party founder Rómulo Betancourt were required to transform Venezuela's changing structural realities into a viable political program. Betancourt traveled the length and breadth of Venezuela in order to understand the national situation, laying the basis for a party headquarters in every region of the country. He and other party leaders then drew up a platform for the Partido Democrático Nacional, the forerunner of AD, which declared "*gomecismo*, the landowners, the usurer banks, and foreign imperialism" to be the enemies of Venezuela and the target of their political action. This position could mobilize and unite the peasants in declining agrarian sectors with the militant oil workers and the emerging middle and industrial classes in Caracas. The party's program was radical, since it took a direct stance against the traditional authoritarian alliance, but the party leaders had the foresight to base it on a broad united front which could include some traditional elites. It explicitly rejected the Communist party's organizing doctrine, which was based upon the notion of class struggle led by workers. Instead, demonstrating a knowledge of Venezuelan reality, AD argued that the industrial working class was too small and weak to lead a regime change and that agrarian reform in a declining sector could be accomplished by peaceful means without alienating traditional urban elites.

Industrialization was the cement which could unite newly emerging social forces with entrepreneurial elites in a party form; thus it became a central aspect of the party platform. Industrialization could avoid a zero-sum struggle by providing practical benefits for all Venezuelans. As the AD program stated:

> We are aiming to put into practice a wide spectrum which will awaken and sustain private initiative through cheap credits and rational protective tariffs to fight the invasion of foreign products. This, and the increase in the buying power of the population through an honest and broad social policy, will increase the domestic market, a necessary step in the development of a national industry and agriculture. We do not make our fervent proclamation for a policy of bettering the conditions of workers and peasants only through loyalty to the principles of social justice. . . . We also recognize a scientific and practical reason: without this improvement, the internal market necessary for a Venezuelan agriculture and industry cannot be created.[8]

Agrarian reform was also a key component of the party's plans for the future, yet the party was careful to avoid references to collectivization or expropriation without compensation of domestic properties, which might frighten Caracas-based elites. Finally, the nationalization of the oil companies, the symbols of foreign domination, was another central element of the party's plan.

The outbreak of World War II boosted AD's industrial vision, since it prompted the first visible change in economic and political attitudes on the part of Venezuela's normally intransigent economic family groups. A large decline in wartime oil sales to Europe had forced the Medina government to implement tight import controls to protect scarce foreign exchange—the first state action of this kind in Venezuela's history. As hardship struck the urban middle classes, leading to increased support for both Acción Democrática and the Communist party, elite fears of social disruption increased. Landowners and the commercial class believed that AD represented a radical future that implied their own demise and nicknamed the party *adeco*, meaning AD–Communist. Yet some farsighted representatives of the economic elite like Eugenio Mendoza, a young entrepreneur and Medina's minister of development, began to call upon Venezuelans to "dress ourselves in our own textiles, take advantage of the production of our nascent industry, and feel noble pride in all that is Venezuelan."[9] Profoundly shaken by wartime scarcity, Venezuelans began to see the value of industrialization.

The war experience and talk of industrialization also began to affect the attitudes of key economic leaders toward the appropriate role for the state. Trade and financial figures such as J. J. González Gorrondona and Rudolfo Rojas, influenced by the New Deal's solution to socioeconomic problems in the United States, discussed planning, protective tariffs, the technification of the state, progressive services such as social security, and indigenous industrial development. Some entrepreneurs began to believe that an interventionist state, a heretical concept in the prewar period, was the only possible guarantee for domestic production and the prevention of social turmoil. In 1944, the nation's most important banker argued: "The state must guarantee the normal development of production, consumption, and trade because if it evades that responsibility and abandons economic activity to the free play of private interests as the liberals argue, this will lead to a systematic repetition of economic cycles, wars, and all types of other disturbances which bring anguish into our social life."[10] While this attitude was fiercely resisted by more conservative agrarian elites, some of their urban counterparts began to see that the political and economic platform of a party like Acción Democrática, while certainly too radical, might hold some possibilities.

World War II also began to affect the ideology of the military in a manner which would ultimately be advantageous for Acción Democrática. Following the death of Gómez, the linchpin of the military hierarchy, disagreements had surfaced within that institution concerning succession, the closed system of advancement, and the conservative bent of Gomecistas such as General López Contreras. As young officers returned from studies and service abroad during the war, they brought newly acquired technical skills, a different conception of a professional military, and fresh ideas originating from their exposure to intense postwar democratic sentiment. They questioned the adequacy of the old army hierarchy for the modernization of Venezuela. In 1954, a group of young officers formed the Union Patriótica Militar and signed a secret oath which proclaimed "the profession of our democratic faith. . . . we advocate the formation of a government that has as its basis the universal and direct vote of the Venezuelan citizenry, a reform of the Constitution . . . and the creation of a truly professional army."[11] Although this democratic faction temporarily lost power in the coup which removed AD in 1948, it remained active in the military and became an important ally of the political parties in the next decade.

The most important political development, however, took place in Acción Democrática during its three years in power. First, AD began to appreciate the value of an organized popular constituency. Indeed, to the dismay of other parties, it took advantage of its control of the state to form and dominate the Confederation of Venezuelan Workers and the Confederation of Venezuelan Peasants. Although both organizations became illegal after the trienio, they provided much of the party's future organizational basis and political clout. The importance of these confederations should not be underestimated. In a mere three years, AD raised the number of organized peasants from 3,959 to 43,302 while increasing the number of legal labor unions from 252 to 1,014.[12] Second, the new party learned the importance of compromise. Isolated and driven underground in 1948, AD understood that it had driven away potential allies during the trienio, especially through its strong actions against Catholic education—a move that alienated both the church and the new Christian Democratic party (COPEI)—and its failure to consult with the other political parties. It would be careful to avoid sectarian behavior in the future.

The trienio government of 1946–48 was premature, a product of elite responses to a changing international context rather than the political product of an emerging mass party. With hindsight, given the weakness of the consensus for increased participation and industrialization, it is easy to see that the first AD government was unlikely to survive. Although "sowing the petroleum" had become a national slogan, an industrial effort and the subsequent creation of socioeconomic forces with a material stake in a party system had yet to occur. Furthermore, as the international oil market recovered, the oil companies reacted to AD's talk of nationalization by threatening to move operations to the Middle East. Fearing another economic crisis, local entrepreneurs withdrew their support for democratic rule. As the fragile consensus fell apart, there was no margin for political error. But Acción Democrática, an inexperienced party, made political errors even as it took advantage of its position in the state. Yet one reality remained: although military rule was promptly restored, the structural transformation of the economy and society had been accelerated during this period, in part through AD's emphasis upon industrial activity. It was merely a matter of time before the disjuncture between an outmoded polity and an increasingly complex economy and society reached crisis point again.

The Politics of Transition: 1957–58

If the vibrant oil-led industrial boom of the 1950s prepared Venezuela for a regime change, the form, timing, and dynamics of its expression were not predetermined. Although demands for participation had grown, sultanistic authoritarianism might have been able to maintain a hold for a longer period if Pérez Jiménez had possessed some degree of political skill. Instead, his systematic and often unnecessary alienation of the key actors in the authoritarian alliance stimulated a breakdown from within—an internal decay which provoked pressure for a transfer of power from within the military institution itself. The fall of Pérez Jiménez, however, does not explain the collapse of military authoritarianism as a system, nor can it account for the subsequent establishment of a political party system. Here other factors intervene. From 1957 to 1958, the fruits of creative and persistent party-building as well as the political experience acquired in the trienio years were finally harvested. Intelligent leadership directing an organized and mobilized civilian population confronted a divided military and an isolated entrepreneurial class. This converted a simple transfer of power among traditional elites into a surrender of power to new historic actors.

The coincidence of a political succession crisis with an economic crisis was the catalyst for regime change. Pérez Jiménez had come to power in a coup in 1948 and had declared himself president by cancelling the elections of 1952. In order to resolve the new leadership dilemma posed by presidential elections scheduled for 1957, Pérez Jiménez rigged a plebiscite sponsored by the legislature and announced his intention to remain in power indefinitely. The outlawed political parties, led by AD, openly protested.[13] A fiscal crisis, appearing on the heels of the plebiscite decision, led the conservative economic elites to join the parties. By 1957, Pérez Jiménez's astounding levels of public spending in the wake of the oil boom of the 1950s had exceeded the nation's capacity to pay. Even industrialists in the construction sector, generally his greatest allies because they received the benefits from public works projects, were left with unpaid bills from the state. Since Venezuela's international credit status suffered, Pérez Jiménez attempted to conceal his overspending and corruption by selling new concessions to the oil companies—a controversial move given widespread nationalist sentiment against the multinationals. As his financial policies brought the economy to the point of crisis in the final months of 1957, well-known entrepreneurs such as Blas Lamberti and Eugenio Mendoza issued public manifestos calling for "the normalization and dignifying of the administration of public monies."[14]

Accusations of economic mismanagement prompted other long-standing complaints from entrepreneurs regarding the lack of protection for national industry as well as the growing role of the state. In 1952, the government had renewed a treaty of reciprocal trade with the United States which permitted a wide range of cheap imported manufactured products to overrun national markets. Non-construction-related industries suffered. Despite repeated appeals to renegotiate the treaty or establish some type of protection for local entrepreneurs, Pérez Jiménez refused to raise tariffs and actually cut industrial credits to all sectors but construction. His simultaneous encouragement of foreign capital inflows, which tripled during his government, threatened local initiative. Pérez Jiménez also began to expand the state into direct production at the expense of the domestic private sector. Although he had originally assured Eugenio Mendoza and other businessmen that the government would not enter the steel sector, the general apparently changed his mind and overruled local proposals for a privately owned mill put forward by the Sindicato de Hierro. In his first open conflict with entrepreneurs, Pérez Jiménez reserved steel, electrification, and petrochemicals for the public sector by establishing state enterprises in each area.[15]

This squeeze on domestic industry was compounded by the lack of formal entrepreneurial access to state decision-making. Since the general favored a particular group of contractors linked to him through corruption, he paid little attention to organized business associations such as Fedecámaras which attempted to represent the entire economic elite. As favoritism grew, important factions of the economic elite felt that they had little access to decisions affecting economic policy. The fixed plebiscite threatened to institutionalize this situation permanently.[16]

The general's intention to remain in power also sparked church opposition. Like the entrepreneurs, the church had been a particular beneficiary of military rule. Virulently hostile to Acción Democrática because of that party's secularizing, anti-Catholic, and reformist policies, it had welcomed the 1948 coup with enthusiasm. Although the local religious hierarchy was content with authoritarian arrangements, changes were occurring within the church at an international level. The papal declarations of Pius XII, urging more sensitivity to social justice, encouraged several Catholic publications to gently remind the government of its duties toward the lower classes in editorials published on May Day. Unused to criticism of any sort, government reaction was swift and overbearing: Minister of Interior Valenilla Lanz summoned the archbishop of Caracas to his office and ordered the church to adopt a lower profile. When the Seguridad Nacional, the political police, detained Padre Hernández, a well-known opposition priest, and harassed other important figures of the church hierarchy on the dictator's orders, the church and the Christian Democratic party (which had never been declared illegal) also moved into the opposition.

As elite civilian support crumbled, the military became the focus of the regime's decay. Pérez Jiménez had initially been careful to placate his own institution, allocating huge funds for military purposes, expanding personnel, purchasing expensive equipment, raising salaries, and virtually creating the navy and the air force. Yet the general's extraordinary levels of corruption, combined with his total reliance upon unpopular civilian ministers such as Valenilla Lanz and Pedro Estrada, alarmed younger officers. More important, he created a parallel military authority through the political police (the Seguridad Nacional), investing it with the power to punish military officers suspected of disloyalty to the government. Discontent crystallized in two factions: the first, mostly higher officers linked to the government, attempted to pressure Pérez into correcting some of the abuses of his rule; the second, composed of younger officers organized in Movimiento para la Liberación Nacional (MLN), sought his overthrow.

Divisions within the military created their own dynamics. As Pérez Jiménez became increasingly suspicious of possible disloyalty, he relied more heavily upon the Seguridad Nacional, using the security forces to arrest officers suspected of treason. As arbitrary use of power against his own military increased, factionalism grew, fueled by the government's activities against Catholics and other civilians. By December 1957, although Pérez Jiménez publicly claimed to have the united support of the armed forces, distrust was so widespread that different divisions had begun to guard each other. When the MLN attempted a futile *quartelazo* to remove Pérez Jiménez on 1 January 1958, it provoked a cabinet crisis in mid-January. On 9 January, Pérez Jiménez's ministers were forced to resign, and a new group was appointed, including known opponents of the general. On 13 January, Pérez Jiménez went on a counteroffensive, appointing himself minister of defense. Amid cabinet reshufflings, coup attempts, and arrests, a new military consensus was formed: Pérez Jiménez had to be removed in order to maintain the unity of the armed forces.[17]

By the time the military and the economic elites finally acted, in January 1958, they had lost their ability to control events or determine the direction of future political change on their own. Initiative had moved to the political parties, who were prepared to exercise political leadership. The organization of each party had strengthened, and their leadership had also matured. Brought together by the common experience of repression and having learned about the dangers of sectarianism from the trienio failure, party representatives agreed to an initiative by the URD and the Venezuelan Communist party to form the Junta Patriótica, the first umbrella organization for all parties, in June 1957. Insisting that all parties must overcome partisan struggles and "act jointly without hate or vengeance," this clandestine organization succeeded in coordinating the opposition activities of parties and student groups which had previously been unable to work together.

But unity had different meanings for different actors. As the Junta Patriótica sought to bring all forces inside Venezuela together in a radical program to oust Pérez Jiménez, some economic and political party elites had a different plan. Fearful that events might spiral out of control, four Venezuelan leaders—Rómulo Betancourt (AD), Rafael Caldera (COPEI), Jovito Villalba (URD), and Eugenio Mendoza—met secretly in New York to discuss the composition and parameters of the government which would follow the demise of Pérez Jiménez. They agreed to abide by some mutually acceptable power-sharing formula and to reject any transition arrangement offered by the military. Furthermore, they quietly decided to exclude the Communist party from claims to equal partnership, despite the party's leading role in the resistance.[18] This arrangement was made without the knowledge of the base of the Junta Patriótica, which continued to work in a broad united front.

On 10 January, in the midst of the cabinet crisis, the Junta Patriótica defied the military by calling a massive civilian demonstration in Caracas. Two days later, it had established itself as the principal organ for the coordination of all civilian action. On 21 January, the Junta Patriótica called a general strike to force Pérez Jiménez from power. AD-led trade unions promptly joined. As people poured into the streets, church bells rang at noon to demonstrate Catholic support for the strike. The Consejo Nacional de Banqueros, the Cámara de Industria, and the Cámara de Construcción, the former bastion of regime support, also backed the general strike, stating:

> The economic structure of Venezuela cannot withstand the political chaos facing the country. The Nation's patrimony is menaced and urgent protective measures must be taken to avoid a crash of commerce, industry, and banking. The return to normalcy can be contemplated only in a climate of security and guarantees, the free play of supply and demand, and equal opportunities to intervene in political and economic activity.[19]

The military refused to leave the barracks to put down the general strike. On 23 January, with the entire city of Caracas mobilized and demonstrations taking place around the country, Pérez Jiménez agreed to leave.

A military junta, led by Admiral Wolfgang Larrazabal and composed of four other officers, attempted to reestablish the authority of the armed forces, but the pressure for democratization was too powerful. The Junta Patriótica declared that further military rule was unacceptable and protested the inclusion of two colonels linked to Pérez Jiménez in the new junta. Crowds again poured into the streets, supporting demands for an end to military rule, only to be fired upon by the Seguridad Nacional. Although Admiral Larrazabal promptly promised elections in the near future, protests continued. With the death toll climbing to over 250, the National Guard joined civilians in a battle against the police. Fearing that the country was on the brink of civil war, the armed forces agreed to change the composition of the new ruling junta. Eugenio Mendoza and Blas Lamberti, another civilian entrepreneur, were asked to join the government and the Perezjimenista colonels were ousted. The Junta Patriótica, dominated by AD and the other political parties, met with the new ruling junta and promised to reestablish social peace in return for democratic elections. On 27 January, Admiral Larrazabal publicly announced the military junta's decision: Venezuela would be democratic.

Negotiating Democracy: The Political and Economic Pacts of Elites

The nature of Venezuela's new democracy was profoundly affected by the manner in which the authoritarian regime broke down. Although long-term structural changes had strengthened emerging social forces at the expense of traditional interests, the ability of new actors to define a different order was always constrained by the persistent power, or the appearance of power, of "nostalgic" elites who sought to limit reform. The definition of democracy which eventually emerged depended largely upon the perceptions formed and the political skills exercised in the immediate context of transition—a context still delineated by traditional elite actors.

The fall of Pérez Jiménez in 1958 plunged the country into acute political and economic crisis. Crowds filled the streets calling for jobs, condemning the oil companies for their support of the past government, and sacking the homes of members of Pérez Jiménez's clique. On the advice of the political and economic leaders who had previously met in New York, the government announced an Emergency Plan consisting of wage subsidies and a massive public works campaign which was intended to defuse the intense mobilization while containing the potentially hostile reaction of economic elites. On 15 February, the unions, following AD's leadership, accepted this proposal and guaranteed labor peace in all major industrial sectors in return for the promise that factory owners would refrain from reducing personnel in their plants. As a quid pro quo, the government consented to pay the outstanding debts left by Pérez Jiménez to the private sector, despite the illegality and corruption of many of the contracts. The cost of this package of agreements, negotiated primarily through Acción Democrática, was enormous. The combination of the Emergency Plan and the payment of $1.4 billion to bankers and industrialists resulted in "a huge dole given on terms that had never been equaled in any other country."[20]

Ironically, the oil revenues which underwrote this arrangement for social peace became an important source of pressure for the limitation of reform. The oil companies, fearful of nationalization and social unrest, threatened to transfer their operations to the Middle East if disruption continued—a powerful warning in the context of the declining oil prices following the end of the 1950s boom. The constant fear of intervention from the U.S. government, which supported the companies, added to the atmosphere of constraint. In March 1958, during an official visit to Caracas, Vice-President Richard Nixon was surrounded by demonstrators, protesting the Eisenhower administration's decision to grant asylum to Pérez Jiménez. This brought a rapid U.S. response: marine and air force transports were sent into the Caribbean "in the event their assistance would be required."[21] In the context of the recent U.S.-directed overthrow of the reformist Arbenz government in nearby Guatemala, as well as the CIA-sponsored coup in Iran, another oil-producing nation with the temerity to confront a regime propped up by the oil companies, the lessons were not lost: the United States would protect the companies if necessary and contain unruly radicalism.

Nevertheless, the most immediate obstacle in the way of a successful transition to democracy as well as overly enthusiastic reform efforts lay closer to home. Right-wing army officers belonging to a group called Pro Fuerzas Armadas Nacionales (PROFAN) refused to accept Admiral Larrazabal's promise to implement a party system that might include AD and perhaps the Communist party. Outraged by the Nixon incident, air force general Castro León, minister of defense in the provisional government, sent troops to control strategic points of Caracas and began a round-up of *adecos* and Communists. His coup attempt was blocked by the combined pressure of Rafael Caldera, Jovito Villalba, and Eugenio Mendoza. Keeping their New York agreement with Betancourt, they told Castro León that there was no civilian support for continued military rule or for a party system which tried to exclude AD. Representatives of Fedecámaras, backing the leading industrialists, warned that commercial and industrial sectors would suspend all operations in the country if the military tried to stop the transition to democracy. Meanwhile, the Junta Patriótica turned 300,000 people into the streets of Caracas to protest Castro León's actions. When senior commanders and unit heads refused to come to his support, his coup attempt failed. Yet *golpistas* continued to act throughout the year, leaving the threat of a coup hanging over the transition process like Damocles' sword.[22]

The conservative pressure from the oil companies, the United States, and *golpista* officers found functional allies among a variety of forces which shared a different yet compatible goal: the desire to limit the power of Acción Democrática. The majority of the armed forces wanted to withdraw from power in order to maintain the institutional integrity of the military. The church, weakened by its long association with authoritarian rule, wanted merely to protect its position. Both forces were anxious to remove themselves from the political arena if they could extract agreements from the parties, primarily AD, guaranteeing their economic and institutional survival. The economic elites wanted their property rights protected, labor controlled, their losses minimized, and the economic situation stabilized. Those with a greater vision, such as Eugenio Mendoza and Gustavo Vollmer, called for state protection for local industrialization—a goal that could provide future earnings as well as diversification away from oil dependence. Yet, driven by fears of populism or socialism, they too sought some formula which could contain any future radicalization arising from AD's leadership in a truly competitive party environment.

The other political parties also wanted to circumscribe the power of Acción Democrática. Although each had a concrete stake in the establishment of a party system, and therefore some incentive to overcome partisan disputes, COPEI and the URD feared the possible hegemonic pretensions on the part of AD given its overwhelming popularity as the "party of the people." Thus, as they sought to limit the future power of AD for their own partisan reasons, they became the de facto allies of the entrepreneurs, the oil companies, the U.S. government, the church, and the military. COPEI, in particular, represented traditional elite interests—a role it played with relative ease owing to its conservative Andean origins. The desire of these parties to delineate carefully the role of Acción Democrática, in conjunction with other traditionally conservative forces, meant the containment of future reform, a reality which would be reflected in the political and economic agreements that formed the basis of the new regime.

In order to accommodate the demands and desires of new politically organized actors without significantly threatening the interests of those who were strong enough to reverse the process of change, democratization required an explicit definition of the new parameters of action and the rules of the game, both formal and informal, which could guarantee the basic objectives of all actors. These institutional arrangements were established through several interlocking elite-negotiated pacts formulated in 1958 and refined during the first years of the Betancourt administration. The Pact of Punto Fijo and "Statement of Principles and Minimum Program of Government," signed prior to the country's first elections by all presidential candidates, bound all signatories to the same basic political and economic program, regardless of the electoral outcome. Only the Communist party was excluded from the two agreements.

The military pact was the first key compromise. In return for accepting a new role, defined as that of an "apolitical, obedient, and nondeliberative body," the armed forces received the state's promise to increase technology and modernize equipment, improve the economic situation of officers and enlisted men, and maintain obligatory military service.[23] In an implicit agreement to remove the question of accountability for its role during the Pérez Jiménez period, the military was assured that all parties would renounce thoughts of trials of military leaders and "recognize the merits and service of the men who made up the Armed Forces and their important collaboration in the maintenance of public peace." This was not mere rhetoric. After 1958 the parties would make a consistent effort to uphold the notion of the military as the repository of national values. The church also received guarantees. While these were not explicit in the original document, the first new AD government immediately altered the church's legal status, granting it greater independence from the state. All political parties also promised to increase their subsidies to the religious establishment.[24]

The political components of pact-making were embodied in the Pact of Punto Fijo. This guaranteed that all parties would respect the electoral process and share power in a manner commensurate with the voting results. In addition, the parties promised to maintain a "prolonged political truce" which would depersonalize debate as well as ensure consultation among the parties. This truce, although not involving explicit power quotas, did require the formation of coalitions and an equitable distribution of state benefits. Regardless of who won the elections, each party was guaranteed some participation in the political and economic pie through access to state jobs and contracts, a partitioning of the ministries, and a complicated spoils system which would ensure the political survival of all signatories.[25] This political formula was the result of intense negotiations among the parties between August and October of 1958, after a previous proposal to put forward a single presidential candidate had been defeated. It would be carefully implemented by President Betancourt.

The political spirit of the Punto Fijo pact was institutionalized in the Venezuelan Constitution of 1961 and thus became an integral part of the state. Reflecting Venezuela's tradition of highly centralized power, as well as the need for a mediator above the parties, the president became the supreme arbiter in the country. The office of the president was given control of the nation's defense, the monetary system, all tax and tariff policy, the exploitation of subsoil rights, the management of foreign affairs, and a variety of other powers; it had the authority to name all cabinet ministers, state governors, and state enterprise officials and declare a state of emergency. In essence, the decision regarding power-sharing belonged to the president, who was supposed to be nonpartisan. A non-reelection clause was aimed in part at weakening party control over the national leader, although it also protected against *continuismo*. The ramifications of this arrangement, however, were felt in the future. Since immediate reelection had been ruled out, Venezuelan presidents would be less responsive to their electoral and party base and more open to the influences of interest groups.

The powers of Congress, on the other hand, were fashioned with the aim of containing political competition. On the one hand, party influence was maximized, since the electoral law provided for a system of proportional representation by party which encouraged partisan control over legislators. The Chamber of Deputies and the Senate were divided into party factions headed by a chairman who was the representative of the party's national central executive committee. On the other hand, the power of the legislature itself was carefully circumscribed in order to limit the perceived dangers which could result from free-ranging competition between the parties. Congressional committees were extremely weak, with few financial or human resources at their disposal; thus it was difficult to initiate legislation or adequately criticize laws originating in the executive. Although parties had finally won a forum for debate and political struggle, the outcome of those struggles in Congress would be relatively insignificant, with the single exception of the five-year electoral cycle.

The possibility of radicalization and partisan conflict stemming from widespread debate was further contained by the Minimum Program of Government, a document which specified the broad outlines of the country's new economic project and exemplified the programmatic compromises conceded by AD. All parties agreed to accept a development model based upon foreign and local private capital accumulation, a basic law codified in the new constitution. They also promised to subsidize the private sector through the Corporación Venezolana de Fomento as well as provide high levels of protection to local industry. The Minimum Program also ruled out the possibility of expropriation. Although it proposed an agrarian reform, it promised that changes in land tenure would be based upon a principle of compensation. Demands for the nationalization of the foreign-owned oil and steel companies were not raised. Although future state policy would insist upon greater participation in revenues from oil and a firm "no concessions" policy, the continued presence of the multinationals in extractive industry was guaranteed in the new democracy—an important retreat from AD's former nationalization policy.

Having granted these substantive assurances to the country's industrial and financial interests, AD and the other political parties received a quid pro quo. The role of the state in the economy was expanded—a development which could only enhance the power of those in control of the political sphere. Although state expansion was a virtual *fait accompli* inherited from the Pérez Jiménez years, it was still viewed with trepidation by the economic elite. Yet the increased job opportunities for politicians, bureaucrats, and technicians were attractive to the large urban middle class, and the implicit nationalism of state ownership of strategic sectors pleased the military. The party system would thus promote a state role in direct production as well as the regulation of the economy.

Political parties also won important new benefits for their organized labor, peasant, and middle-class base. The Minimum Program promised to pursue full employment, a major housing program for the poor, a new labor code, and widespread social legislation in health, education, and social security. Recognizing that "work is the fundamental element of economic progress," the democratic regime granted trade union rights and the freedom of association. In practice this meant that the state would intervene in the process of collective bargaining in favor of the Confederation of Venezuelan Workers as well as the Peasant Federation, both closely linked to Acción Democrática. In addition, the state would provide various subsidies in food, housing, and welfare for the popular sectors.

The Minimum Program of Government and the Pact of Punto Fijo thus represented a classic exchange, primarily between AD and the entrepreneurs, of "the right to rule for the right to make money." The party system implemented did have the power to channel elite demands through political parties, but fundamental policies toward industry, the petroleum companies, labor, and the peasantry were decided *before* any elections were held, thus changing potential issues into established parameters by removing them from the electoral arena. In essence, the overall rules of production were determined prior to a national debate, while future partisan conflict was confined to a largely powerless Congress. This depoliticization of broad economic questions was guaranteed to continue as long as the basic compromise served to bind all parties. Although the signatories could struggle over issues not included in the Minimum Program, they could not cross previously accepted economic boundaries.

Structure and Statecraft in Venezuela's Democratization

Despite the intelligence of the democratic design, the viability of Venezuela's democracy by pact always rested upon the existence of a structurally created opportunity for democracy providing the political and economic space for the accommodation of divergent interests. Without this structural opportunity, the will, intentions, and political experience of individuals could not alone have produced the desired outcome. Petroleum stands out as the most important element here. In the short run, petrodollars financed an emergency plan that calmed the atmosphere during the transition to democracy. In the long run, petroleum provided the fiscal revenues upon which democratic administrations depended to maintain the ambiguous, and expensive, situation of fomenting the growth of a private sector while simultaneously granting favors to the middle and working classes. Concretely, each government granted extensive subsidies, contracts, and infrastructure to entrepreneurs while charging the lowest taxes on the continent and allowing some of the highest profits. At the same time, democratic governments could afford to support collective bargaining for the highest wages on the continent, price controls, huge food subsidies, and an agrarian reform.

Oil revenues paid the bill for Venezuela's pacted democracy, subsidizing both business and the popular sectors. They protected the country from the inflation and balance-of-payments problems that plagued other party systems with similar economic projects. Indeed, Venezuela had a persistent advantage that earlier democracies like those of Argentina and Chile lacked: if it needed more revenues, the state could always pressure the foreign-controlled oil industry rather than its own population. Since capital accumulation actually took place through the transfer of resources from the oil sector to other parts of the economy, this fiscal avenue mitigated those economic tensions that would eventually have required a reduction in wages and benefits for labor—a situation that generally spelled the demise of political democracy.

Over time, as we have seen, the impact of petroleum also produced a social class formation conducive to democratization. Given Venezuela's small size, this had particular advantages that have not yet been mentioned. Oil-induced development delayed the formation and organization of all social classes. Subsequently, the small number of elite actors produced, in part, by this phenomenon was essential to the process of accommodation, since this facilitated interelite bargaining as well as the control which leaders like Betancourt or Mendoza could exercise over their constituencies. The small entrepreneurial class, for example, was characterized by unusually high levels of concentration and centralization of capital, strong links with foreign investment, a low level of competition, and few of the political or economic divisions found among non-oil-based elites—factors which contributed to their united stance in pact-making. A slowly emerging working class and a dying landlord class largely explained the weakness of the Right and the Left—another favorable condition for democratization through pact-making.[26] Their lack of strength meant that the perceived costs of their partial exclusion were relatively low. The peculiar characteristics of petroleum development also facilitated the communication and discipline of the political parties. The parties could capture the loyalties of a rapidly growing urban middle class with little competition from weak or nonexistent interest associations.

Yet oil-based development was only part of the structural conditions that favored democratization. In the early 1960s, the international state system encouraged a democratic outcome while simultaneously limiting the degree of democracy in the new party system. This was largely the result of the timing of Venezuela's regime change, rather than intentionality on the part of hegemonic powers. The Eisenhower administration, worried by radicalism close to important oil fields, initially adopted a "wait and see" attitude toward Venezuela's new government.[27] Yet the mere presence of a hegemonic power willing to intervene in Latin America and in oil-producing nations provided an important obstacle to profound reform. When AD decided to refrain from insisting upon the nationalization of the oil companies, fear of a potential U.S. government response was the decisive element in party discussions. Later, in the crucial period of regime consolidation from 1959 to 1961, President Kennedy's election and the shift of attention toward the upheaval in Cuba changed the parameters of U.S. activity in the hemisphere in favor of democratization. In the sudden search for palatable alternatives to revolution, Venezuela's party system stood out like a shining star; thus the United States became a bulwark of the new regime.

These structural conditions favorable to democratization had to be understood and taken advantage of in order to be politically meaningful; thus the presence or absence of statecraft at various moments has been an essential component of the Venezuelan transition. During the decline of the authoritarian system, Pérez Jiménez's lack of skill, particularly with regard to the military and the church, was notable. To some extent, good leadership could have prolonged the unity of the military and avoided the fiscal crisis of 1957. Where statecraft did exist, its benefits were obvious. The pacts depended upon skillful political engineering, the product of an understanding on the part of important Venezuelan leaders that had its roots in the trienio. Betancourt, for example, understood the importance of compromising with traditional interests as well as with other political parties. Eugenio Mendoza had the foresight to recognize that AD's capacity to organize and direct large segments of labor and the peasantry could be valuable to entrepreneurs seeking to control the work force. In general, pact-making among elites requires this intelligent interpretation of the present as well as the future. Pacts depend upon the organizational resources that key actors bring to the bargaining table at a particular moment, their perception of those resources, their understanding of their opposition's strengths and weaknesses, and their ability to control their constituencies.

The truest indicator of statecraft can be seen through the granting of concessions. While compromise involves an explicit recognition of existing power structures, the necessity for concessions is more difficult to realize, since these often require some vision of the future. Concessions demonstrate the ability to *underutilize* power while simultaneously overrewarding weaker forces in order to create a durable system. Betancourt understood that well-timed strategic concessions could bring long-term benefits. By agreeing to the programmatic restrictions in Punto Fijo and the Minimum Program, the country's dominant political leader explicitly renounced the full effect of AD's remarkable mobilizational capacity as well as some of its future electoral clout. Later, as president, Betancourt agreed to a partitioning of state ministries and a formula of power-sharing in the unions with COPEI and the URD, thus helping to ensure the future growth of the other parties. By curbing its own influence while strengthening a loyal opposition, AD granted these parties the potential to win elections in the future—an act which would guarantee their commitment to a defense of the party system.

Certain conclusions concerning the successful transition from an authoritarian regime to a polity based upon party competition can be drawn from the Venezuelan case. Since a regime characterized by elections institutionalizes the resolution of conflict by means of contests whose winners are not predetermined and whose subsequent activities cannot be prescribed, winning the support of traditional elites for this uncertain form of rule is difficult. Conversely, as we have seen, the combination of crises that can lead to the collapse of authoritarianism—the coincidence of serious economic difficulties with a political succession dilemma—weakens those very elites normally hostile to accommodation, that is, the military and the economic elites. Thus, in the immediate circumstances, they may be drawn by necessity into compromises with new social forces. A central task for the designers of a new democracy is to limit the uncertainty of a political transition and the subsequent democratization in order to facilitate this historic compromise.

A pacted democracy is a form of limiting this uncertainty that has both advantages and disadvantages for democratization. If stability is the primary measure, pacts among elites can be highly successful. Venezuela, for example, has experienced five popular elections and three transfers of power between opposition parties, a unique phenomenon in Latin America. Formal coalitions closely following the spirit of the pacts existed in the AD administrations of Betancourt and Leoni; during the COPEI government of Rafael Caldera, they were abandoned for a set of informal working arrangements between parties which are still partially in effect. Pact-making has functioned as a mechanism for conflict regulation. Whenever intense political struggles have strained the limits of acceptable party competition, tensions have been resolved by "summit meetings" between the original designers of Venezuelan democracy, particularly Betancourt and Caldera. In the end, the most important legacy of the transition period has been a style of governance based upon an ongoing "pact to make pacts" in the future.

Yet the cost of the stability of pact-making has been the abandonment of greater democratization. Elite pact-making, an inherently antidemocratic form of interest representation, is predicated upon exclusion as well as inclusion. In the Venezuelan case, the agreement to exclude important social forces and organizations was initially exemplified by the decision to isolate the Communist party, abandon mobilizational tactics by purging overly reformist party leaders, and forego attempts to organize unorganized groups in the country. That exclusion, combined with substantive compromises with the military and the economic elites, has resulted in a modified economic and political program that places grave limits upon the possibilities for reform. Not surprisingly, this was bitterly resented by the Communist party as well as by militant AD youth. In April 1960, the entire youth branch of AD left in protest after their leaders had been expelled from the party as well as from labor and peasant federations, and launched the largest guerrilla movement in Latin America to that date. While Daniel Levine is correct in his claim that their defeat was the single most important factor in the consolidation of the democracy headed by AD,[28] this also led to the permanent demobilization of the popular sectors, the freezing of initial efforts toward redistribution of wealth, and the loss of lives and valuable political leadership. If Venezuelan democracy performed well as regards stability, its original goals of equity and participation suffered.[29]

Even stability, the measure of Venezuela's success, could become problematic in the long run. The durability of pacts has limits which are intrinsic to the pact itself. In part, these limits are generational. Pact-making relies upon a high degree of communication and implicit understanding that often arises from the process of accommodation itself. Shared assumptions and interests create a new community in the act of negotiation which permits the spirit of an original pact to be recaptured in the future. The decision to enter an initial pact is a "pact about making pacts," but this spirit of accommodation can be difficult to sustain once the original negotiators have departed from the scene. In Venezuela, for example, the "spirit of Punto Fijo" that permeated the first three administrations was absent from the government of Carlos Andres Pérez (1974–79) and Luis Herrera Campins (1979–84).

In addition, the very success of pacts undermines their durability. While pacts depend upon the existence of a particular structurally determined space, the political stability they produce creates the opportunity for future socioeconomic transformation. Thus pacts permit socioeconomic structures to change over time while freezing a set of relationships in place. In the Venezuelan case, these agreements have created the conditions for the emergence of new, politically relevant social actors which are unrepresented by the elite agreements of the past. As the country becomes more industrialized and complex, the ability of particular elites to maintain control over their constituencies is thrown into question. Thus, oil-mediated development undermines the bases for existing political pacts just as it once destroyed the social foundations of authoritarian rule. Meanwhile, the mere passage of time and the healing effects of staying out of power have cemented a new unity within the military, establishing a possible future alternative to a party system.

Finally, the viability of a *democracia pactada* is related to the cost of the maintenance of the pacts themselves. Ironically, the state-owned petroleum that provides a fiscal advantage also has powerful disadvantages associated with it. Since the state is the center of accumulation in an oil-producing country, pact-making is based upon agreements that carve up the state through a complicated spoils system which, in the end, has a deeply corrosive influence upon the efficacy and productivity of the state itself. At the same time, these pacts fuel and depend upon the fulfillment of constantly rising, albeit unequal expectations, since the implicit assumption of inexhaustible oil revenues underlies the demands of every social group represented in the pact-making process. Whatever sacrifice must occur in this spiral of inefficiency and growing demand is extracted disproportionately from excluded groups—the unorganized urban and rural poor or independent unions—who have few political or economic resources with which to defend their interests.

A type of complicity develops between the diverse organized sectors included in pact-making, as they allocate oil benefits to themselves regardless of the long-term impact on state efficiency, equity, and political legitimacy. Yet if this new social alliance, certainly broader and more inclusive than anything previously seen in Venezuela, represents "a nation of accomplices" (in the words of the Venezuelan poet Thomas Lander), this complicity is built upon a fragile structure—a nonrenewable resource which is slowly being depleted. Since petroleum has played a fundamental and unique role in the formation and maintenance of this party system, the long-term viability of this form of pacted democracy and its value as a model for other countries may become clear only when the oil money begins to disappear.

Notes

Chapter 1 Introduction to the Latin American Cases

1. For a first statement on this subject, see my *Modernization and Bureaucratic-Authoritarianism: Studies in South American Politics* (Berkeley: University of California, Institute of International Studies, 1973). For a more recent discussion, see my *El estado burocrático-autoritario: Argentina, 1966–1973* (Buenos Aires: Editorial de Belgrano, 1982; forthcoming in English from the University of California Press).

2. Valuable contributions to this theme can be found in two recent volumes: Julian Santamaría, ed., *Transición a la democracia en el Sur de Europa y América Latina* (Madrid: Centro de Investigaciones Sociales, 1982), and Howard Handelman and Thomas Sanders, eds., *Military Government and the Movement Toward Democracy in South America* (Bloomington: Indiana University Press, 1981).

3. For interesting discussions of the characteristics and perspectives of the Nicaraguan revolution, see especially Richard Fagen, "The Nicaraguan Revolution" (Working Paper no. 78, Latin American Program, The Wilson Center, Washington, D.C., 1981), and Xabier Gorostiaga, "Dilemmas of the Nicaraguan Revolution," in *The Future of Central America: Policy Choices for the U.S. and Mexico*, ed. Richard Fagen and Olga Pellicer (Stanford: Stanford University Press, 1983), pp. 47–66.

4. About these regimes, see especially David Collier, ed., *The New Authoritarianism in Latin America* (Princeton: Princeton University Press, 1979).

5. Robert Dahl, *Polyarchy: Participation and Opposition* (New Haven: Yale University Press, 1971).

6. The previous post–World War II waves of democratization were strongly (and very explicitly) promoted by U.S. governments. This impulse, although quite efficient in its short-run goals, probably undermined the long-run viability of the new democracies, by increasing the hostility toward them from the Left and the extreme Right. Today, even if some still quite recent democratizations like those of Peru, Ecuador, and especially the Dominican Republic were supported by the Carter administration, under the presidency of Reagan, U.S. public policies are quite ambiguous with respect to democratization in Latin America. Somewhat paradoxically, this circumstance may help the breadth and consistency of support for democratization within Latin America.

7. These considerations are inspired by the "possibilistic" approach developed by Albert Hirschman; see especially his *A Bias for Hope* (Cambridge, Mass.: Harvard University Press, 1979).

Chapter 2 Political Cycles in Argentina since 1955

1. Guillermo O'Donnell, "Estado y alianzas en la Argentina, 1956–1976," *CEDES Documento de Trabajo*, no. 5. An English translation of this article appeared in 1977 in *Journal of Developments Studies*. O'Donnell's writings evince a certain amount of economism. In particular, the mechanisms of formation and confrontation of social alliances, offensive and defensive, partly overlook the political aspects. In my discussion of the three currents of thought on economic policy which appeared within post-1955 anti-Peronism, below, I outline an alternative approach.

2. The partial exception is, of course, that of the 1973 Peronist government, in which, as I discuss later in the chapter, there coexisted attempts at democratic stabilization and attempts to "deepen" authoritarianism.

3. Non-Peronist reformist populism, in fact, took the class conciliation scheme further than Peronism itself. The pampa landowners had suffered confiscation of an important part of their profits so that income redistribution and import substitution, which took place between 1945 and 1955, could occur. After 1955 it was unclear, therefore, what could be done to restore economic incentives to the landowners without affecting the interests of the urban classes, bourgeoisie or proletariat or both.

4. As a result of the proscription of Peronism the political parties were put under a double pressure. Toward the end of the 1920s the Argentine political system had attained levels of electoral participation comparable to those of the most advanced capitalist countries. Moreover, during the Peronist regime the working class had attained full citizenship, and the government had extended the right to vote to women. Therefore, the Argentine political reality of the mid-1950s rendered unviable the attempts by "democrats" to establish "democracy" solely for themselves.

5. The army had traditionally been the most powerful branch, and the navy's alliance with precisely the sector that would be defeated in the 1962–63 confrontations—the colorados—further consolidated the army's dominant role.

6. Quoted in Marcelo Cavarozzi, "Sindicatos y política en Argentina 1955–1958," Estudios CEDES (Buenos Aires) 2, no. 1 (1979): 62.

7. Symbolically, the buildings belonging to the parties were confiscated by handing them over to the Ministry of Education, while the brand-new National Security Council was installed at the National Congress building.

8. For analysis of the characteristics and interactions of these currents see Guillermo O'Donnell, El estado burocrático autoritario: Argentina, 1966–1973 (Buenos Aires: Belgrano, 1982), p. 72 and passim.

9. O'Donnell, El estado burocrático autoritario, p. 257.

10. The assumption of supreme state power by the commanders in chief of the three branches of the armed forces reflected the learning process of the Argentine military, who wanted to avoid a repetition of Onganía's experience as a caudillo occupying the presidency not subject to any type of formal or institutional control by the armed forces.

11. Adolfo Canitrot, "Teoría y práctica del liberalismo: Política anti-inflacionaria y apertura económica en la Argentina, 1976–1981," Estudios CEDES 3, no. 10 (1980): 26. An English translation of this article was published in World Development 8, no. 11 (November 1980): 913–28.

Chapter 3 Bolivia's Failed Democratization, 1977–80

1. I have elaborated on these themes in "The State and Sectional Interests: The Bolivian Case," European Journal of Political Research (Amsterdam), June 1975, and "Politics and the Military in Bolivia," Society of Latin American Studies Bulletin, no. 26 (1977).

2. See my "Bolivia Swings Right," Current History, February 1972, and "Banzer's Bolivia," Current History, February 1976.

3. With 75 percent of the vote tabulated by 19 July, the official totals just before nullification were as follows: Pereda, 763,204 (50.1%); Siles Suazo (UDP), 320,223 (21.8%); Paz Estenssoro (MNR), 164,652 (11.2%); the Christian Democrat René Bernal, 155,165 (10.6%). On this occasion the Socialist, Quiroga Santa Cruz, was credited with less than 1 percent of the vote. Paz Estenssoro and Juan Lechín both publicly estimated that 60 percent of the recorded votes were fraudulent, and most other observers gave similar opinions. One indication of the character of the fraud comes from comparing the official tally one and two days after the election·

	10 July	11 July
Pereda	153,211	283,824
Siles Suazo	129,063	103,527
Paz Estenssoro	52,364	82,324
Bernal	26,148	98,930

Since Pereda was not likely to obtain an absolute majority in Congress (where Siles Suazo would be strongly represented), his bid for the presidency required an outright majority of the popular vote, which may explain the last-minute scramble to inflate his support. On 11 July 1978, Siles Suazo proclaimed himself president-elect.

4. Compare the official results four days after the election, with 67 percent of the vote tabulated, with those finally confirmed at the end of July:

	5 July	31 July
Siles Suazo	469,575	528,696
Paz Estenssoro	374,843	527,184
Banzer	214,657	218,587

Just as the support of Pereda and Bernal was inflated in 1978 in order to block Siles Suazo, so in 1979 the Paz Estenssoro vote may have been artificially boosted for the same reason. Siles Suazo again proclaimed himself president-elect on 16 July 1979. The supporters of Paz Estenssoro replied that the army was deeply split, and that there would be a coup unless the government handed power to them.

5. A senior Bolivian official interviewed by Yves Hardy, *Le Monde*, April 1981.

6. Argentine journalists held the following interview with General Banzer on 3 July 1980, which appeared in *Clarín* (Buenos Aires), 4 July 1980.

Q: What can you say about the alleged interference by the Department of State and the U.S. Ambassador in recent events?
A: I am really sorry about it.
Q: Do you disapprove of the State Department's declaration of support of the democratic process in Bolivia?
A: I do not disapprove of the declaration of support, that is interest, but I do disapprove of any declaration implying interference with Bolivian freedom, like saying "we will not permit that."
Q: By that phrase you mean not permitting a coup?
A: I mean whatever it refers to . . . !
Q: Even in reference to a coup?
A: Whatever it refers to! Even referring to a coup.

7. Official Results:

	1978	1979	1980
Siles Suazo (UDP)	484,383	528,696	507,173
Paz Estenssoro (MNR)	213,622	527,184	263,706
Pereda/Banzer	986,140	218,587	220,309
Quiroga Santa Cruz (Socialist)	< 10,000	100,000	113,959

8. *O Estado de São Paulo*, 3 July 1980. García Meza also referred to peasant complaints about the large number of votes received by Siles Suazo, asserting that the armed forces had the support of the peasantry, who made up 70 percent of the population. Siles Suazo made clear that on assuming office he would replace the high command of the armed forces. The coup began on 17 July 1980 in the garrison at Trinidad, which was then being visited by García Meza. This was the capital of the one department carried by Banzer in the 1980 elections. Extremely underpopulated and with an economy based on cattle-raising, this area was untouched by land reform or peasant organization. A key demand of the Trinidad garrison was "to reaffirm the military-peasant pact."

9. *La Prensa* (Lima), 9 July 1980.

Chapter 4 The "Liberalization" of Authoritarian Rule in Brazil

Author's Note: I am indebted to Guillermo O'Donnell for his valuable suggestions and critical comments regarding the first version of this chapter.

1. By degree of institutionalization I mean the ability shown by the regime to solve problems of its "internal economy" (the building up of a decision-making structure, ideological coherence, rules of succession, etc.) and its ability to solve authoritatively the basic systemic problems which it confronts.

2. This (analytical) distinction cannot be understood, of course, as if the authoritarian regime should be viewed as something *apart* from society. However, the very nature of authoritarian situations—where the exercise of power rests immediately on discrete structures and cliques (the military, the secret police, the palace entourage, and the like) and where, at the same time, the rulers are not politically accountable to society— creates within the regime a sort of "inner world" with specific interests, tensions, and rules of equilibrium. These elements are said here to constitute the "internal economy" of the regime in the sense that, first, the regime's operational capability greatly depends on how these elements interact, and, second, they do not necessarily correspond to the existing social interests, tensions, and rules of equilibrium prevailing in the society. In this sense—and only in this sense—the authoritarian regime can be examined as something separated, although not apart, from society.

3. A somewhat folkloric, but nevertheless authentic, version of the regime's ideology can be found in General Figueiredo's discourse. Example: "Now, you tell me, are the Brazilian people ready for the vote?" "No, the Brazilian voter does not yet have the American or French voter's level." Cf. *O livro de pensamentos do General Figueiredo* (São Paulo: Alfa-Omega, 1978), p. 82. For a slightly more sophisticated version see the *Manuais* of the Escola Superior de Guerra.

4. For instance, during 1966–76 more state enterprises were created in Brazil (about 600) than in the previous sixty years; also, between 1960 and 1974 the union's budget increased by 348 percent in real terms. Moreover, extrabudget revenues of the union were higher than the budgetary ones by the end of 1974. Data are from my "A Expansão do estado no Brasil; Seus problemas e seus atores" (Rio de Janeiro: IUPERJ/FINEP, 1977, mimeo).

5. Concerning Gramsci's (not always clear) concept of hegemony see, for instance, Perry Anderson, *Sur Gramsci* (Paris: Maspero, 1978).

6. Although an actual slowing-down of the economy occurred only at the end of the 1970s, the first oil shock (1974) was quickly perceived by the business community as a factor of potential crisis. The same could be said concerning the contradictory goals established by Geisel's Second Plan of Economic Development. The potential economic crisis did not play a role in the decision to "liberalize," but has conditioned the subsequent behavior of influential entrepreneurs. See also the chapter by Fernando Henrique Cardoso, in Volume 3 of this series.

7. This reality is obscured by the constant reference, in official discourse, to the regime's "democratic" goals. But this reference must be understood in the context mentioned before: the goal can be attained in the long run only through the consolidation of capitalism and the elimination of the generic "Communist" threat.

8. For instance, 1977 fiscal subsidies are estimated to have represented 6 percent of the GDP, and corresponded to *half* (Cr$121 billion) of total revenues of the treasury in that year. See "Subsidios governamentais e a expansão da base monetaria," *Conjuntura Economica* 33, no. 3 (March 1979): 93–107. More recently, data released by the president of the Central Bank show that subsidies plus fiscal incentives reached 80.32 percent of the federal tax revenues in 1979, and 99.28 percent in 1980. This corresponds to 6.18 percent (in 1979) and 7.61 percent (in 1980) of the GDP.

9. According to a four-star general who was a member of the army high command for more than four years in the mid-1970s, the high command has never discussed any

economic or other major public policy—not even nuclear policy. This information has been confirmed by one of the top figures in the Geisel government. My interviews, Rio de Janeiro, March 1981.

10. This "segregation" was overcome only through the practice of incorporating officers into the payroll of private firms—not in the majority of cases because of their specific competence, but because of their military positions. This practice began after 1964. By the end of 1980, the number of military in private jobs was estimated, by military sources, at about five thousand, although this figure obviously cannot be verified.

11. The most prominent leader of *novo sindicalismo*, Luis Inacio da Silva, "Lula," was dismissed by the government as the head of the metallurgical union and prosecuted under the National Security Law for his participation in the strike. Later on he was condemned jointly with other union leaders to a (suspended) three-year jail term.

12. This interpretation is based on fragments of Golbery's statements, government leaks to the press, and interviews with political leaders, in the best tradition of the "kremlinological" approach.

13. To be granted the "provisional registration" required to compete in an election, the new political parties were made to fulfill rather complex requirements following a very precise schedule. To achieve the full status of a political party (and congressional representation), each party has to obtain in the next election a minimum of 5 percent of the total national vote and a minimum of 3 percent of the vote in at least nine states of the Federation (Law No. 6.767, 20 December 1979).

14. After a more or less grotesque judicial dispute, in which the hand of the government was evident, the label PTB was awarded, not to Brizola, but to his rival (and Golbery's proxy), Vargas's heir (Ivette Vargas). Brizola then named his party Partido Democrático Trabalhista, PDT.

15. A bomb was to be placed in the Riocentro stadium during a popular show to celebrate May Day. However, the bomb exploded in the laps of a sergeant and a captain on active duty, who were working for the Secret Service of the First Army. The sergeant's funeral (the captain survived) was attended by the highest military hierarchy in Rio. An official military investigation concluded that the bomb was "placed" by leftists in the car occupied by these military personnel.

16. The lower house results were as follows: PDS, 36.6 percent; PMDB, 36.4 percent; PDT, 4.9 percent; PTB, 3.7 percent; PT, 3.0 percent; blank/null, 15.1 percent. Although the difference between PDS and PMDB was only 0.2 percent, the former won 235 seats and the latter 200 seats (49.0% and 41.7% respectively). This is because the apportionment system overrepresents the poor states (where clientelistic voting prevails, and the government party normally wins) and underrepresents the more industrialized ones (where the opposition wins).

17. In the state of São Paulo, for instance, the number of PMDB mayors rose from 37 to 309; in Paraná, from 14 to 168; in Minas, from 50 to 263.

18. A case in point is the November 1983 rejection (due to the vote of some PDS dissidents) of economic measures proposed by the government to comply with the policies imposed by the International Monetary Fund. A modified bill was subsequently approved as a result of a tradeoff with the PDS's dissidents and with one of the opposition parties (PTB).

19. The gravity of the crisis can be evaluated, for instance, through its impact on the economy of São Paulo, where most of Brazil's economic activity is concentrated. According to official data released by José Serra, secretary of economy and planning, the performance of the *paulista* economy can be summarized as follows for the years 1980–83; GDP fell by 11 percent, industrial production by 18 percent, and per capita income by 19.6 percent; a total of 847,000 jobs were eliminated in the same period, which means that for every twenty individuals employed in 1980, one had lost his job by the end of 1983. The same source estimates that if the *paulista* economy could grow by a

highly optimistic 5 percent a year from 1984 onwards (and supposing a demographic expansion of 3.6% a year), sixteen years would be needed to regain the per capita income of 1980 (*Folha de São Paulo*, 8 December 1983, p. 8).

20. In June 1983, for the first time in Brazilian history, civil servants and employees of state firms led a march of 50,000 people in the streets of Rio to protest insufficient salaries, the government policies, and the IMF intervention. Meanwhile, the assassination of a journalist linked to the secret services exposed the latter's involvement in other illicit acts and financial scandals (the Cruzeiro and Capemi affairs).

21. Two high government officials (the president of the Central Bank and the minister of social welfare) resigned, expressing unheard-of criticism of government policies and dignitaries. General Golbery "discovered" that Figueiredo had no political qualifications. Figueiredo, in turn, threatened to resign as president of his own party because of his difficulties in managing his own succession. (See the Brazilian press, July–November 1983).

22. By October–November 1983, the same ladies' organization which led the public demonstrations against the government of João Goulart was again in the streets, this time protesting against the regime.

23. On this point see Claude Lefort, *L'invention démocratique* (Paris: Fayard, 1981).

24. I am inclined to think that the consolidation of social hegemony of capitalism in Brazil is underway, regardless of the economic contradictions of the present model of growth, or the gravity of the present economic crisis. The deep penetration of a capitalist ethos within the state apparatus is a good example of this, as shown, for instance, by the adoption of a "private" capitalist management mentality by the state enterprises. Another indicator is the fact that, although the criticism of the actual model of growth has become widespread, a socialist alternative is not the object of any political debate—not even as a utopia.

25. Alain Touraine, *Les sociétés dépendantes* (Paris: Duculot, 1976).

Chapter 5 The Political Evolution of the Chilean Military Regime and Problems in the Transition to Democracy

1. On the unions see A. Angell, *Partidos políticos y movimiento obrero en Chile* (Mexico City: ERA, 1974). On the student movement in recent decades, see M. A. Garretón, "Política y universidad en los procesos de transformación y reversión en Chile, 1967–1977," *Estudios Sociales* (Santiago), no. 26 (1981).

2. I have called this the "backbone" of Chilean society. See *El Proceso político chileno* (Chile: FLACSO, 1983).

3. On this concept see, for example, J. Graciarena and R. Franco, "Social Formations and Power Structures in Latin America," *Current Sociology* 26, no. 1 (1978).

4. This move from a strictly military regime to an authoritarian type of regime is what official circles term "transition." I propose that it should be called "institutionalization" and that the term "transition" be reserved for the process of change of regime.

5. An important group of Christian Democratic leaders and activists were radically opposed to the military coup. On this, see the documents published in *Revista Análisis*, March 1982.

6. See this development in G. Arriagada, "El marco institucional de las Fuerzas Armadas" (Working Paper, Latin American Program, The Wilson Center, Washington, D.C., 1980).

7. The culmination of these confrontations between 1973 and 1980 was the removal of General Leigh and of almost all the Air Force General Staff. That showed the

extent to which the highest political leadership could have been split at any moment; however, at the same time it also showed the power which Pinochet enjoyed to bring the armed forces as a whole behind his position in disciplined and orderly fashion.

8. This vision appears in synthesis in Pinochet's inaugural speech at the beginning of the 1979 academic year at the University of Chile.

9. E.g., Orlando Saenz, ex-president of the Sociedad de Fomento Fabril (SOFOFA), which represents industrial employers.

10. The *duros*, or "nationalists," expressed their points of view through columns in the *Diario La Tercera*. Some came out of the Fascist Patria y Libertad movement, whose activity between 1970 and 1973 was important. Many had links with officers connected to DINA. Several have been related to the Corporación de Estudios Nacionales, headed by Pinochet's daughter. Others were government consultants and took part in some of its commissions.

11. This was the conception of these sectors as expressed in the 1981 Constitution. Groups linked with the economic team, a large number of the mayors appointed by the regime, the *gremialista* sector which had come out of the Catholic University Students' Federation (FEUC), and certain groups related to *El Mercurio* company were among the main elements of this sector. They were grouped around magazines like *Realidad* or institutions like the New Democracy Group.

12. See H. Fruhling, "Strategies of Repression and Legal Strategy for the Defense of Human Rights in Chile: 1973–1980," *Human Rights Quarterly* 5, no. 4 (1983):510–53.

13. On the "modernizations" see Pinochet's messages of 11 September 1978 and 1979. The periodical *Chile-América* (Rome), nos. 74–75 (October–December 1981), has a complete analysis.

14. Governing Military Junta, *Declaración de Principios del Gobierno de Chile* (March 1974).

15. The constitution provides that Pinochet will stay in power until 1989. At that date the junta will propose an uncontested presidential candidate (this could be Pinochet) to serve until 1997. Only after the plebiscite will some form of legislative representation (congress, etc.) be constituted. See *Constitución de 1980: comentarios de juristas internacionales* (Santiago: Centro de Estudios Sociales, 1984).

16. On the referendum's irregularities, see the deposition by P. Aylwin and others, "Presentación ante el Colegio Escrutador," *El Mercurio*, 3 October 1980.

17. It is evident that there are different types of crisis administration, ranging from the attempt at direct regulation to a laissez faire policy concerned only with staying in power. On the other hand, it is worth emphasizing that there is no single direction for these processes: a crisis administration regime may take up its transformative dimension again. We should also note that, with regard to the study of these regimes, the importance of the developments which have been pointed to lies in the shift of analytical emphasis from the regime and the overall process to the study of the emergence and dynamic of specific social actors.

18. These were *gremios* of industrialists, merchants, farmers, truckers, and small businessmen. The political importance of these sectors dates from the disintegration of the Chilean political system during the Popular Unity government. Since these sectors were not part of the traditional political structure, they lack a clear political identity. In April 1982 the journal *Análisis* reported on some of these groups under the heading "The Other Opposition." In the case of the professional colleges there has been a more clearcut evolution toward the opposition.

19. I refer to Sergio Onofre Jarpa, who was president of the National party when it dissolved itself in support of the military regime.

20. These are regimes which, without intending to, give rise to opportunities and political spaces in which various forms of dissidence or opposition can be expressed, albeit within strict limits and at the risk of repression. To some extent, this bears out the concept proposed by Juan Linz, "An Authoritarian Regime: Spain" in *Cleavages, Ideolo-*

gies, and Party Systems, ed. E. Allard and Yrjö Littuven (Helsinki: Westermarck Society, 1964) but with a caveat against overuse for ideological purposes of the term "authoritarian regimes," as occurs, for example, in the writings of former U.S. Ambassador to the U.N. Jeane Kirkpatrick.

21. The change of archbishop in 1983 probably signified a switch by the church from a posture of critical opposition to one of mediation between the government and the opposition, while still exercising a degree of criticism. Although in some ways a setback, this switch has not diminished the church's crucial role as an independent source of testimony and as the sole institutional channel for the expression of the mass discontent that appeared during that year.

22. The journal *Chile-América,* published in Rome, has documented the recent evolution of the Chilean Left. In September 1980 the general secretary of the Communist party put forward the necessity of adopting every form of struggle, including that of "acute violence." This created problems even within the CP, because it was a sharp change from this party's traditional thinking. Although it is debatable how far this policy has been carried out in practice, the very declaration provoked a heated debate among the various political groups of the Left. The Frente Patriótico Manuel Rodriguez, an armed group, has its origins in the CP although it is not considered its "armed arm" and has increasing autonomy from the former.

23. Elsewhere I have characterized the coexistence of the patterns of political action in the Left. On the one hand, there is the classical pattern which predominated in all left-wing political organizations in the 1960s and early 1970s. This pattern started with the view of each class as the bearer of a societal project; it conceived of the party as vanguard and the party's activity as the class's direct projection on society; power rested only in the state as sole reference point for political activity; theory was seen as a body of truths of which the party and its activists were the depositories. On the other hand, in recent years a pattern of action less well-endowed with certainties has emerged. In this pattern there is not "a" class bearing a theoretical and historical truth that has been defined once and for all, but rather a diversified popular subject which must discover and constitute itself historically; the party is not the bearer of a "theory," nor does it have a sacred character, but is just one instrument in this process of constitution; politics is redefined in every sphere of social life; there is not "a" theory but a historical learning process making use of different theoretical camps. See M. A. Garretón, *El proceso político chileno* (Santiago: FLACSO, 1983).

24. These were the Alianza Democrática (composed of a sector of the democratic Right, the Christian Democrats, the Social Democrats, the Radical party, and one of the Socialist parties); the Bloque Socialista (composed of the same Socialist party and the new groups of the socialist Left, such as MAPU, Izquierda Cristiana, and Convergencia); and the Movimiento Democrático Popular (composed of the Communist party, the other Socialist party, the MIR, and other socialist factions).

25. In 1985, the transition to democracy in Chile seemed blocked. First, no transition initiated from above had occurred. In November 1984 the state of siege had been promulgated in order to end the protest movement; it lasted until June 1985. No new "opening" has been announced since then, and the government is aiming to create the conditions to arrive at 1989 and elect Pinochet, combining repression with economic cooptation of different sectors of the bourgeoisie and petty bourgeoisie. Secondly, neither has the opposition been able to unleash a process of transition, although some progress was made with the Acuerdo Nacional (promoted by the church and signed by all the opposition parties, with the exception of Movimiento Democrático Popular, which was excluded, and two important parties of the Right that supported the regime until recently). Two problems faced by the opposition are the difficulties of linking social mobilization with a concrete formula of transition and the exclusion of the Communist party and some socialist sectors. Different sectors of the Right and U.S.

policy attempt to maintain the status quo until 1989, but avoiding the election of Pinochet in that year. Thirdly, the conflict between dictatorship and opposition has not been resolved because of the absence of political space (such as elections), a mediating institution—such as the king in Spain (although the Church is moving toward playing this role), and the lack of an "external" event (such as a war or the death of Pinochet). All are factors that contribute to that impasse. Therefore, the challenge for the opposition is how to change the institutional framework before 1989 and how to combine mobilization with negotiation while avoiding the exclusion of certain parties.

Chapter 6 Political Liberalization in an Authoritarian Regime: The Case of Mexico

Author's Note: Much of this chapter is based on field research conducted in Mexico in 1980, 1982, and 1983. I wish to thank the Office of Research and Graduate Development and the President's Council on International Programs, Indiana University–Bloomington, for financial support for field research in June–August 1982. The Center for U.S.-Mexican Studies, University of California–San Diego, provided valuable research support during the final revision of this chapter. I would like to thank Douglas Bennett, David Collier, Maria Cook, Julio Cotler, Richard R. Fagen, Gary Gereffi, Albert O. Hirschman, Juan Linz, Abraham F. Lowenthal, Guillermo O'Donnell, and Laurence Whitehead for their comments on earlier versions.

This chapter was revised for publication in December 1984. It does not examine more recent political events in Mexico, including the 1985 mid-term elections for the federal Chamber of Deputies and state and local offices.

1. This characterization of the Mexican system draws on Linz's more general theoretical discussion of authoritarian regimes; see Juan J. Linz, "Totalitarian and Authoritarian Regimes," in *Handbook of Political Science*, ed. Fred I. Greenstein and Nelson W. Polsby, vol. 3 (Reading, Mass.: Addison-Wesley, 1975), esp. pp. 264–69.

2. For a perceptive and suggestive discussion of the relationships among political legitimacy (the belief that existing political arrangements are better than others that might be established, and that they can therefore command obedience), efficacy (the capacity of a regime to find reasonably satisfactory solutions to basic problems), and effectiveness (the capacity actually to implement chosen policies to achieve the desired results) in democratic systems, see Juan J. Linz, "The Breakdown of Democratic Regimes: Crisis, Breakdown, and Reequilibration," in *The Breakdown of Democratic Regimes*, ed. Juan J. Linz and Alfred Stepan (Baltimore: Johns Hopkins University Press, 1978), pp. 11–13, 16–23.

3. See Pablo González Casanova and Enrique Florescano, eds., *México, hoy* (Mexico City: Siglo XXI, 1979), for an examination of Mexico's contemporary socioeconomic problems.

4. Comisión Federal Electoral, *Reforma política*, 9 (Mexico City: 1982): 129. In the 1973 federal legislative election the officially recorded abstention rate reached 39.7 percent. It is important to note that official electoral statistics may significantly underestimate the rate of voter abstention.

5. Luis Medina, *Evolución electoral en el México contemporáneo* (Mexico City: Comisión Federal Electoral, 1978), pp. 14–21, 38, 40; Javier López Moreno, *La reforma política en México* (Mexico City: Centro de Documentación Política, 1979), pp. 62–70, 72.

6. In addition to Reyes Heroles, other cabinet members who supported the political reform project included José Andrés Oteyza (minister of national property and industrial development), Emilio Mujica Montoya (minister of communications and transporta-

tion), and Carlos Tello Macías (minister of planning and budget). They were joined by Echeverristas (supporters of former president Luis Echeverría, 1970–76) and old-line Cardenistas (supporters of former president Lázaro Cárdenas, 1934–40). However, given the heterogeneity of the PRI (especially its "popular," or middle-class, sector, the National Confederation of Popular Organizations), it is otherwise difficult to identify other groups or factions in the "official" party that actively backed the political reform except in terms of individual political leaders who stated their position regarding the liberalization measure.

7. This section is based largely on interviews conducted with labor leaders, government officials, and political party representatives in Mexico in June–July 1980.

8. See, for example, Carlos Sánchez Cárdenas, *Reforma política: Estrategia y táctica* (Mexico City: Editorial Extemporáneos, 1979), p. 155.

9. For evidence of younger CTM leaders' support for the political reform, see *El Día*, 26 February 1979, pp. 1, 6–7, and *Crítica política* 4 (15 May 1980): 17.

10. Interview with cabinet member in López Portillo administration, 29 November 1984. Also see the highly accurate predictions made by political columnist Manuel Buendía shortly after Reyes Heroles's 1 April 1977 address in *El Sol de México*, 17 April 1977, reproduced in Comisión Federal Electoral, "Comentarios," *Reforma política*, 2 (1977): 86–89.

11. All thirty-one states eventually introduced reform legislation providing opposition parties with proportional representation in state legislatures. Although the proportional representation formula established at the federal level by the López Portillo reform served as the basic model, specific provisions varied somewhat from state to state.

12. The reform law and its implementing legislation are reproduced in Comisión Federal Electoral, *Ley federal de organizaciones políticas y procesos electorales* (Mexico City, 1978).

13. However, in order for minority parties to participate in party-list circumscriptions, they were required to present candidates in at least one hundred of the single-member districts. Once minority parties were accepted for participation in party-list circumscriptions, they were required to complete regional lists in all party-list circumscriptions formed by the Federal Electoral Commission for a given election (3 in 1979 and 4 in 1982, but the reform law allowed up to 5). A party winning more than sixty seats in single-member districts was barred from competing in party-list circumscriptions.

14. The López Portillo reform also altered the role of the judiciary in the electoral process. Under previous legislation the Supreme Court was the final authority in disputes regarding the legality of electoral proceedings. The 1977 reform permitted the Supreme Court to examine the legality of the electoral process on appeal and offer a nonbinding declaration regarding its findings, but the Chamber of Deputies remained the final authority on the validity of electoral results. The electoral college had previously consisted of the full Chamber of Deputies; under the 1977 reform law it was composed of sixty "majority" (PRI) and forty "minority" (opposition) deputies. The Federal Electoral Commission's powers were also substantially increased under the 1977 reform law. The commission, in which progovernment members hold a decisive majority, became the effective final authority on several important matters concerning the electoral process.

15. Comisión Federal Electoral, *Ley federal de organizaciones políticas y procesos electorales* (Mexico City, 1982), articles 68(I), 70. The reforms implemented in January 1982 affected 35 of the 250 articles in the law. For the most part, these changes involved minor revisions in electoral procedures and reflected the practical lessons offered by the 1979 electoral process.

16. Comisión Federal Electoral, *Reforma política*, 9:128–29. Total opposition support does not include votes for unregistered candidates. The decline in opposition party support in the 1976 election for the federal Chamber of Deputies was apparently due to

the absence of a major opposition presidential candidate in these elections and the presence of a significant abstention movement within PAN.

17. Ibid., pp. 133–39.

18. Rafael Segovia, "Las elecciones federales de 1979," *Foro Internacional,* 79 (January–March 1980): 409–10.

19. The 100 proportional representation seats were distributed as follows: PAN, 50; PSUM, 17; PDM, 12; PST, 11; PPS, 10. In this case the Hagenbach–Bishöv system benefitted PDM and PST at the expense of PAN. PAN also won one single-member district, for a total chamber representation of 51 seats. PRT's share in the proportional representation vote was 1.47 percent, less than the minimum 1.5 percent required to qualify for representation in the Chamber.

20. *Excelsior,* 26 June 1980, p. 14.

21. *Unomasuno,* 17 July 1982, p. 7; *El Día (Metrópoli),* 5 July 1982, p. 1. Voter abstentation data in this section are drawn from Comisión Federal Electoral, *Reforma política,* 9:129.

22. Interviews with Federal Electoral Commission official, 7 July 1982; with opposition party leader, 7 July 1982; and with Federal Electoral Commission official, 3 August 1982. In addition, the Ministry of the Interior paid for all parties' radio and television announcements. Although PAN formally rejected all government subsidies except free access to radio and television, there is some evidence that the party received other material support from the government as well (interview with Federal Electoral Commission official, 3 August 1982).

23. *Unomasuno,* 6 July 1982, p. 3.

24. Interviews with opposition party leader, 7 July 1982, and with PSUM party leader, 28 July 1982.

25. *Excelsior,* 6 July 1982, p. 4; 27 July 1982, p. 26; 28 July 1982, p. 23; interview with Federal Electoral Commission official, 3 August 1982.

26. Wayne A. Cornelius, "The Political Economy of Mexico under de la Madrid: Austerity, Routinized Crisis, and Nascent Recovery," *Mexican Studies/Estudios Mexicanos* 1, no. 1 (Winter 1985): 99–101.

27. Ibid.

Chapter 7 Military Interventions and "Transfer of Power to Civilians" in Peru

1. Julio Cotler, *Clases, estado, y nación en el Perú* (Lima: Instituto de Estudios Peruanos, 1978).

2. Alfred Stepan, *The State and Society: Peru in Comparative Perspective* (Princeton: Princeton University Press, 1978).

3. Cotler, *Clases, estado, y nación.*

4. Julio Cotler, *Democracia e integración nacional* (Lima: Instituto de Estudios Peruanos, 1980).

5. A. Lowenthal, ed., *The Peruvian Experiment* (Princeton: Princeton University Press, 1975); A. Lowenthal and Cynthia McClintock, eds., *The Peruvian Experiment Revisited* (Princeton: Princeton University Press, in press).

6. Carlos Amat, *La economía de la crisis peruana* (Lima: Fundación Ebert, 1978); Banco Central de Reserva, *Reflexiones en torno a un programa de estabilización: La experiencia peruana, 1978–1980* (Lima, July 1980); Cesar Humberto Cabrera, *Perú: La crisis y la política de estabilización* (Lima: Fundación Ebert, 1978); Felipe Portocarrero, *Crisis y recuperación de la economía peruana* (Lima: Mosca Azul, 1980); Rosemary Thorpe and Alan Angell, "Inflation, Stabilization, and Attempted Redemocratization in Peru, 1975–1979," *World Development* 8, no. 11 (November 1980); Oscar Ugarteche, *Teoría y práctica de la deuda externa en el Perú* (Lima: Instituto de Estudios Peruanos, 1980).

7. Alberto Couriel, *Perú: Estrategías de desarrollo y grados de satisfacción de las necesidades básicas* (Santiago: PREALC, 1978); E.V.K. FitzGerald, *The Political Economy of Peru, 1956-1978: Economic Development and the Restructuring of Capital* (Cambridge: Cambridge University Press, 1979).

8. Exposition by the executive president of the Banco Central de Reserva in IPAE, 25 January 1979.

9. Barbara Stallings, "Peru and the U.S. Banks: Privatization of Financial Relations," in *Capitalism and the State in U.S.-Latin American Relations*, ed. Richard R. Fagen (Stanford: Stanford University Press, 1979).

10. Ibid.

11. The interlocking strategies of the main political parties are traced in Sandra L. Woy-Hazleton, "The Return to Partisan Politics in Peru" (Paper presented to the Latin American Studies Association Conference [LASA], Bloomington, Ind., October 1980).

12. Oscar Ugarteche, *La banca transnacional, la deuda externa, y el estado: Perú, 1965-1978* (Lima: Instituto de Estudios Peruanos, 1981).

13. N. Asheshov, "Peru's Flirtation with Disaster," *Institutional Investor* 11, no. 10 (October 1977): 181-90.

14. Aldo Ferrer, "El monetarismo en la Argentina y Chile," *Ambiente Financiero*, 22 August 1980; Oscar Ugarteche, "El Perú es el Cono Sur?" *La Revista*, no. 4 (April 1981).

Chapter 8 Uruguay's Transition from Collegial Military-Technocratic Rule

Author's Note: This chapter reflects research in progress in Uruguay funded by the Inter-American Foundation, the Social Science Research Council, and the American Council of Learned Societies, with grants from the Ford and Mellon Foundations and the National Endowment for the Humanities. My debts of gratitude to countless Uruguayan journalists, politicians and academics are enormous, but too numerous to mention. I should like to thank V. G. and R. G.

1. Romeo Pérez, "La Izquierda en la fase postautoritaria," in *Uruguay y democracia*, vol. 2 (Montevideo: Banda Oriental, 1985) argues that the Left underestimated the depth of support for the traditional parties in the 1960s, as has been shown by their survival under the authoritarian regime. The complex electoral system, which discourages the multiplication of parties and promotes factionalism within them instead, is described in Alberto Pérez Pérez, *La ley de lemas* (Montevideo: FCU, 1971).

2. M.H.J. Finch, *A Political Economy of Uruguay since 1870* (London: Macmillan, 1981), applies the notions of Uruguay's leading historians Barran and Nahum with respect to the relative autonomy of the political class to a discussion of the country's development from booming prosperity to stagnation. Uruguay nevertheless remains one of the most developed and least inegalitarian countries in Latin America.

3. Two books which give an impression of the grass-roots operation of patronage politics in the traditional parties are Germán Rama, *El club político* (Montevideo: Arca, 1971), which estimates there were 8,000 political clubs in Montevideo at the time of the election, and Juan Carlos Fa Robaina, *Cartas a un diputado* (Montevideo: Alfa, 1972), a compilation of requests for help received by a deputy. Quantitative work using survey data has been done by Robert Biles in "Patronage Politics: Electoral Behavior in Uruguay" (Ph.D. diss., Johns Hopkins University, 1972), and "Political Participation in Urban Uruguay," in *Political Participation in Latin America*, ed. J. A. Booth and M. Seligson, vol. 2 (New York: Holmes & Meier, 1978).

4. The evidence that the vote for the Left was not much less multiclass than that for the other parties, although it was more urban, is in César Aguiar, "La Doble escena," *Uruguay y democracia*, vol. 1 (Montevideo: Banda Oriental, 1984).

5. Charlie Gillespie, "The Breakdown of Democracy in Uruguay: Alternative Political Models" (Working Paper no. 143, Latin American Program, The Wilson Center, Washington, D.C., 1984). My analysis is criticized by Juan Rial, *Partidos políticos, democracia y autoritarismo*, vol. 2 (Montevideo: CIESU-EBO, 1984), unfortunately on the basis of wrongly attributing to me three views which I explicitly rejected in the above essay: (1) that patronage was the only prop by which traditional parties survived; (2) that the symptoms of the crisis in themselves explain the structural flaws of the democratic system which led to its collapse; and (3) that conjunctural factors played no part in the breakdown. An important factor in the subsequent low support for the authoritarian regime was precisely the low level of "threat" to the capitalist order compared, for example, to Chile, as K. L. Remmer and G. W. Merkx argue in "Bureaucratic Authoritarianism Revisited," *Latin American Research Review* 17, no. 2 (1982): 3–40.

6. One of the very few published essays on the military is María del Huerto Amarillo's contribution to *Uruguay y democracia*, vol. 1. My account relies on the excellent article, "Les transformations institutionelles de l'Uruguay (1973–78)" by François Lérin and Cristina Torres in *Notes et etudes documentaires*, November 1978, pp. 4485–86.

7. See the articles by Howard Handelman in the book he edited with Thomas Sanders, *Military Government and the Movement toward Democracy in South America* (Bloomington: Indiana University Press, 1981).

8. For a summary of the institutional acts in English see *Uruguay: Generals' Rule* (London: Latin America Bureau, 1979).

9. Horacio Martorelli's "La maquinaria de la dictadura en la transición democrática del Uruguay," in *Transición a la democracia* (Montevideo: Banda Oriental, 1984), makes a convincing critique of those who ascribe the logic of authoritarianism purely to the needs of capitalism. He sets out, in effect, a Weberian model of the authoritarian institutions as they attempt to mold and discipline society in their image.

10. Luis Macadar, *Uruguay, 1974–1980: Un nuevo ensayo de reajuste económico?* (Montevideo: EBO-CINVE, 1982).

11. See Jorge Notaro, *La política económica en el Uruguay, 1968–84* (Montevideo: EBO-CIEDUR, 1984), and the compilation of articles by economists at CINVE, *La crisis uruguaya y el problema nacional* (Montevideo: CINVE-EBO, 1984).

12. Luis González, "Uruguay, 1980–81: An Unexpected Opening," *Latin American Research Review* 18, no. 3 (1983): 63–76.

13. For the background to the primaries see my "From Suspended Animation to Animated Suspension" (Paper presented to the annual meeting of the American Political Science Association, Chicago, 1983), which investigates the ecological pattern of voting. Survey data are reported in my "Activists, Apathy, and the Floating Voter: The Unheeded Lessons of Uruguay's 1982 Primaries," in *Elections and Democratization in Latin America, 1980–85*, ed. Paul Drake and Eduardo Silva (San Diego: Center for Iberian and Latin American Studies, forthcoming).

14. As Luis González argues in "Political Parties and Redemocratization in Uruguay" (Working Paper no. 163, Latin American Program, The Wilson Center, Washington, D.C., 1984), an important and often neglected feature of the electoral system is that candidates for president and Assembly appear on the same preprinted ballot, one for each party faction, and ticket-splitting is thus not allowed (even between national and local office). This prevents tactical voting, for example, should the Left choose to support the Blancos against the Colorados. Since no one liked their suggestion that indirect elections might be fairer, the Blancos now favor a run-off election, as in France.

15. Angel Flisfisch, "Partidos y dualismo en la transición" (Paper presented to the conference Procesos de Democratización y Consolidación de la Democracia, Santiago, 9–12 April 1984).

16. Aldo Solari, "Algunas reflexiones sobre los resultados electorales," *La Semana de El Día*, no. 301 (1-7 December 1984). Further analysis of the elections may be found in my "Electoral Stability and Redemocratization: The Uruguayan Case" (Paper presented to the Conference on Latin American Elections, San Diego, 21-22 February 1985).

17. For an analysis of competing theories on the causes of democratic transitions and their applicability to the Uruguayan case see my *"Democradura or Reforma Pactada?* Perspectives on Democratic Restoration in Uruguay" (Paper presented at the Thirteenth World Congress of the International Political Science Association, Paris, 1985).

18. Carlos Filgueira, *El dilema de la democratización en el Uruguay* (Montevideo: CIESU, 1984).

19. Martín Gargiulo, "Movimiento sindical y estabilidad democrática," *Cuadernos del CLAEH* (Montevideo) 30:17-38.

20. González, "Political Parties and Redemocratization in Uruguay."

21. The 300th issue of *La Semana de El Día*, 24-30 November 1984, is entirely devoted to articles on the Uruguayan party system by Solari, Rial, González, Franco, Otero, and myself. The problem of party government is discussed by Giuseppe Di Palma, "Governo dei partiti e riproducibilità democratica: Il dilemma delle nuove democrazie," *Rivista Italiana di Scienza Politica* 13, no. 1 (April 1983): 3-36. Di Palma, however, sees executive domination of the legislature as an indispensable condition of party government. In fact, there is a need to distinguish parliamentary from presidential democracies. The virtue of the former is that they supersede the old rigid doctrine of "separation of powers," and while the government gains full control of the legislative agenda and normally insists that representatives toe the party line, it is also subject to the will of the legislature in order to stay in office. By its very personalization of political power, the presidential system is inimical to party government.

Chapter 9 Petroleum and Political Pacts: The Transition to Democracy in Venezuela

Author's Note: I would like to thank Philippe Schmitter, David Collier, Richard Fagen, Alexander George, and Robert Keohane for their comments on an earlier version of this chapter. The Center for International Affairs, Harvard University, generously provided institutional support.

1. Peter Merkl, "Democratic Development, Breakdowns, and Fascism," *World Politics* 34, no. 1 (October 1981): 114-35.

2. The debate over the relative importance of structure versus "process" variables like leadership or party organization can be followed in Guillermo O'Donnell's classic study, *Modernization and Bureaucratic Authoritarianism* (Berkeley: Institute of International Studies, University of California, 1973), as well as in subsequent essays in David Collier, ed., *The New Authoritarianism in Latin America* (Princeton: Princeton University Press, 1979). Also see the series edited by Juan Linz and Alfred Stepan, *The Breakdown of Democratic Regimes* (Baltimore: Johns Hopkins University Press, 1978).

3. See the analysis of David Blank, *Politics in Venezuela* (Boston: Little, Brown, 1973). The approach here is based upon Albert Hirschman's essay "A Generalized Linkage Approach to Development, with Special Reference to Staples," *Economic Development and Cultural Change* 25, Supplement (1977): 67-98.

4. Daniel Levine, *Conflict and Political Change in Venezuela* (Princeton: Princeton University Press, 1973). Also see his essay "Venezuela since 1958: The Consolidation of Democratic Politics," in Linz and Stepan, *The Breakdown of Democratic Regimes:*

Latin America. On consociational democracies, see Hans Daalder, "Building Consociational Nations," in *Building States and Nations,* ed. S. N. Eisenstadt and Stein Rokkan (Beverly Hills: Sage, 1973), vol. 2; Arendt Lijphart, *Democracy in Plural Societies: A Comparative Exploration* (New Haven: Yale University Press, 1977); and Eric Nordlinger, *Conflict Regulation in Divided Societies* (Cambridge: Center for International Affairs, Harvard University, 1972).

5. See Edwin Lieuwen, *Petroleum in Venezuela: A History* (Berkeley and Los Angeles: University of California Press, 1954); Domingo Alberto Rangel, *Capital y desarrollo,* vol. 2 (Caracas: Universidad Central de Venezuela, 1970), and his *Los Andinos en el poder: Balance de una hegemonía, 1899–1945* (Caracas, 1964).

6. For a discussion of the impact of the commercialization of agriculture on social and political change see Barrington Moore, *The Social Origins of Dictatorship and Democracy* (Boston: Beacon, 1966); Jeffrey Paige, *Agrarian Revolution* (New York: Free Press, 1975); and Theda Skocpol, *States and Social Revolutions* (Cambridge: Cambridge University Press, 1979).

7. James Petras, *The Nationalization of Venezuelan Oil* (New York: Praeger, 1977), pp. 6–7.

8. Acción Democrática, *Doctrina y programa* (Caracas: Secretaría Nacional de Propaganda de Acción Democrática, 1962).

9. *Las empresas Mendoza* (Caracas: Fundación Mendoza, n.d.), p. 59.

10. Speech of J. J. González Gorrondona in *La libertad económica y la intervención del estado: Ciclo de conferencias organizado por el Partido Democrático Venezolano* (Caracas: Tipográfica de la Nación, 1945), p. 91.

11. Philip Taylor, *The Venezuelan Golpe de Estado of 1958* (Washington, D.C.: Institute for the Comparative Study of Political Systems, 1968), pp. 41–42.

12. John Duncan Powell, *The Political Mobilization of the Venezuelan Peasant* (Cambridge, Mass.: Harvard University Press, 1971), p. 79.

13. In the plebiscite, Venezuelans were asked to vote whether they "were in agreement with the executive actions of the regime and consequently considered that the person actually exercising the Office of the President should be reelected." Given the repressive nature of the regime and the use of open balloting, it is not surprising that the majority of Venezuelans decided to support Pérez Jiménez. See Luis Herrera Campins, "Transición política," in *1958: Tránsito de la dictadura a la democracia en Venezuela,* ed. J. L. Salcedo-Bastardo et al. (Barcelona: Ariel, 1978), pp. 94ff.

14. Cited in Andres Stambouli, "La actuación política de la dictadura y el rechazo el autoritarianismo" (Paper presented at the 1979 national meeting of the Latin American Studies Association, Pittsburgh).

15. On the Sindicato de Hierro, see ibid., p. 28, as well as the forthcoming doctoral thesis by Julie Skurski and Fernando Coronil, University of Chicago, and Corporación Venezolano de Fomento, *30 Años* (Caracas: CVF, 1971).

16. For the importance of lack of business access to state decisions during this period, see Robert Clark, "Fedecámaras en el proceso de formulación de políticas en Venezuela" (mimeo, Caracas, n.d.).

17. This description of military events is based upon Taylor, *The Venezuelan Golpe;* Stambouli, "La actuación política"; and Winfield Burgraff, *The Venezuelan Armed Forces in Politics, 1935–1959* (Columbia: University of Missouri Press, 1972).

18. Party leaders often deny that Mendoza actually took part in this New York meeting, but his visit coincided with that of the party leaders, and he did participate in conversations with them. Interview with Eugenio Mendoza, Caracas, 1978.

19. Stambouli, "La actuación política," p. 34.

20. See Robert Alexander, *The Venezuelan Democratic Revolution* (New Brunswick, N.J.: Rutgers University Press, 1964), p. 59. For more on the immediate economic situation, see James Hanson, "Cycles of Economic Growth and Structural Change since

1950," in *Venezuela: The Democratic Experience*, ed. John Martz and David Myers (New York: Praeger, 1977).

21. See Herrera Campins, "Transición política," pp. 111–16. Juan Pablo Pérez Alfonzo, Benito Raul Losada, Carlos D'Ascoli, and other party leaders interviewed in Caracas in 1978 confirmed that fears of a possible coup attempt strongly conditioned the responses of AD leaders in the early years of the democracy.

22. For a day-by-day accounting of these events, see Salcedo-Bastardo et al., *1958*, appendices.

23. The Pact of Punto Fijo was signed on 31 October 1958 by the URD, AD, and COPEI. The signatories included *copeyanos* Rafael Caldera and Lorenzo Fernando; *adecos* Rómulo Betancourt, Raul Leoni, and Gonzalo Barrios; and Jovíto Villalba from the URD. Significant portions of these documents are reproduced in Herrera Campins, "Transición política."

24. See Daniel Levine, "Democracy and the Church," in Martz and Myers, *Venezuela*, p. 160.

25. The wording of Punto Fijo is particularly instructive here. It calls for (a) security that the electoral process and the public power that stems from it will correspond to the results of the vote; and (b) assurances that the electoral process will not merely avoid any rupturing of the united front but will also strengthen this unity through a prolonged political truce, the depersonalization of debate, the eradication of interparty violence, and the definition of norms to facilitate the formation of a government and a deliberative body that equitably reflects all sectors of Venezuelan society. See Herrera Campins, "Transición política," p. 131.

26. See Stuart Fagen, "The Venezuelan Labor Movement: A Study of Political Unionism" (Ph.D. diss., University of California, 1974), and Rodolfo Quintero, *Sindicalismo y cambio social en Venezuela* (Caracas: Universidad Central de Venezuela, 1966), for Communist party attempts to organize the unions.

27. There are indications that the State Department was under pressure from the oil companies to "do something about Acción Democrática." But John Foster Dulles, secretary of state at the time, was more preoccupied with events in Europe. Then, within a short period of time, events in Cuba overshadowed any possible preoccupation with Venezuela. Interview with former State Department official now in Creole Oil, Caracas, 1978.

28. See Levine, "Venezuela since 1958," p. 98.

29. Terry Karl, "The Political Economy of Petrodollars in Venezuela" (Ph.D. diss., Stanford University, 1982), p. 123.

Index